THE KREMLIN, SEAT OF RUSSIAN GOVERNMENT

An Introduction to Russian History and Culture

by

IVAR SPECTOR

University of Washington

SECOND EDITION

D. VAN NOSTRAND COMPANY, INC.

TORONTO   NEW YORK   LONDON

NEW YORK
D. Van Nostrand Company, Inc., 250 Fourth Avenue, New York 3

TORONTO
D. Van Nostrand Company (Canada), Ltd., 25 Hollinger Rd., Toronto

LONDON
Macmillan & Company, Ltd., St. Martin's Street, London, W.C. 2

PRINTED IN THE UNITED STATES OF AMERICA
BY GEORGE S. FERGUSON COMPANY, Philadelphia, Pa.

To
My Father
VLADIMIR LVOVITCH

Preface

THIS work is a product of twenty years of teaching undergraduate beginners in the field of Russian history and civilization in the Far Eastern Department of the University of Washington. In its present form, it represents a thorough revision and expansion of the 1949 edition.

As a result of World War II, new emphasis has been placed not only on formal history but on the cultural background of the people whose history is the object of study. The writer therefore has presumed to devote considerable space to Russian and Soviet culture. This is particularly important because, as explained in this text, current events and culture in Russia are so closely interwoven.

In America, where a constitutional system of government has always prevailed, where Party platforms and Congressional debates have reflected the thinking and needs of the people at large, and where daily events have been chronicled by a free press, it is possible to teach formal history and still provide a key to an understanding of the American people. In Russia, however, where there has never existed a strictly civilian government, where policies both domestic and foreign reflected not the will of the people so much as the will of the ruler, we must turn to the novels, dramas, poems, music, and art—in other words, to Russian culture—for an understanding of the history of the Russian people and their achievements. That is why no study of Russian history can be complete without a parallel study of Russian culture.

Although there has long been a need for a Russian history for American undergraduates, since the texts already in use have been designed largely to meet the requirements of advanced students with a broader background, it will be readily understood that under present circumstances it was by no means easy to write such a book. Strangely enough, even historians, not to mention the public at large, who would never dream of demanding that a history should be favorable to or critical of England, France, Japan, or almost any other country, are inclined to expect one thing or the other of a book on Russia, especially if it stresses the contemporary period. It should therefore be understood that this book has not been written to praise or blame the Soviet Union but rather to provide the knowledge and understanding of that country and its peoples which Americans must have if they are to cope successfully with the problems that confront them in the world today.

In view of the current need for greater emphasis on the Soviet Union, this book has been organized for reasons of simplification and convenience into two parts with 1917 as the dividing line, and the writer has made an effort to preserve a balance between the prerevolutionary and the postrevolutionary periods.

In conclusion, the writer wishes to express his thanks to all those professors and instructors who have used this book and taken the trouble to offer suggestions for its improvement, as well as to Professor Andrei Lobanov-Rostovsky of the University of Michigan for his advice and encouragement with regard to its publication. Warm acknowledgment is made to Margaret Marion Spector, the author's wife, without whose assistance it could not have been completed.

I.S.

March, 1954
University of Washington

Contents

List of Illustrations

(All photographs in the book unless otherwise credited are used with the permission of Sovfoto Agency, New York.)

xi

Geography and Population

THE USSR embraces a territory of about 8,500,000 square miles, approximately one-sixth of the world's land surface, with a population of about 212,000,000. Including as it does the greater part of Europe and all of northern Asia, the USSR is as large as the United States, Alaska, Canada, and Mexico combined. In area it is nearly two and two-thirds times the size of the United States. Stretching from the Carpathian Mountains and the Baltic Sea on the west to the Pacific Ocean on the east, from the Arctic Ocean on the north to the Mongolian plains, the Pamirs, the Caucasus and the Black Sea on the south, the Soviet Union encompasses a vast and contiguous land mass with great diversity in topography, in climatic conditions, mineral resources, and vegetation. Thus in the north the USSR has to contend with the icy wastes of the Arctic, while in the south there are not only deserts and mountains, but also subtropical or irrigated areas where cotton and tea plantations, as well as citrus fruit orchards, flourish. The dominant feature of the topography of this vast land mass is the great plain, most of which is less than 1000 feet above sea level, that stretches from the western borders of the USSR east to the Yenisei River in Asiatic Russia, and is broken only by the Ural Mountains. The greater part of the country, most of which lies in the same latitudes as Canada, has a continental climate marked by extremes of heat and cold. In breadth the USSR spans 160 degrees of longitude, stretching almost halfway around the world. Travel from Leningrad to Vladivostok requires nine and one-half days via the Trans-Siberian Express.

The USSR, which is rich in strategic and industrial minerals and in raw materials, holds first place in the world for its resources of iron ore (with quartzites), oil, manganese, apatite, phosphorites, magnesium salts, niobium and peat, for its water power and timber reserves; it ranks second in coal, lead, zinc, and nickel.

In spite of its vast size and great natural wealth, however, large areas of the Soviet Union remain unproductive, either because they are too cold, too arid, too marshy, too mountainous, or too isolated from existing transportation facilities. The USSR has been handicapped in the past by its lack of ice-free ports, such as Murmansk, and by the fact that most of its long coastline fronts on the Arctic Ocean. Many of the greatest rivers of the Soviet Union, such as the Dvina, the Ob, the Yenisei, and the Lena flow into the Arctic, while the mighty Volga flows into the Caspian Sea, the largest landlocked body of water in the world. The USSR has partially overcome some of these obstacles by the development of the Northern Sea Route, by the use of ice-breakers to keep its harbors open, by air traffic to isolated regions, and by the construction of a highly important series of canals, still in process of completion, to link its major European rivers, the Dnieper, the Don, and the Volga with the Baltic and White Seas.

The Soviet Union is a multinational state, which comprises between 170 and 180 ethnic groups, with as many languages and dialects, although the basic element is Slavic and the Russian language predominates. Actually, three-quarters of the population are Slavs, while the rest are of Mongoloid, Iranian, or Turkic origin. The Russian people proper are the eastern branch of the Slavonic group. Being the largest member of the Slavic family, they are in turn subdivided into three distinct groups, namely, Great Russian, Little Russian (Ukrainian), and Byelorussian (White Russian). Among nearly 168,000,000 Slavs in the USSR, the Great Russians number more than 116,000,000, the Ukrainians about 40,000,000, and the Byelorussians 12,000,000. The Great Russians inhabit most of European Russia and Siberia, with scattered colonies in other parts of the Union. The Ukrainians live, for the most part, in the south and southwest regions of European Russia, bordering on Poland, Czechoslovakia, Hungary, Rumania, and the Black Sea. The White Russians are located in the west, adjacent to Latvia, Lithuania, Poland, and the Ukraine. The Mongoloid peoples of the Soviet Union are to be found mainly in the Baikal area and on the lower Volga. The Turkic peoples are in Central Asiatic Russia, the Volga valley, and Yakutia; those of Iranian extraction are mainly in the Caucasus and South Central Asia.

The USSR is a federation of sixteen republics, some of which include subsidiary autonomous republics. Although on paper these republics have certain powers delegated to them, including even the right to secede from the Union, in practice their association as members of the USSR is far from being voluntary. Their domestic and foreign policies are in reality controlled by Moscow. Attempts at independent action have resulted in drastic purges of key local officials and their replacement by Russian officials subservient to Moscow.

By far the largest of these republics is the Russian Soviet Federated Republic (RSFSR), which comprises 74 per cent of the area of the

USSR and over 50 per cent of its population, or 116,000,000 people, including more than 100 nationalities and ethnic groups. Non-Slavic elements in the population number about 45,000,000. The two principal cities of the RSFSR are Moscow, capital of both the USSR and of the Russian Republic, with a population of about 5,100,000, and Leningrad with a population of 3,300,000 (1950). The borders of the RSFSR extend from the Arctic Ocean, the Baltic states and the Ukraine, to the Mongolian plains and the Pacific Ocean. On the eve of World War II it produced about 70 per cent of the industrial and agricultural output of the USSR, about 20 per cent of the oil, more than 40 per cent of the coal, about 40 per cent of the pig iron, over 50 per cent of the steel, two-thirds of the electric power, and the greater part of the output of machinery, timber, textiles, grain, technical crops, and food products. The Ural Mountains, 1200 miles in length, ranging in height from approximately 1000 to 6200 feet, divide the European areas of the RSFSR from the Asiatic. Such large industrial centers as Sverdlovsk, Tchelyabinsk and Magnitogorsk are located here. World War II greatly hastened a process already emphasized in the prewar Five-Year Plans: the rapid development of the vast mineral wealth of the Ural region, as well as the industrial and agricultural development of Siberia, including the Soviet Far East. As of October 1945 the RSFSR was subdivided politically into 6 *Krais* (territories), 45 *Oblasts* (regions), 12 Autonomous Republics representing small nationalities, one Autonomous *Oblast* (Tuva), and the Koenigsberg *Okrug* (area) in what was formerly East Prussia, and which was acquired as a result of World War II.

The Ukrainian Soviet Socialist Republic, with an area of 223,000 square miles and a population of 40,000,000 (1940) ranks second in importance only to the RSFSR. The Ukraine, which is larger than France, is divided into 24 *Oblasts*. It includes many important cities, including Kiev, the capital (900,000), Kharkov (833,432), Odessa (604,223), and Dnepropetrovsk (300,000), the home of the famous Dnieper Dam. This republic has rich mineral resources and a fertile black soil. Before World War II, according to official figures, it produced 54 per cent of the coal, 60 per cent of the pig iron, 48 per cent of the steel, and 35 per cent of the manganese ore of the entire USSR. As a granary of major importance, it produced about half of the winter wheat and nearly three-quarters of the sugar-beet crop of the Union. In 1939, after the occupation of Southeastern Poland by the Red Army, the Ukraine acquired an additional 7,000,000 citizens. In 1940 it absorbed Northern Bukovina and part of Bessarabia, while in 1945, by agreement with Czechoslovakia, it took over the Carpatho-Ukraine (Ruthenia), with a population of some 725,000.

The Byelorussian Soviet Socialist Republic, which compares with Kansas in size, covers an area of 89,000 square miles and has a population of 12,500,000. Its main industrial centers include Minsk, the capital (239,000), Mogilev, Vitebsk, and Gomel. This republic is noted for its vast reserves of timber and peat, for its dairy farms and other agricultural processing industries. Like the Ukraine, it suffered major damage as a result of the Nazi invasion and occupation. The Byelorussian Republic almost doubled its size and population in 1939 when the White Russian areas of Northeastern Poland were taken over. White Russia includes most of the famous Pripet Marshes where extensive drainage projects have been undertaken to increase agricultural production. Postwar plans include the reclamation of 15,000 square miles of marsh land—an area larger than the Netherlands.

The region once known as the Transcaucasian SRR was in 1936 divided into three Union Republics: the Azerbaijan, Georgian, and Armenian Republics. Azerbaijan, with an area of 33,000 square miles and a population of 3,210,000, occupies the eastern part of Transcaucasia and lies on the border between the USSR and Iran. In size it is comparable to Maine. Its capital, Baku, on the Caspian Sea, which has a population above 600,000, is one of the greatest oil-producing centers in the world. The republic is also famous for its cotton production, its orchards, vineyards, tobacco plantations, silk and tea cultivation, and caviar output. The large industrial city of Kirovabad is known for its textile mills.

The Georgian SSR, situated in western Transcaucasia adjacent to Turkey, has an area of 27,000 square miles and a population of 4,000,000. Its capital is at Tbilisi, formerly known as Tiflis (530,000). Georgia is famous as a health resort, for its vineyards, and its subtropical crops of tea, lemons, and other citrus fruits. The extensive swamps of the Colchis lowland—the Soviet Riviera on the Black Sea— are being drained, and the reclaimed land transformed into citrus groves, tea plantations, and eucalyptus forests. The great manganese mines of Chiatura, once operated by an American syndicate headed by W. Averill Harriman, which the Germans tried to seize in World War II, are reputed to contain one-third of the world's deposits of this strategically important mineral. Today Georgia has important industries, including machine-building plants, textile mills, and boot and shoe works; a large new iron and steel mill, the first in the Trans-caucasus, is now under construction. The famous Georgian Military Highway is a favorite route for Soviet tourists.

The Armenian SSR, with an area of 12,000 square miles, about the size of Belgium, and a population of 1,500,000, is located in the Caucasian highlands on the borders of Turkey and Iran. Its capital, Yerevan (200,000), lies in the shadow of the famous Mt. Ararat. In Armenia irrigation is extensively practiced for the growing of cotton, grapes, fruit, tobacco, and silk. A vast new power and irrigation project will harness the waters of Lake Sevan and the Zanga River. The republic has extensive reserves of copper and molybdenum and is also exploiting its resources of iron ore, chromite, and building materials. Its cotton and wine industries are expanding. To facilitate the further development of the country, the Soviet Union has encouraged the return of Armenians from abroad, especially from Turkey, Greece, Syria, and the United States.

In spite of the exploratory work undertaken by the Soviet Government in the Northern Caucasus, a leading Soviet engineer now a refugee in the United States, has stated that the republics in this area remain basically agrarian, with the present state of industry differing "very little from that which prevailed 32-33 years ago." [1]

An extensive area of the USSR east of the Caspian Sea and south of Siberia in Central Asia is now divided into five republics: the Turkmen, Uzbek, Tadjik, Kazakh, and Kirghiz Soviet Socialist Republics.

The Turkmen SSR, with an area of 187,000 square miles and a population of 1,500,000, is situated on the frontiers of Iran and Afghanistan. The Kara-Kum (Black Sands) Desert covers nearly 80 per cent of the territory of the republic, the capital of which is Ashkhabad (140,000). Although, under the tsarist regime, this region was inhabited mainly by nomadic tribes, extensive new irrigation projects have eliminated nomadism and led to large-scale production of cotton, silk, *kok-sagyz*—a rubber-bearing plant—fruits, etc., in addition to stock raising. The construction of the first unit of the Bolshoi Kara-Kum Canal, one of the largest irrigation projects not only in Turkmenistan but in the USSR, has already begun. It is expected to increase the total area of irrigated land in the southern and southeastern Kara-Kum by some 95,000 acres. Industry has now superseded agriculture in the Turkmenian economy, with new cotton and silk mills, shoe factories, and meat-packing plants taking precedence. Mineral deposits include sulphur, salt, and oil.

---

[1] *Construction Materials of the Northern Caucasus.* New York, Research Program on the U.S.S.R., Mimeographed Series, No. 20, 1952, p. 72.

The Uzbek SSR, which occupies a plateau in the heart of Central Asia, and extends to the Tien-Shan and Pamir Mountains on the frontier of Afghanistan, has an area of 160,000 square miles and a population of 7,500,000. Tashkent, the capital, was a city of nearly 600,000 in 1939. Irrigated agriculture is practiced on a large scale in Uzbekistan. The Great Stalin Ferghana Canal, 168 miles in length, provides irrigation for 1,250,000 acres of land. In 1947 the total length of the irrigation network reached over 120,000 miles. The canals alone extend over 600 miles. Among the new projects under construction is the Amu-Darya Canal (300 miles). Already the Uzbek Republic has more land under irrigation than the other Central Asiatic republics combined. As a result of the irrigation program, the Uzbek Republic has become the cotton belt of the Soviet Union, producing more than 60 per cent of all its cotton fiber. The republic is also noted for its stock breeding and for its caracul sheep. Today Uzbekistan has its own steel and rolled iron industries, its chemical, machine-building, textile, and food-processing industries. Its new industrial centers include Tchirtchik, with its chemical, power, and machine-building plants, Yangi-Yul, with its food production and light industry, Angren, the Uzbek "coal-pit" not far from Tashkent, and Kuvasai, a center for building materials. The ancient cities of Samarkand and Bokhara have well-developed silk and cotton industries respectively. Included among the minerals of the Republic are oil, copper, coal, and many rare metals. The new Tchardzhou-Kungrad Railroad, begun in 1947, will link the Kara-Kalpak ASSR, the Khorezm region of the Uzbek SSR, and the Tashauz region of the Turkmen SSR. The national economy of the Uzbek SSR is said to be developing faster, on the average, than that of the Union. This republic is often referred to in the Soviet press as the socialist beacon of the East.

The Tadjik SSR, with an area of 55,000 square miles and a population of 1,600,000, is situated in picturesque mountainous territory on the borders of Afghanistan and western China. It became a Union Republic in 1929. Its capital, the modern industrial city of Stalinabad, the youngest of the Soviet capital cities, has a population of 95,000. Regarded as one of the most ancient peoples of Central Asia, the Tadjiks are of Iranian origin. Soviet scientists have conducted many exploratory expeditions in the Pamirs, and an important program of road and railroad construction has been carried out. A new arterial highway runs from Stalinabad to the new town of Khorog in the Pamirs on the Afghan frontier. Stalinabad is linked with the Soviet Union by railroad. New air routes connect the capital with Khorog, with Leninabad, the center of the canning and silk-processing industries, and with the cotton area of the Vakhsh Valley. Extensive irrigation projects, such as the Vakhsh, Great Ferghana, and Gissar Canals have greatly increased the area under cultivation. In irrigated areas Egyptian cotton, fruits, and even sugar-cane are produced. By 1941 Tadjikistan was harvesting six times as much cotton as before the Revolution. The existence of more than 100 "millionaire" *kolkhozi* is indicative of the growing proseprity of agriculture in this republic. Important indus-tries, including the textile, food, building materials, and mining in-dustries, have been developed under the Soviet regime. More than 270 deposits of rare and nonferrous minerals have been discovered by Soviet geologists, seventy of which were already being exploited in 1947. Stalin Peak (25,600 feet), the highest mountain peak in the Soviet Union, is located in eastern Tadjikistan.

The Kazakh SSR, with its now famous capital of Alma-Ata, the Soviet Hollywood, covers an area of 1,560,000 square miles and has a population of 9,000,000. It stretches from the Caspian Sea to the Altai Mountains and the borders of Sinkiang. Kazakhstan, which became a Union Republic in 1936, ranks second in area among the republics of the USSR and is approximately one-third the size of the United States. More than 60 per cent of the republic consists of moun-tain and steppe pasture lands, with the result that Kazakhstan is one of the largest stock-raising regions in the USSR. Mechanized agri-culture and irrigation projects have made it possible to reclaim exten-sive arid regions, including the virgin soil of sections of the Golodnaya (Hungry) Steppe. As a result cereals, sugar-beets, cotton, hemp, sun-flower, tobacco, rubber plants, and other crops are now being cultivated. The Syr-Darya and Amu-Darya Rivers, which flow into the Aral Sea, fourth in size among the salt lakes in the world, are the center of important power projects for the republic. The completion in 1953 of the Ust-Kamenogorsk Hydroelectric Station, the largest in the republic, on the Irtysh River, will provide power for eastern Kazakhstan. Im-portant industrial centers have sprung up in Kazakhstan, including Karaganda, Balkhash, Leninogorsk, Ust-Kamenogorsk, and others. During the Stalin Five-Year Plans great railroad trunk lines, such as the Turkestan-Siberian (Turksib), the Akmolinsk-Kartaly, and the Akmolinsk-Karaganda-Balkhash have been constructed. New airlines, radio, and telegraph communications have contributed to the progress of the republic. Kazakhstan ranks first in the USSR as a center for nonferrous metals and third in coal. In the Altai Mountains large de-posits of lead, zinc, tin, silver, gold, copper and rare metals are being mined. Much of Kazakhstan's mineral wealth is still unexploited. The Karaganda coal basin north of Lake Balkhash and the important Emba oil fields northeast of the Caspian Sea are of great strategic importance for the Soviet Union.

Another Central Asiatic Republic, the Kirghiz SSR, has an area of 78,000 square miles and a population of about 1,700,000. Kirghizia, often termed the birthplace of the human race, is situated in the mountainous Tien-Shan range on the borders of Sinkiang. Its population, formerly nomadic, is now engaged in cattle-breeding, agriculture, and fruit production, or in such industries as the textile and meat-packing. Kirghiz industry is expanding rapidly. Such items as water-turbines, silk and woolen fabrics, agricultural machinery, sugar, canned goods, and cigarettes are now being produced. The city of Osh is the center of the republic's thriving silk industry. Rich mineral resources, including coal, oil, mercury, wolfram, lead, and antimony are being exploited. The construction of new irrigation canals in Kirghizia has increased the area under cultivation by 75 per cent. The Great Tchu Canal, now in process of construction, is expected to open up additional areas to agriculture and cattle-raising. The Great Kirghizian Highway leads from Frunze (100,000), the capital, into China.

Along the western frontiers of the USSR, as a result of Soviet seizure of former tsarist territory from 1939 to 1940, five additional Union Republics have been established: the Karelo-Finnish, Esthonian, Latvian, Lithuanian, and Moldavian. The Karelo-Finnish SSR, which is situated between the Baltic and White Seas adjacent to the Finnish frontier in a region studded with lakes, has an area of some 92,000 square miles and a population of about 500,000. The capital is Petrozavodsk (70,000), the location of the Onega Metal Works, established in the time of Peter the Great. Because of the dense pine, fir, and birch forests characteristic of this region, timber is the basis of the republic's economy. The Stalin White Sea-Baltic Sea Canal, 140 miles in length, was completed in 1933 and constitutes one of the major achievements of the Five-Year Plans. Granite, marble, diabasis, and mica are mined.

The Esthonian SSR, with an area of 18,000 square miles and a population of 1,131,000, became a Union Republic in August, 1940. It is strategically located on the Baltic Coast between the Gulfs of Finland and Riga, with Tallin (147,000) as the capital. The production of food, shipbuilding, fishing, and the oil-shale refining industry constitute the principal occupations of Esthonians.

The Latvian SSR, the most industrialized of the Baltic Republics, has an area of 25,000 square miles and a population of 1,971,000. Riga

(385,000), the capital, is an important Baltic port. The republic has important textile and metal industries.

The Lithuanian SSR has an area of 24,000 square miles and a population of 2,880,000. The breeding of dairy cattle and pigs, as well as the cultivation of cereals, constitute the main branches of the country's economy. Vilnius (250,000), the capital, was the subject of a long dispute with Poland after World War I. Memel is the chief Lithuanian seaport of the Baltic.

In August 1940, after the recovery of the former Russian province of Bessarabia from Rumania, the Moldavian SSR was established, with its capital at Kishinev (110,000). The area of Moldavia is 13,000 square miles and the population numbers 2,300,000. Located southwest of the Ukraine on the borders of Rumania, this republic is a fertile black soil region, where cereal crops, sugar beets, and vineyards flourish.

As a result of World War II the distribution of Soviet industry and population underwent drastic changes. Not only was there enormous destruction of Soviet cities and villages, of Soviet industry and agriculture in European Russia as far east as Stalingrad and the suburbs of Moscow, but there was a great migration of industries and population eastward to Soviet Asia, beyond the reach of enemy attack. During the war years there was a veritable boom in Siberia, Soviet Central Asia, and even in the Soviet Arctic. Accurate statistics reflecting these changes are not yet available. It nevertheless appears that the redistribution of the population of the USSR, undertaken as an emergency measure in World War II, was continued as an integral part of the Stalin or Fourth Five-Year Plan (1946-1950). This redistribution was motivated by strategic as well as by economic factors. A careful examination of materials available to date suggests that a Slavic belt has been established along the borders of the USSR, especially on the Baltic coast and in Asiatic Russia. In the Baltic Republics, as a result of widespread deportation of the inhabitants during the postwar years, it is virtually impossible to estimate with any degree of accuracy how much of the native population remains. In some of the Central Asiatic Republics, the Slavs already outnumber the native inhabitants by as many as two or three to one. Whereas, in the prewar Five-Year Plans, emphasis was placed on the decentralization of industry as a security measure, the Fourth and Fifth Five-Year Plans, in addition to the above, seem to be accomplishing a permanent decentralization of population for economic and strategic reasons.

Geographical conditions in the Soviet Union are thus dynamic rather than static. Where a government has absolute power to determine which resources shall be developed and to distribute labor forces and specialists wherever necessary to accomplish this purpose, much can be done, albeit at great cost in terms of human values and efficiency, to change the face of nature. Since World War II, the Soviet Government has undertaken extensive, long-term afforestation and irrigation projects under what is known as the Stalin Plan for Remaking Nature, which it hopes will eventually banish drought and famine from large areas in the Volga-Don region and parts of Central Asia.

Americans who are impressed by the wealth and diversity of natural resources in the Soviet Union and by the nature of its dynamism should bear in mind that in spite of the herculean efforts of the Soviet Government the USSR is still far behind the United States in the exploitation of these resources, in the development of transportation and industry, and in the standard of living it is able to provide for the average citizen.

I

RUSSIA from 862 to 1917

The Rurik Dynasty
862 to 1598

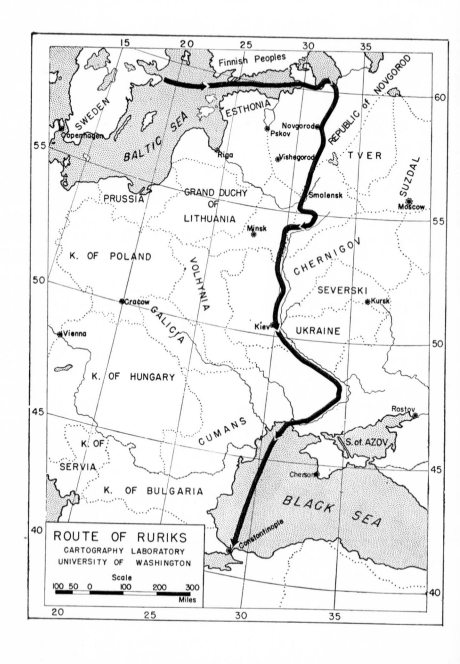

ROUTE OF RURIKS
CARTOGRAPHY LABORATORY
UNIVERSITY OF WASHINGTON

Scale
100 50 0   100   200   300
                                    Miles

I

From Rurik to the Mongols
862-1243

LTHOUGH much has been written concerning the origin of the Russian people and the formation of their state, very little is known for a certainty about these vital facts of their history. Even the origin of the name "Russia" has been for many years a subject of speculation among native and foreign scholars, who have failed to reach any definite conclusions. We do know that the people who gave Russia its earliest rulers, and perhaps its name, were called *Rūs,* but who they really were has been a matter of conjecture. Some historians have maintained that they were Russian Slavs, whereas others have held that they were Norsemen or Varangians. Later authorities have stated that the Slavs used the term *Rūs* as a general designation for all Varangians. The Greeks used the name *Rūs* to identify Slavs and Norsemen living by the Black Sea, whereas they (the Greeks) called the Norsemen, who were in Greek service, Varangians. It is apparent that the name was loosely applied and that there has been no uniformity of opinion concerning the actual identity of the people. An examination of the works of distinguished historians concerning the earliest stage of Russian history reveals, at best, only theories based upon conjectures, hypotheses, and guesses.

Obviously the lack of authentic source material is responsible for the vagueness and obscurity which shroud early Russian history. The first account that purported to be historical was the *Original Chronicle,* traditionally ascribed to a certain monk, Nestor (1056-1114), of the Pechersky monastery at Kiev. Modern scholars, however, regard it as a compilation, the product of several generations of writers, which assumed its present form in the early part of the twelfth century

3

as the *Collection of Chronicles* or the *Chronicle of Ancient Years.*[1] The *Chronicle* covers the period roughly from the middle of the ninth century to the second decade of the twelfth century.

According to the *Chronicle,* the Russian state had its beginnings about A.D. 862 when the Slavonic tribes of Russia had fallen into disorder and confusion. Realizing their inability to promote peace and establish justice among themselves, they sent messengers to the tribe, *Rūs Varangians,* the implication of the *Chronicle* being that they were a Scandinavian people living in the north, requesting that a prince might be sent to govern their rich and vast dominion. The *Chronicle* reports their message in these words: "Our land is great and rich, but there is no order in it; come and rule and govern us." Three brothers took advantage of this opportunity, and with their kinsmen and retainers speedily established themselves in the land of the Slavs. Rurik, the eldest, settled in Novgorod, Sineus, the second, on Lake Byeloozero, and Truvor, the youngest, in Izborsk, near Pskov. The sovereignty, thus divided, became concentrated after their deaths in the hands of Igor, the son of Rurik.

The foregoing account is distinguished chiefly for its inaccuracy and obscurity. For instance, the date of the first arrival of the *Rūs,* A.D. 862, conflicts with the fact that at least twenty years earlier they were known to have been in the neighborhood of the Black Sea, engaged in warfare with the Greeks, and that in June 860 they had laid siege even to Constantinople. These facts alone suggest that they came from the south rather than from the north. Furthermore the designation "Varangian" implies that they (the *Rūs*) were of Scandinavian origin, which is at variance with the foregoing facts and also with the distinction which the Greeks and Arabs of the period made between the two peoples, namely, the *Rūs* and the Varangians.

---

[1] The principal Russian editions of the chronicle are St. Petersburg, 1767, and 1809-1819; Moscow, 1824. "In addition to numerous Russian editions, the *Chronicle of Ancient Years* was translated and published abroad. Excerpts from it were quoted by Herberstein; in 1771 a German translation was made in Göttingen (Schlözer, vol. I, p. xxi); in 1860 it was published in Latin in Vienna by Fr. Miklošič. At the same time Kotkowsky in Kiev published it with a translation in the Polish language. A German translation was made by Josef Miller in Berlin in 1812, a French translation in Paris in 1834 by Louis Paris, a Swedish translation in Helsingfors in 1849; it was translated into the Czech language in 1864 by Jaromïr Erben in Prague, into the Danish language in 1859 by Smith in Copenhagen. Louis Leger translated part of the annals in 1868 into French as an appendix to his doctor's dissertation, *The Nestor Annals.* He also made a complete translation of these annals in 1884 and that same year they came out in Lvov in Latin, the translation having been made by K. Luchakovsky. The *Chronicle* was also translated into English in 1930 by S. H. Cross." (Academician B. D. Grekov, *The Culture of Kiev Rūs,* pp. 118-119.)

THE LANDING OF RURIK

Many theories have prevailed as to the origin of the Slavs and the location of their ancient habitat. The famous Russian historians of the nineteenth century, S. M. Solovyev (1820-1879) and V. O. Klyutchevsky (1841-1911) were strongly influenced by the *Chronicle*. According to Klyutchevsky, the lands along the Danube were the original habitat of the Slavs, who later migrated to the northeastern foothills of the Carpathian Mountains, where their recorded history begins in the sixth century. The Russian historian and philologist, A. A. Shakhmatov (1864-1920) advanced a different theory. According to him, the original home of the Slavs was on the coast of the Baltic Sea, in the basin of the Western Dvina and the Lower Niemen Rivers, whence they migrated to the Lower Vistula, after the exodus of the Goths at the end of the second and the beginning of the third centuries. Finally, Shakhmatov believes that in the fourth century, following the expulsion of the Goths by the Huns from the steppes bordering on the Black Sea, the Slavs moved south to fill this gap. It should likewise be noted that the well-known Czech scholar, Lubor Niederle (1865-1944), placed the original habitat of the Slavs in parts of what is contemporary Poland, White Russia, and the lands on the right bank of the Dnieper. The consensus among outstanding German scholars, including Gustaf Kossinna (1858-1931), was that the proto-Europeans (Aryans) were originally located in northern Germany, Jutland, and southern Scandinavia, from which center they migrated and scattered throughout Europe and Asia as far as India, mixing with the native non-Aryan populations and thereby laying the foundation of the various Indo-European peoples (Aryans), including the Slavs.

Soviet scholars, on the basis of extensive archeological investigation in European Russia, have established a new school of thought with regard to the early beginnings of the Slavs.[1] They have refuted earlier accepted theories of the Scandinavian origin of the term *Rūs* and of a mass migration of Norsemen into what is now Russia. According to them the name *Rūs* was well established in South Russia as early as the fourth century and therefore antedates by some five centuries the use of the term by the Norsemen. The Slavs, according to Soviet interpretation, did not migrate to this region, but their ancestors were the autochthonic population of Central and Eastern Europe, dating back at least to 3000 B.C. It is their contention that neither the

---

[1] See Professor A. D. Udaltsov, "The Origin of the Slavs," *Voprosy Istorii*, No. 7, July 1947, pp. 95-100; *ibid.*, No. 9, September 1948, pp. 97-108; V. Mavrodin, "The Basic Stages of the Ethnical Development of the Russian People," *Voprosy Istorii*, No. 4, April 1950, pp. 55-70; see also, B. D. Grekov, *The Culture of Kiev Rūs.*

Goths nor the Scandinavians brought civilization to the *Rūs,* but rather they acquired a higher civilization from the *Rūs* and were absorbed by them.

Soviet archeological studies have indicated that there was an unbroken process of development of society in the Dnieper area, between the Carpathians and the Don, from the Scythians to the establishment of the Kiev state in the ninth century. Unfortunately, our knowledge of these ancient Scythians is not very extensive. The Greek historian, Herodotus, speaks of them at some length, but his account is superficial and unreliable. Archeological excavations in South Russia have revealed some details with regard to their civilization.[1] It has been established, for instance, that their territory lay between the Danube and the Don and thence extended inland to the edge of the forest region. The Scythians had numerous colonies, the chief of which were: Olbia, situated at the mouth of the Bug River; Tanais, at the mouth of the Don; Chersonesus, located approximately on the site of modern Sevastopol; Panticapea, now the city of Kertch; and Phanagoria, situated on the Taman peninsula. In these Scythian colonies, the inhabitants so thoroughly assimilated Greek culture that they became known as Greeks or Greek-Scythians. Although certain of the aforementioned sources of information would lead us to infer that the Scythians were regarded by their neighbors as the wildest of all barbarians, archeological discoveries tend to refute this and reveal them as a people of not inconsiderable cultural development. Their ill repute as barbarians may have arisen from an attempt on the part of their enemies to cast discredit upon their activities in war. Inasmuch as they early came in contact with at least three peoples of an advanced degree of culture, namely, the Arabs, the Hebrews, and the Greeks, it is unlikely that they remained in a state of extreme barbarism.

Arabic culture reached them through merchants of that race. Semitic influence was powerful not only upon the Scythians, but throughout the various Slavonic tribes, as is witnessed by the fact that the entire ruling class of the Khazars, together with some of their subjects, embraced Judaism in the eighth century. The Greek influence reached the Scythians chiefly through the Metics, or aliens residing in Athens, who included Thracians, Phrygians, Paphlagonians, Galatians, Lydians, Syrians, Egyptians, Hellenized Arabs, and He-

---

[1] See M. Rostovtzeff, *Iranians and Greeks in South Russia;* also by the same author, *A History of the Ancient World,* pp. 250 ff.; I. Tolstoy and N. Kondakov, *Russian Antiquities in the Monuments of Art,* Serials II, III, IV, 1889, 1890, 1891, St. Petersburg (in Russian); and George Vernadsky, *Ancient Russia.*

brews. These Greeks of foreign extraction brought with them elements of culture, distinctly Greek, which left an impress upon the Scythians, by whom they were shortly absorbed.

Although archeological research has not established a direct connection between the Scythian period and the history of the Eastern Slavs, scientists nevertheless believe that the Slavs are genetically related to the Scythians, and there is evidence of Scythian influence on the Slavs. Scythian ritual designs have been perpetuated in later Russian folk embroidery. On the banks of the Dnieper the burial mounds of the Scythian ploughmen, 1000 years older than the Slavonic barrows but similar to them, have been discovered, which afford additional evidence of the tenacity of Scythian influence.

Large numbers of Roman coins of the second and third centuries, discovered in the Dnieper region, indicate that active trade relations were established with the eastern provinces of the Roman Empire. But the barbarian invasions that brought about the fall of the West Roman Empire likewise led to mass migrations of peoples across the Danube into the Eastern Empire as Goths, Avars, and Huns occupied or swept across what is now the Soviet Ukraine.

Whether the Slavs as such were the descendants of these earlier peoples who occupied the southern plains of Russia, whether they were the basic stock of this region and had been subjugated by successive waves of invaders, or were newcomers who moved into a land already subjected to the depredations of barbarian tribes, are still matters of controversy. Irrespective of the various theories as to its origin, it is apparent that Slavonic civilization does not date, as was long assumed. from the ninth to the tenth centuries but actually had its beginnings much earlier. Modern archeological research has established the fact that an independent East Slavonic or *Rūs Ante* civilization had assumed form in the Dnieper region during the sixth to the eighth centuries. There is evidence to the effect that trade with Byzantium, and with the East via the Khazar Khanate on the Volga, flourished. Excavations at Sarskoye Gorodishche (the predecessor of Rostov) have disclosed a fortified city, where spinners, carpenters, tanners, jewelers, potters, smiths, and founders plied their trades in the seventh and eighth centuries. Many such city fortresses existed in South Russia and even as far north as Smolensk and Lake Ladoga at this time—cities which appear to have been at one and the same time centers of trade and places of refuge for the population of the surrounding countryside in the event of attack. It therefore seems clear that the highly developed civilization of Kiev *Rūs,* which long puzzled historians, was not a sudden development but was based on foundations laid many centuries earlier. This may well explain why the Norsemen, who came in the ninth century, and who, in other parts of Europe, rarely founded pioneer settlements, were attracted to the Dnieper region by the flourishing towns which already existed, as well as by the urge to push on to Byzantium. The Icelandic sagas lend support to the thesis that such wealthy, organized and fortified centers existed in Russia prior to the Viking settlements. Unfortunately there are no Russian written records prior to the coming of the Norsemen. As a result the *Chronicle,* highly traditional and far from complete as it is, of necessity has continued to serve as the main primary source for the beginnings of Russian history until almost the present day.

The history of the Russian state from its earliest beginnings to the Revolution of 1917 may be divided roughly into two dynasties, the Rurik and the Romanov. The first began with Rurik in A.D. 862 and ended with Tsar Fyodor, son of Ivan Grozny, in 1598. The Romanov dynasty began with Michael in 1613 and continued until the deposition of Nicholas II in 1917.

The founders of the Rurik dynasty were, as already indicated, of the *Rūs* tribe, later known as *Rūs*-Varangians. Under this dynasty the Russian state experienced both signal advances and bitter reverses, while two events of the most vital importance took place—the adoption of Christianity and the Mongol invasion. The greatest weakness of the Rurik government was the lack of centralization of power, resulting from a peculiar order of succession and feudal particularism. This led to bitter quarrels and endless dissension among claimants to the throne and caused the state to break up into a multiplicity of principalities. The lack of unity hastened and was, in a measure, responsible for the 240 years of Tartar domination, since the state was unable to meet attack with united strength.

The first ruler, Rurik (862-879), from whom the dynasty took its name, and whom succeeding princes, despite their mutual hostility, regarded as their common progenitor, appears to have been a man of foresight and considerable ability in statecraft. A good organizer, he left behind him a machinery of government which, considering the time and the difficulties which confronted him, was indeed excellent. At his death in 879 his son, Igor, had not attained his majority; hence a relative, Oleg, became regent and continued the policy of Rurik. This policy had been twofold: first, to establish order within his immediate jurisdiction and, second, to weld into an organized unit all the scattered and unorganized Slavonic tribes. Rurik succeeded in a measure in accomplishing the first, but it fell to the lot of his son, Igor, under the guidance of Oleg, to lay the foundation of the Russian state with Kiev, "Mother of Russian Cities," as the capital.

For this reason the reign of Igor, as directed by Oleg, is of the utmost importance in early Russian history. Oleg was the first ruler to make a determined effort to check invasion by acquiring territory at the expense of the invaders. So successful was he in his conquests that in 907 he was able to organize a flotilla of some 2000 vessels and appear before Constantinople, forcing the Greeks to purchase immunity from further depredations. This expedition resulted in a commercial treaty, which granted Russian merchants special privileges at Constantinople. In 945 a more comprehensive treaty was negotiated by Igor which regulated all commercial and political relations between Kiev *Rūs* and Byzantium. Oleg's policy of eastern expansion was likewise followed by later rulers, who regarded Asia as the source of all the troubles and evils that beset *Rūs*. Because of Oleg's military success, Russian folklore abounds in tales of his prowess, while his deeds form the subject of many poems. In the nineteenth century, the famous Russian poet, Pushkin, wrote "The Lay of Oleg" (1822), a poem memorized and sung by generations of Russian children.[1] After his death Oleg came to be known by the name "Vieshchy," which means "the sage" or "the seer," and indicates that his contemporaries attributed to him unusual wisdom. Igor, deprived of the regent's ability and guidance, accomplished little.

Upon Igor's death, his widow, Olga, took control of the government on behalf of her infant son, Svyatoslav. Her assumption of power is an interesting revelation of the liberality of the Slavonic laws, which accorded to women a position considerably in advance of that enjoyed by them in other lands at this period. The *Chronicle* reveals that Olga was both astute and ruthless in her exercise of this power. Perhaps the most significant event of Olga's reign was her conversion to Christianity. In 957 she was baptized with the name of Helen, journeying for this purpose to Constantinople where the ceremony took place in the Byzantine court. The "Ceremonial Book" of Emperor Constantine Porphyrogenitus gives a detailed description of her reception. The account of the ceremony, which relates that certain honors were withheld because the convert was a woman, gives further evidence that Greek law was considerably less liberal than Slavonic law with respect to women, and that they enjoyed fewer privileges in the Byzantine

---

[1] For an English translation of this poem, see Yarmolinsky, A. (Editor), *The Works of Alexander Pushkin*, N. Y., 1936, pp. 55-58.

Empire than in Russia. Despite Olga's example, however, Christianity did not immediately became established in *Rūs*. Even her son, Svyatoslav, refused to adopt the new religion, for fear the *druzhina* (retainers) would laugh at him.

With the accession of Svyatoslav in 962, Russian expansion began in earnest, and the state was so increased that it can be compared in extent with the dominion of the Huns in the fourth and fifth centuries. It was at this time that considerable parts of the forest regions were added to the steppes. Svyatoslav's conquests extended from the stone Byzantine fortress of the Khazars at Sarkel on the Don to the Bulgar base at Pereyaslavets on the Danube, where he established his headquarters, and from which he was able to menace the cities of the empire and to march against Byzantium. According to the *Chronicle,* Svyatoslav preferred Pereyaslavets to Kiev as the center of his dominion, for it was an important crossroads where he could obtain silver, cloth, fruit, and wine from Greece, silver and horses from Bohemia and Hungary, furs, wax, honey, and slaves from *Rūs*. His imperialistic designs were retarded by the Pecheniegs, a Slavic-Turkish tribe, who even laid siege to Kiev during his absence, and were definitely checked by Emperor John Tsimiskes, a brilliant military leader of Byzantium, who paid tribute to Svyatoslav but forced him to abandon war against the empire in favor of an alliance. In 972 Svyatoslav was killed in battle by the Pecheniegs. According to the *Chronicle,* a prince of the Pecheniegs tribe fashioned a drinking cup out of his skull.

After a prolonged struggle over the succession among the three sons of Svyatoslav, one of them, Vladimir (980-1015), entered Kiev in triumph and was recognized as "Grand Prince." His reign is of especial importance from the religious and cultural standpoints, for during this period Christianity became the official religion not merely of the princely house but of the entire Kievan state.

Although there is evidence that the Greeks had tried to spread Christianity among the Scythians in the first centuries of the Christian era, and legend, as recorded in the *Chronicle,* claims that the Apostle Andrew visited Kherson on the Black Sea and ascended the Dnieper to the site of Kiev, *Rūs* paganism long resisted the pressure of the Christian faith. The chief pagan gods of *Rūs* included Peroun, the patron deity of the feudal-military class, Volos, the god of cattle, who became the god of the merchants, Dazhbog, the sun god, Khors, the sun god of the peoples of Central Asia, and Mokosh, a goddess of the Finnish tribes to the north. There is evidence to the effect that Vladimir, before he accepted Christianity, had established a kind of pantheon in Kiev and Novgorod with his personal deity, Peroun, at the head.

How far Christianity had spread among the people of *Rūs* by the time of Vladimir is not clear, but it seems evident that they were acquainted with the state religion of the Eastern Empire and that Olga was by no means the only convert. That Christians were subject to some persecution seems apparent from a record which reveals that in 983 two Christians were killed by a mob for failure to observe certain pagan rites.

As Christianity spread throughout Europe, there was considerable competition between Rome and Byzantium as to which should win the Kievan state. By the reign of Vladimir the missionary efforts of the Roman Church extended north to Scandinavia and the Poles had accepted Roman Christianity from the Germans. The Eastern Church, less aggressive than Rome in its efforts to propagate the faith, was nevertheless reaching out into the Balkans to include Bulgaria and the Black Sea coastal region.

The *Chronicle* relates that in 986 four faiths attempted to win the prince Vladimir through their missionaries. The Bulgars of the Volga presented the claims of Mohammedanism; Roman Catholicism was represented by German emissaries, and Judaism by members of the Khazar tribe. The Greek Orthodox Church sent one of its philosophers. After listening to the arguments advanced, Vladimir sent envoys into the various countries to investigate and verify what the missionaries had said. These envoys returned, greatly impressed by the beauty and solemnity of the Greek service at St. Sophia in Constantinople, and submitted reports which in 987 led Vladimir to decide in favor of the Greek Orthodox. Accompanied by his Varangian mercenaries, he thereupon descended upon Kherson on the Black Sea and compelled the Emperor Basilius to provide him with a Greek bride, part of the bargain being that Vladimir himself should be baptized in the Christian faith. About 988-989 Vladimir enforced a general baptism on the people of Kiev *Rūs,* and the Church was officially established. The Roman Church apparently refused to recognize the decision as final, however, for papal missions were sent to Vladimir in 991 and 1000. Vladimir, in response, despatched his own envoys to Rome in 994 and 1001. The fact that Vladimir's wife, the Greek princess Anna, was the aunt of Holy Roman Emperor Otto III may have led to increased contacts, and the breach between the Eastern and Western Churches was not yet recognized as final. Vladimir nevertheless pursued his original course. There is a record of taxes collected by the Church in

996, and a statute with regard to Church courts appears in 1010. It may be assumed, therefore, that by the beginning of the eleventh century Orthodox Christianity was firmly established in *Rūs*.

It has been generally assumed that Christianity was responsible for the introduction of a written language among the Slavs. The Soviet scholar, B. D. Grekov, however, thinks that the *Rūs* may have had a written language in the eighth century, prior to the adoption of Christianity, using Latin and Greek characters, and that the Greek bishops, Kirill and Methodius, provided the Slavs with a Slavonic alphabet rather than a written language. Christianity, he claims, only increased the need for a written language and led to the improvement of the alphabet by the inclusion of Slavonic letters to represent sounds that could not be reproduced through the Latin and Greek alphabets.

Whether or not it was to the advantage of *Rūs* to cast its lot with Byzantium has long been a subject for debate. The decision, for one thing, led to religious division among the Slavs, some of whom, notably the Croatians, Czechs, Slovaks, and especially the Poles, accepted Roman Catholicism. There is every reason to believe that the antagonism of centuries between the Poles and the Russians was based to a very considerable degree on religious differences. On the favorable side, it has been suggested that the Byzantine Church, more tolerant than the Roman, permitted greater religious autonomy, which led to the rise of independent national churches among the Eastern Slavs. That the choice of Byzantium was the natural one for the *Rūs* there can be little doubt. Byzantium was still far in advance of the West as the foremost center of culture and wealth in the Christian world. Commercial contacts between Kievan *Rūs* and the capital of the Eastern Empire were already well established. The ancestors of the *Rūs* had many points of contact with the Greeks whereby they borrowed and shared elements of culture. The adoption of Orthodox Christianity, for a time at least, produced even closer ties with Byzantium. No doubt the Greek alliance enhanced the prestige and importance of Vladimir and the Kievan state among the countries of Europe, although historians have long speculated as to whether Vladimir, by his marriage with the Greek princess Anna and his baptism in the Orthodox faith, became a vassal or an ally of the emperor at Constantinople.[1]

After Vladimir's adoption of Orthodox Christianity, Byzantine influence was strong in Kiev *Rūs*. Greek priests and monks, sculptors,

---

[1] See Vasiliev, A. A., "Was Old Russia a Vassal State of Byzantium?" *Speculum,* Vol. VII, pp. 350 ff.

ikon painters, architects, and teachers flocked to Kiev. The metropolitan of Kiev, the head of the Church, was a Greek. The first of the
great churches of Kiev, the Desyatinnaya (Church of the Tithe), was
constructed of brick by Greek architects. Vladimir is said to have
established a state school in Kiev to provide "book learning" for the
children of the aristocracy. Church services, however, were held in
Church Slavonic rather than in the Greek language—a factor of no
inconsiderable importance in paving the way for a national church.

Following another bitter controversy over the succession—this
time among the sons of Vladimir—Yaroslav, prince of Novgorod,
later known as Yaroslav the Wise (1036-1054), finally gained possession of Kiev. Yaroslav was the first Russian ruler to establish an
international position of some considerable importance in Europe.
During his reign the princely house of Kiev was united with the royal
lines of other Christian nations. His sister married Kazimir I of
Poland. His wife was a Swedish princess. He married his daughters
into the ruling families of France, Hungary, and Norway. Three of
his sons married German princesses whereas a fourth married a relative of Constantine Monomachus, emperor of Byzantium.

It was Yaroslav's ambition to free himself from the dominance of
Constantinople which, especially after the adoption of Christianity,
was felt in all fields—religious, economic, and social. To this end he
even launched an unsuccessful expedition against the Greeks in 1043.
He sent traders to Germany, France, Hungary, and the Scandinavian
countries. He invited and encouraged foreign artisans to settle in Rūs.
He was instrumental in disseminating education, at least among members of the ruling class. He opened religious schools in connection with
the churches and was probably the first Russian to establish a "Sunday School." The famous Pechersky monastery at Kiev, founded during Yaroslav's reign, came to have great political significance, since it
supported his campaign for an independent Church and established a
seminary for the training of Russian Church leaders. In 1051 Yaroslav even ventured to appoint the first Russian metropolitan, Hilarion,
a highly educated man particularly well versed in homiletics, as is
shown by one of his sermons yet extant. Despite the temporary appearance of a native metropolitan, however, Byzantium continued to send
Greek metropolitans to Kiev until the thirteenth century.

Since it was his ambition that Kiev should vie with Constantinople
in splendor, Yaroslav embellished it with many beautiful churches of
stone, notable among which was the splendid cathedral of St. Sophia.
That Kiev did more than just copy the patterns of Byzantium is evi-

dent from the fact that the Kiev Sophia had thirteen cupolas, and a fresco on the wall of this same cathedral depicted St. Nicholas not as a Greek but as a typical Russian. The tendency toward Russification was apparent in art as well as in politics. Other fine churches were built in Novgorod and in other cities of Kievan *Rūs*. Yaroslav also constructed the "Golden Gates of Kiev." It may be said that under him medieval Russian culture reached its zenith and that it was by no means inferior to that of the West.

Of great significance from the standpoint of internal policy was the promulgation by Yaroslav, first in Novgorod and later in Kiev, of the earliest Russian code of laws, the famous *Russkaya Pravda*,[1] which incorporated both Norse and Slavonic customs. This code restricted the hitherto prevalent exaction of blood vengeance for murder, substituting court procedure and payment of fines. It provided severe punishment for such crimes as theft, abduction, and concealment of slaves. As amended and expanded by Yaroslav's successors, this code became the most important written guide for the civil and Church courts of *Rūs*. The Yaroslav *Pravda*, as the historian George Vernadsky points out, affords many parallels with Frankish (Salic) law and with Anglo-Saxon law as depicted in the Wessex Code of Alfred the Great. Yaroslav's sons introduced provisions that afforded more protection to the princes and landholders.

At his death in 1054 much of the progress due to Yaroslav's efforts was lost when dissension of unusual bitterness broke out among the princes and continued with only occasional lulls until the reign of Ivan Grozny (1533-1584), who was strong enough to put a stop to it. During this long period of political confusion, the contending princes, with a total disregard for the interests of the country as a whole, often sought the alliance of foreign powers, such as Hungary and Poland, in their quarrels with one another. In consequence the principalities suffered severely from every standpoint, political, social and cultural, and the foundations were laid for the separation of the *Rūs* into three main branches, namely, Great Russians, White Russians, and Ukrainians (Little Russians). Had it not been for the dissension following the death of Yaroslav, it is doubtful if *Rūs* would ever have become so divided.

In 1113 the people became weary of continual confusion and, disregarding all rules of succession, elected a prince of their own choice,

[1] For an English translation, see Vernadsky, George, *Medieval Russian Laws*, N. Y., 1947, pp. 26-29. Revised and expanded versions of the same are also included, pp. 29-56.

Vladimir Monomakh (1113-1125), a grandson of Yaroslav. He was sixty years of age at the time of his election, wealthy and experienced and essentially a man of peace. Nevertheless he had displayed prowess in war against the Polovtsy (Cumani), a Turkish nomadic people from the steppe, which caused him to be feared and respected. He showed himself able to maintain order, and the people were loyal to him. During his reign education flourished; Vladimir himself was the author of several epistles which served as guides for conduct. In fact it is sometimes claimed that the *Chronicle* itself was a product of the intellectual activity characteristic of Vladimir's reign. The *Chronicle* places great emphasis upon the achievements of Vladimir, on his importance as the rallying point for all native elements against the foreign aggressor, on his role as a peacemaker, and as a popular hero. Additions to Yaroslav's *Pravda* in the Statute of Vladimir afforded protection to middle-class burghers and landowners of moderate means by limiting and regulating interest rates on short-term and long-term loans. In this connection it seems clear that in the commercial society of Eastern Europe the Orthodox Church failed to achieve the same results in regard to usury as did the Roman Catholic Church in the West.

After the death of Vladimir II, however, disorder broke out again. The city of Kiev began to decline, since it was frequently pillaged in civil wars among the princes. Kiev suffered a serious decline in 1169 when it was captured by Prince Bogolyubsky (1169-1174). Moreover, the raids of the warlike tribes of the Polovtsy against the lower Dnieper interrupted the trade via the "Varangian" route to the Black Sea and Constantinople. In 1204, when Constantinople was sacked by the Crusaders (the fourth Crusade), Kiev, being economically dependent upon the latter city, suffered even more severely. During the Mongol period (1240-1480), its glory definitely departed; and the political and cultural capital was transferred from the democratic "Cradle of Russia" in the south to autocratic Moscow in the north. Indeed, Moscow is said to have been founded by George Dolgoruky, the son of Vladimir Monomakh, as early as 1147.

For many years the throne of Kiev was regarded as the highest and most desirable position in the entire Russian state, and its occupant was recognized as the chief ruler, or grand prince. Consequently the eldest son in each successive ruling house did everything in his power to secure for himself the coveted honor. However, there were always other claimants who regarded themselves as at least eligible to the title and the power; hence there arose the jealousy and conflicts of the interested princes, which, as has already been noted, were especially bitter following the death of Yaroslav. As a result, by the middle of the twelfth century, instead of one strong national center at Kiev, there were a number of secondary centers or principalities, wherein disgruntled and disappointed aspirants to the title of "Grand Prince" sought solace in exercising local control. The most important of these were the Galician principality in the west, Novgorod in the north, and Vladimir-Suzdal in the northeast. In the south Kiev maintained its sway despite a constant decline in importance and population. Many of its inhabitants were attracted to other principalities and migrated there, not the least of the reasons being that the possession on the part of these principalities of forest lands offered a greater natural protection against invasions. Constantly the object of attacks which all too often ended in its defeat, and suffering from periods of economic depression, Kiev, nevertheless, remained the center of the Russian state in the real sense of the word. The history of the Russian people up to the time of the Mongol invasion is really the history of Kiev.

Before discussing the Mongol invasion and its disastrous effects, let us consider briefly the political, social, and religious structure of Russia preceding the cataclysm.

In all principalities the political structure was modeled upon that of Kiev, although there were minor variations due to local interests. In all cases, however, the government was semimonarchial, semiaristocratic, and semidemocratic. The monarchial element was represented by the ruling prince. His chief function was military, that is, it was his duty to protect the principality from outside foes. In addition judicial power was vested in him. For the exercise of this responsibility, he appointed special representatives to render judgment in litigations arising among his subjects.

The aristocratic element of the political structure was centered in the Council of the Prince, composed of the higher officers of his *druzhina*. This body discussed the most important matters of government and was instrumental in formulating the laws.

The democratic element found its expression in a popular gathering known as the *vieche,* almost the oldest of all socio-political Slavonic institutions and hence the one nearest to the hearts of the people. This gathering was not a representative assembly but was merely a meeting of all the adult males of any given town. The decision on any question had to be unanimous, the men indicating their wishes by shouts. In the event of any difference of opinion, the matter was settled by fisticuffs. This structure is reminiscent of the political organization of the

Homeric state wherein an uncrowned king represented the monarchial element, the Boule, the aristocratic, while the democratic element came into prominence in the assembly of the common citizens.

Although the three elements were always present, in the various regions one frequently took precedence over the others. Thus the monarchial element had ascendancy in northeastern Russia. The aristocratic element was predominant in southwestern Russia in the principalities of Galicia and Volyn. Here the *boyars,* or early nobility, influenced no doubt by ideas of Western feudalism reaching them through Poland and Hungary, compelled the ruling prince to make a choice between submitting to them or fighting them. The democratic element found its highest development in Novgorod[1] where there came to be a permanent assembly known as the *Vieche House,* through which means the principality attained complete and independent self-government with the *vieche* as the sole governing body.

During the tenth and eleventh centuries, Novgorod was governed from Kiev by the grand prince who appointed a viceroy, usually his son. After the death of Vladimir Monomakh in 1125, Novgorod took advantage of the fact that civil war had weakened the power of the princes and demanded and secured the privilege of electing its own prince. Through the *vieche* the principality was also rich and powerful enough to secure the right of appointing its own bishop from its own clergy. Up to the middle of the twelfth century this appointment had been made by the metropolitan of Kiev, but thereafter this authority was lost to him and he retained only the power of investiture.

The social structure of early Russia was composed of three groups, namely, freemen, semifreemen, and slaves. To the first group belonged the Churchmen, the *boyars,* that is, army officials and rich landowners, the townsmen who followed the crafts and trades, and the peasants. The semifree, or *zakupy,* were debtors who were obliged to work in order to repay debts contracted. There was a strong feeling among the *Rūs* that if a man could not pay in money, he must cancel his obligations by surrendering a portion of his personal liberty; hence there came into existence this semifree group. Originally the third group, the slaves, was composed mainly of prisoners taken in war, but, as time went on, slavery became a well-established institution and absorbed many of the native citizens as well; the usual reason advanced for its continuance was that it was necessary for the progress of civilization.

[1] For a translation of the Novgorod Charter of 1471, see Vernadsky, George, *op. cit.,* pp. 83-92.

As a rule, in a country which suffers from frequent invasion and devastation, agriculture does not occupy a very prominent place. Industry is likely to be more developed. Nevertheless in Kievan *Rūs* agriculture was a leading if not the most prominent occupation, and, in consequence, the peasants made up the bulk of the population. Agriculture did not, however, develop at the expense of industry, which, especially in the field of foreign trade, flourished remarkably.

To what extent the feudal system, which flourished in Western and Central Europe during this era, was characteristic of the Kievan state is still open to question. Soviet scholars, including B. D. Grekov, in recent years have devoted considerable attention to the study of this problem. The well-known historian, George Vernadsky, points out,[1] however, that serfdom was by no means universal in Kievan *Rūs*, whereas slave labor was used extensively; and that the Russian *boyars* and princes depended not only on agriculture but on trade, especially foreign trade, for their livelihood—all of which involved the growth of a money economy, as opposed to barter and services. He likewise contends that, although there was a marked development of political feudalism, as indicated by the relationship between suzerain and vassal in Suzdal (northeast) and Galicia (west) by the middle of the twelfth century, there was in reality a greater similarity between Kievan *Rūs* and the Byzantine Empire than between it and Western Europe.

Of highest importance, however, in pre-Mongol Russia was the Church, which had a vital and far-reaching influence upon the lives of the people. In common with other members of the Greek Orthodox faith, the Russians recognized as the head of the Church the patriarch of Constantinople. Directly subordinate to him was the metropolitan of Kiev who had jurisdiction over the bishops. They, in turn, had charge of the lower clergy. Thus there existed a closely knit ecclesiastical organization.

The Russian Church calls itself the Holy Catholic Apostolic and Orthodox Church. It has, with certain differences in administration, the same seven sacraments as the Roman Catholic Church, namely, baptism, confirmation, holy eucharist, penance, unction, holy orders, and matrimony. While the two Churches separated originally on minor questions of discipline, the gulf between them widened in the course of time with respect to questions of dogma. For example, the Orthodox Church denies the Dogma of Immaculate Conception in the sense that it is accepted by the Roman Church. According to the latter, all human

---

[1] See Vernadsky, George, *Kievan Russia,* Yale University Press, 1948, pp. 163-172, 209-212.

beings at birth bear the taint of original sin with the exception of the Holy Virgin. Further the Orthodox Church rejects the infallibility of the pope and refuses to recognize his authority over the Church as a whole. It affirms that the sole head of the Church is Jesus Christ, who has no vicar on earth. Thus the pope is the patriarch of the West but has no universal control. Considering the matter in the light of comparative religion, the Orthodox Church appears to approach Protestantism with respect to dogma, whereas in ritualism, it has more in common with the Roman Catholic faith.

In Orthodox worship the ikon plays an important role. Although the ikon portrays pictures of the holy family or saints or scenes from their lives, it is not regarded as a picture, but as a symbolic object of worship and veneration. Placed in a prominent position, with a lighted taper before it, it becomes the central point for the exercise of religious service. It is ever regarded as a symbol or reminder of the spiritual world, its purpose being to arouse noble spiritual aspirations.

It is impossible to overemphasize the importance of the spiritual life of Russia as it found expression in the Church of the period. The Church, like the spirit within a body, invisible yet all pervading, was the center from which all life both spiritual and secular radiated. Not only matters of a strictly religious nature but mundane affairs as well were discussed and decided within the Church. Yet the Church attempted no dominance. Such compulsion as was felt came from the efforts of overzealous princes. The Church itself was not the tool or instrument of any class or order but was the common possession of the people of all ranks and stations. In their devotion and mutual service to the institution, all met on a basis of equality. The pre-Mongol period may, therefore, be called the "honeymoon" of Orthodox Christianity in Russia.

Great credit is due the clergy of the period for the beneficial influence exerted by the Church. The Greeks sent their most capable and intelligent spiritual leaders, the very elite of the clergy. Yet the spiritual life remained in no sense an extraneous element in national life but immediately took on distinctly Russo-Slavonic characteristics. Thus the language of the Church service, which in the beginning was Greek, was gradually supplanted by Slavonic Bulgarian, which at that time was the dialect best adapted to translation from the Greek. As time passed, it assumed more and more Russian characteristics through the impress of Russo-Slavonic temperament. The service was often simplified, but at the same time a higher meaning was attributed to the symbolism, thereby sublimating it from the Slavonic standpoint.

A RUSSIAN IKON OF VIRGIN AND CHILD

In consideration of what has been said, it occasions no surprise that the first literature emanated from the Church and took the form of liturgies and prayers, mostly translations from the Greek. Secular literature, chiefly the epic, soon flourished side by side with it. Many literary critics have observed here a conscious effort on the part of secular literature to free itself from Church influence. This, however, was not the case. As has been stated previously, the Church made no effort to dominate secular life, hence there was no necessity for secular literature to free itself from a clerical control which never existed. It merely pictured a different phase of life and exhibited a variation from ecclesiastical literature. The best known of these secular epics, still in existence, is the *Tale of the Host of Igor*,[1] an account of a heroic but unsuccessful campaign which Igor made against the Polovtsy in 1185. Many other epics or "bylinas," proverbs and various forms of folk-lore originated in this period, but with the coming of the Mongols, material of incalculable value was lost.

Russian art, which was essentially religious, remained subordinate to the Orthodox Church until the time of Peter the Great. It was the Church which brought the ikon, and Russian monks, taught by the Greeks, developed the art of mural painting. Architecture was marked by greater diversity during the Kievan period. The cube-shaped churches of Novgorod and Pskov to the north, with their oval cupolas, high gabled roofs, and narrow windows were distinct Russian adaptations of Byzantine forms, and in decoration they even reflected the influence of Persia and India.[2] While Church influence prevailed, that is, until the close of the seventeenth century, there was no development of Russian sculpture. The iconoclastic struggle which rocked the Greek Orthodox Church in this respect left its imprint upon its Russian counterpart.

The pre-Mongol period in Russia was distinguished by great spiritual activity and not a little political and social progress. The stage was set for great cultural development, which might have had a far-reaching and beneficent influence not only upon Russia but upon the entire Western world. Outside foes, aided by internal discord, interrupted and retarded its development for many years to come.

---

[1] Now available in an English translation by Samuel H. Cross. See *Annuaire de l'Institut de Philologie et d'Histoire Orientales et Slaves*, Vol. VIII, pp. 151-179.

[2] For illustrations see Cross, S. H., *Mediaeval Russian Churches*, Cambridge, Mass., 1949.

2

The Mongol Period

1240-1480

THE Mongol or Tartar invasion and domination of *Rūs*, which began in the first half of the thirteenth century and lasted until the latter part of the fifteenth, is of vital importance in the history of the country, the effects thereof being felt even to the present day. During this long period of foreign control and influence, the face of Russia was entirely changed. Not only were there territorial alterations, but the physical and mental characteristics of the people were transformed to an almost unbelievable extent, so that the break between Russian culture and Western culture became complete. To be sure, this separation had begun automatically with the acceptance of the Greek Orthodox form of Christianity. This was especially true after 1054, when the final division between Roman and Greek Catholic Churches took place, marking the culmination of the original division of 867. The Tartar period, however, brought about a change which was much more vital and complete. It caused a division of the Russian people proper into the Eastern group, subjugated by the Mongols, and the Western group, overcome by Lithuanians. Upon the conquered peoples, the usurpers imposed their domination sometimes subtly, sometimes by force; they succeeded not only in eradicating many of the spiritual values which *Rūs* had attained through the adoption of Christianity, but it is sometimes claimed that they effected an actual physical change in the people.

They accomplished these ends in several ways. In the first place, the Mongol conquerors continuously practised polygamy and maintained many harems, which included Russian women. In addition intermarriage between Tartars and Russians was of frequent occurrence. Then there was the shifting of population and consequent racial transformation by the slave trade. Not only were slaves imported in

23

large numbers from other countries, but Russians were sold into slavery in the central market of Kaffa (Crimea) to be distributed thence to all parts of Asia Minor, Africa, and even Europe. This export trade in slaves arose from the Tartar practice of brutally crushing all opposition to their rule. Thus if a Russian prince had the temerity to indulge in disobedience, his territory was invaded and the inhabitants were sold into slavery.

So extensive was this slave traffic that in al-Zahra the Umayyad Caliph of Cordova surrounded himself with a bodyguard of 3750 Slavs. Although the term *Slav* seems to have been applied at first to slaves and prisoners captured by the Germans and others from among the Slavonic tribes and later sold to the Arabs, it was later used to denote all purchased foreigners, whether Franks, Galicians, Lombards, or others.[1]

The Tartar influence upon the religious and spiritual life was more subtle but no less powerful. The Russian Church suffered comparatively little from interference or intolerance; nevertheless many customs, practices and ceremonies, distinctly Oriental, left their impress upon religion and daily life, and by reason of long duration they came to be regarded as of Christian origin.[2] For example, the free Russian woman of the pre-Mongol period was reduced to the status of the Mohammedan woman. She adopted the veil and began to lead a more and more secluded life. Thus when Peter the Great attempted by force to abolish this and other Asiatic practices, he encountered the most stubborn resistance, since they had become so completely ingrained in the daily life of his subjects that they were considered national customs of immemorial antiquity.

Although Tartar hordes brought misfortune and devastation to many other peoples and countries, the harm which they inflicted upon Russia was the greatest of all.

The prologue to the Mongol domination of Russia began in 1223 when wild hordes, headed by Chingis Khan (Jenghis Khan) and under the leadership of two brilliant generals, Djebe and Subutai, appeared in the southeast. Here they defeated the Polovtsy at the Khalka on the Dnieper and likewise put to rout a Russian army, which hastened to repel the invaders. During this battle the prince of Kiev was killed.

---

[1] See Hitti, Philip K., *History of the Arabs*, p. 525.
[2] See, however, Lobanov-Rostovsky, A., *Russia and Asia*, pp. 23-24, 305. See also Buslayev, F., *Sketches of the History of Russian Folklore and Art*, Vol. II, pp. 233-237. Compare Kunitz, Joshua, *Russian Literature and the Jew*, Columbia University Press. 1929, pp. 2-3.

The "evil Tartars," however, did not follow up their victory but disappeared as quickly as they had come. Of them the Chronicler wrote: "Only God knows whence they came and whither they went." For many years *Rūs* heard nothing further of the Mongols, but in 1240 they reappeared in Russian territory, better organized and in greater numbers than before.

Our knowledge of the career of Chingis Khan (1155-1227), the leader of the Mongol invasion of 1223, is extremely limited. Even the real meaning of his title *Chingis* (or *Jenghis*) is unknown, although many scholars and historians have suggested translations and interpretations. The following scanty facts may be regarded, however, as more or less authentic.

He was born of a Mongol father and a Turkish mother at Delium-Boldak on the Onon river and died in August 1227, while engaged in a campaign against the Tanguts. He was buried on Mount Burkan-Kaldun. Like the majority of his countrymen, he practiced polygamy extensively, having four senior wives, a great number of junior wives, and in addition numerous concubines and maid servants. As a military organizer he had unusual ability, but his genius alone would have been insufficient to institute and inspire the great Mongol invasion. He was the able warrior, but the driving and controlling spirit of the movement was supplied by another man, Ye-liu Chu-tsai, whom Chingis Khan met in Peking in 1215.

Ye-liu Chu-tsai was a statesman of great renown, possessed of a sound liberal education. Learning of Chingis Khan's plans for conquest of western territory, he became deeply interested, but from a motive which from his standpoint was ethical—the domination of the territory in question by a higher and more ancient culture. It was through the inspiration of this Chinese statesman and philosopher that the Mongol invasion and devastation of the world assumed in the eyes of the invaders the aspect of a Mongol "mission," and their conquests, from their point of view, assumed the form of crusades.

It is not too much to say that the invasion of Europe by an alien people was a reverberation of the Christian Crusades of the eleventh to the thirteenth centuries, an actual boomerang, in fact. Tales of chivalry, heroism, and adventure of both the Christian knights and the Arabian emirs and sheiks had spread through the entire world and had stirred up a desire for like exploits not only among the Mongols but among all races and peoples. The Mongols were supplied with a great military leader in Chingis Khan. All that was needed further was to give to the movement a spiritual significance—to make a holy cause—and this was done by Ye-liu Chu-tsai. In establishing their ascendancy over European territory, however, the Mongols attempted no religious "conversion." As far as religious conversion was concerned, they were completely indifferent and tolerant. Their "mission" took a different direction, dominance being their sole aim.

When Chingis Khan died in 1227, he was succeeded by his son, Ugedey. The change in military leadership, however, meant very little, for the motivating spirit was still Ye-liu Chu-tsai, who, although keeping himself in the background, guided and directed the course of the entire Mongol invasion. His most significant accomplishment was the transformation which he brought about in the army. From an invading horde, whose chief purpose was the acquisition of booty, he converted it into a military force with the mission of bringing the world under one control and one scepter.

In 1235, therefore, after lengthy and careful preparations, the Mongol forces began their advance toward their various objectives. Subutai, Chingis Khan's brilliant general, had over-all command of the invasion, while the Russian expedition was in charge of Batu, a nephew of Ugedey. Naturally Kiev was the most important point of attack in Russia, and Batu moved against it with a force of about 150,000 horsemen. After withstanding several assaults, the city surrendered to the invaders in 1240. Batu rapidly pushed forward, so that within another year he had gained control of the south Russian steppes, the northern forests, and even the region of the lower Danube. By the middle of the thirteenth century, the Mongol Empire embraced a vast expanse of territory, reaching from the Pacific Ocean to the Adriatic Sea.

Although Kiev fell in 1240, the Mongol period proper did not begin for Russia until 1243, when the "Golden Horde" was established with its capital at Sarai on the lower Volga not far from the now famous city of Stalingrad, which site was selected for strategic reasons. The Tartars had shown no disposition to interfere with the political organization of Russia into principalities. Indeed the Mongol Empire tended to adopt a similar organization and to become divided into principalities, or *ulus,* under the control of the various descendants of Chingis Khan. Russia became part of the Djuchi's *ulus,* or the "Golden Horde." In the principal Russian towns, representatives of the "Golden Horde" were stationed and shared jurisdiction with the native princes. These representatives collected taxes and organized an army from enlisted men, who later took part in the conquest of southern China as directed by Kublai Khan, emperor from 1257 to 1298 (Chinese records 1260-1294).

The Tartars, likewise, made no attempt to impose their own religion upon the subjugated Russians. Even after 1341, when Islam became the official religion of the Khans of the "Golden Horde," no effort was made to eradicate the Orthodox worship. The "Golden Horde" even permitted a Russian bishopric to be established in the city of Sarai, where the bishop not only enjoyed full freedom in holding services but was also allowed the privilege of proselytism.

Tartar rule was not entirely detrimental to Russia, especially during the first century of control. Comparative peace and order were maintained. Diplomatic and trade relations were established with many countries, and agreements concerning these relations were honorably kept. Trade routes were developed, which gave merchants assurance of safe transportation of their wares. In consequence a lively commerce grew up and flourished, and the country enjoyed a fair degree of tranquillity and prosperity. The stamp of Tartar rule, however, was upon everything and the country chafed because of the submergence of its nationalism.

Among the Russian princes, two attitudes prevailed toward the Tartar conquerors. The princes of one group gave apparent co-operation, biding their time until the foreign yoke could be thrown off. Meanwhile they availed themselves of Tartar assistance in repelling attacks from European neighbors, whose encroachments they feared even more than they did the Tartar dominance. Thus Prince Alexander Nevsky (died 1263) of Novgorod was aided by the Tartars in repulsing attacks of the Swedes, Finns, and Lithuanians against whom he won an outstanding victory on the River Neva (hence the name Nevsky) in 1240. He won a second triumph against the Germans (Teutonic Knights) in the famous "Battle of the Ice" at Lake Peipus in 1242 and drove the Lithuanians from Novgorod territory in 1245. The Russian Orthodox Church, which viewed Alexander Nevsky's victories as a decisive triumph over Roman Catholicism, later canonized its hero. His fame has been revived under the Soviet regime in the well-known film *Alexander Nevsky,* produced by the late Sergei Eisenstein. Even as Grand Prince of Vladimir, to which position he succeded in 1246, Alexander Nevsky continued to recognize the dependence of the new Russia on the Tartars. When confronted simultaneously by danger from both the East and the West, he is reputed to have said: "The Mongol can wait." His example, in giving priority to European over

Asiatic affairs, has often characterized Russian and even Soviet foreign policy.

Another group of princes turned toward the West for assistance in freeing themselves from Tartar control. These princes, whose realms occupied most of northwestern Russia and Moscow, either made overtures to Western powers or adopted a policy of nonresistance toward Western invaders. One of their number, Daniel of Galicia, went so far as to offer to recognize the authority of the pope if the latter would start a crusade against the Tartars. When the help was not forthcoming, however, he relinquished his plans for securing Western aid and joined the Tartophile camp.

Of the Western powers, the one to make the most frequent raids upon Russian territory was Lithuania. The Lithuanians were aided in their invasions by the aforementioned policy of nonresistance on the part of those Russian princes who preferred them to the Tartars, and who believed they saw in the Lithuanian inroads an opportunity to rid themselves of their subjugators. They were aided, likewise, by the violent internal dissensions which by the middle of the thirteenth century had begun to disrupt the "Golden Horde," various pretenders quarreling for sovereignty very much as the native Russian princes had formerly contended for supremacy of Kiev. The Lithuanians were quick to take advantage of the weakening of the "Horde" and shortly brought under their control a considerable portion of Western Russia.

Originally the preference of the Russian princes for the Lithuanians as opposed to the Tartars or to other Western powers had been occasioned by the fact that the pagan Lithuanians had been very susceptible to Greek Orthodox influence, and the Orthodox Church had exerted considerable control over them. Toward the end of the fourteenth century, however, a change came about in religious policy. At that time the Lithuanian grand duke, Jagiello, was offered and accepted the Polish throne, which brought Lithuania under Polish influence. Moreover in 1386, the grand duke embraced Roman Catholicism, his example being rapidly followed by the pagan nobility of Lithuania. Even a part of the Russian nobility residing in Lithuanian territory became converted to the Roman faith.

The Russian princes, who had foreseen the political changes in Lithuania, now adopted a new policy whereby Tartophiles and their opponents joined forces to attain two objectives. In the first place, they resolved to take advantage of the quarrels among the Khans, attack them and drive them out from Russia as the Mongols were

expelled from China in 1368.[1] This done, they planned to direct their
energies toward winning back Russian territory from the Western
invaders, the Lithuanians.

The first step was taken in 1380 when Dimitri, Grand Duke of
Moscow (1350-1389), met and defeated the forces of Khan Mamai
at Kulikovo Meadow on the Don River. Although the victory was
not decisive and was followed by reprisals, including the ruthless sack
of Moscow in 1382, the psychological effect upon the Russians was
enormous. Heretofore the Tartars had been regarded as invincible,
but now that this armor of invincibility had been pierced, the "Golden
Horde" could never again inspire the same awe and terror as before.
The year 1380, therefore, marks a turning point in the Mongol
hegemony. The battle at Kulikovo Meadow had for the Russians
the same significance that the battle of Marathon in 490 B.C. had for
the Athenians, when their forces under Miltiades defeated the
Persians, for "up to this time the very name of Medes was to the
Hellenes a terror to hear." In recognition of this victory, Dimitri was
given the surname Donskoi (of the Don). Among his other accomplishments, Dimitri is credited with the introduction of firearms into
the army, and during his reign silver money came into general use.
During the last years of his reign the Black Death, which had previously deprived him of his father, once again brought dire distress and
want to the population of Russia. The Grand Duke Vasily (1389-
1425), son of Dimitri, was forced to recognize once more the over-
lordship of the "Horde," but he cleverly availed himself of their aid
against the Lithuanians. In a battle by the River Vorskla near Poltava in 1399, the Lithuanians were overwhelmingly defeated and their
control of Russian territory ceased forthwith.

Dimitri's accomplishments, therefore, were twofold and of the
greatest importance. In the first place, he proved that the Tartars
could be defeated, and, secondly, his son and successor, Vasily, by
playing one foe against another (also following the Chinese example),
rid his land of Western invaders and was no longer a vassal of the
"Golden Horde." Fully one hundred years were needed to rid the
land entirely of Tartar dominance. This was accomplished in 1480
by Ivan III, known as Ivan the Great (1462-1505), who proved to be
a statesman of outstanding ability.

---

[1] The Mongol period in China lasted from 1268 to 1368. Kublai Khan (1216-
1294) was the first emperor of the Mongols in China. He made Buddhism the state
religion.

RUSSIAN MONK VERSUS TARTAR CHIEFTAIN AT THE BATTLE OF KULIKOVO (1380)

In Russia's struggle for survival against the Tartar hordes, the Church played a militant part. The painting, by Victor Vasnetsov, shows the monk Peresviet in single combat with the Mongol chief Tchelibey

By the accession of Ivan III the principality of Moscow had emerged out of the confusion and disintegration to the extent that its grand prince was recognized as the leading suzerain of north Russia. His was not yet an extensive domain. Most of the south and south-west of Russia had been appropriated by Poland and Lithuania. On the south the principality of Moscow reached only as far as the River Oka on the edge of the steppes. To the east, Kazan was dominated by the Great Khan, who still claimed to be the overlord of Moscow, and to the north lay Novgorod, only nominally subject to the Grand Prince of Moscow.

Ivan III undertook to round out and consolidate his domain. From 1471-1479 he accomplished the complete subjugation of Novgorod, then a prosperous outpost of the Hanseatic League, which had entered into an alliance with Casimir of Poland and declared its independence of Moscow. This was followed, from 1484-1485, by the annexation of Tver and Ryazan. In 1480, Ivan having refused to pay tribute to the "Golden Horde," the Khan Akhmat invaded the principality of Moscow to enforce recognition of his suzerainty. The khan suddenly abandoned the field to his opponent, and the "Golden Horde" never reasserted its power over Moscow.

In 1472 Ivan III married Sophia Palaeologue, a niece and heiress of the last of the Byzantine emperors, who had taken refuge in Italy after the fall of Constantinople to the Turks in 1453. He then as-sumed the coat of arms of the former Byzantine Empire, namely the double-headed eagle, and began to regard himself as a "tsar" and suc-cessor to the Byzantine emperors. The expectations of the papacy and of some European sovereigns that, as a result of the marriage, he would join a Christian crusade against the Turks and effect a union of the Orthodox and Roman Catholic faiths, did not materialize.

Ivan did, however, enter into diplomatic relations with the West. He dispatched emissaries to Rome to secure armorers, engineers, artists, and artisans for Russia. In 1486 the Holy Roman Empire sent its first ambassador to Moscow. In 1493, following the subjugation of Novgorod, he entered into treaty relations with Denmark, another country which had contributed to the decline of the Hanseatic League and its trade monopoly in the Baltic. In reaching out to the West, and in particular toward the Baltic, he paved the way for his grand-son, Ivan IV.

The dearth of public building during the Mongol period com-pelled Ivan III to devote considerable attention to the reconstruction of Moscow. Since Russian architects had become so ignorant, in the meantime, of the principles of good masonry that several churches collapsed before completion, Ivan brought Italian architects to Moscow, including Aristotle Fioravanti of Bologna and Pietro Antonio Solari of Milan. It was natural that the various churches and cathedrals restored by Italian artists should in many respects reflect the influence of the early Italian Renaissance. Since the Russians refused to abandon the old Russian-Byzantine forms, however, the chief contribution of the Italians seems to have been a better technique of construction. From them the Russians learned how to make better bricks and mortar and to reinforce their structures with iron instead of wood. Fioravanti reconstructed the Uspensky Cathedral (Cathedral of the Assumption), which became the Coronation Church of the tsars. Solari helped to build the first stone palace in the Kremlin and part of the Kremlin walls. The Cathedral of the Annunciation (Blagoveshchensky), which served as the Royal Chapel, and the Cathedral of the Archangel Michael, the burial place of the grand princes and tsars, were the work of Milanese architects, of whom the most notable was Aloisio da Carezano. In fact, the Kremlin was basically the work of the Italian colony of artists in Moscow.

In his reorganization of the administration, the army, and the system of land tenure, Ivan the Great contributed immensely to the centralization of authority and laid the foundations for Russian autocracy of the sixteenth century. The influence of Byzantine models and precedents in this respect is evident. Soviet scholars now regard the revival of Byzantine law and culture in Russia in the second half of the fifteenth century as something akin to a Renaissance. One phase of this revival was the renewed emphasis on jurisprudence, which resulted in the issuing in 1497 of a new code of laws, the *Sudebnik,* based upon the *Russkaya Pravda* of Kievan *Rūs.*

To handle the vastly increased amount of clerical work which his domestic and foreign program involved, Ivan drew heavily upon the ecclesiastical schools for trained secretaries and clerks. The Church, which became an important prop for the state, helped to lay the foundations of the tsarist bureaucracy. Like the Mongols, Ivan also maintained a highly efficient system of communications throughout his realm by the construction of post roads and the establishment of post stations to facilitate travel. Baron Herberstein, the emissary of the Holy Roman Emperor, Charles V, in Moscow from 1526 to 1533, who has left a first-hand account of his Russian sojourn, commented that his servant was able to travel from Novgorod to Moscow—a distance of some 600 *versts* (about 400 miles)—in seventy-two hours, with frequent changes of horses at the post stations.

Of special significance for the centralization of authority in the hands of the grand prince was the land policy instituted by Ivan III. Following the seizure of Novgorod and the wholesale slaughter and eviction of the *boyars* there, Ivan granted the land thus obtained to his subordinate officers on condition of constant service. This policy, which was pursued in the case of future annexations, built up a loyal and well-trained cavalry force, entirely subject to the grand prince. Although Russian scholars have termed this procedure a "manorial system" it might be more adequately defined as "royal feudalism" of the type instituted in England by William the Conqueror after 1066. No such military force had been available to the rulers of Kievan *Rūs*.

It should perhaps be noted here that at the very time when Ivan III was pursuing measures to centralize authority in his own hands, in the neighboring state of Poland the Polish aristocracy was successfully wresting authority from the hands of the monarch. Ivan III laid his foundations so well that they survived even the difficult period of the minority of his grandson, Ivan IV.

Russia emerged from her long Mongol subjugation (1240-1480) an entirely altered land. The capital had moved by stages from Kiev to Moscow, which had, likewise, become the ecclesiastical center, the metropolitan having taken up his residence here in preference to Kiev. The semidemocratic government of the Kievan period had been replaced by a rule of harsh autocracy. The Russian princes, following the example of the Tartars, whose government had been one of implacable despotism, had come to regard themselves as absolute monarchs.

Perhaps an even more disastrous result of the Mongol period was its influence upon the Church. Previous to the Tartar invasion, the Church, as already indicated, was a guiding and directing force toward the highest spiritual aims. Leading rather than compelling, it permeated all life to the extent that it became in reality the life of the people. It emerged from the Mongol period, however, as just one more autocratic institution, seeking supremacy. Like the Russian princes, the Church wished to make its authority felt; hence, having similar aims with the state, a close autocratic union developed between the two institutions.

Another result of Tartar rule was the development of monasticism, which in Russia was not so much a borrowed institution as an outgrowth of national distress. Although records show that there had

THE EASTERN FACADE OF THE CATHEDRAL OF OUR LADY OF
SMOLENSK AT THE NOVODYEVITCHI MONASTERY IN MOSCOW

been monasteries in Russia even before the Mongol invasion, they were few in number. Many individuals as well as groups, who chafed under the Tartar regime, often met outside the towns for the purpose of seeking solace in another environment. Here they frequently indulged in prayer and religious discussion, until by long continuance this led to the establishment of a religious organization, which developed later into the Russian monastery. While monasticism was responsible for many worthwhile accomplishments and even made valuable contributions to Russian culture, it began to decline in importance in proportion as Russia became independent of foreign influence. At no time did it enjoy particular favor from the government. Peter the Great began the practice of closing the monasteries, and those which remained down to modern times were closed by the Soviet government.

To sum up, the situation at the death of Ivan III in 1505 was as follows: Moscow, with a large mixed population of native Russians and assimilated Tartars, had transformed the Russian princes into despots, who punished with torture and death the least disobedience on the part of their subjects. Although the supremacy of the Tartars was forever broken, they still held control in several regions, especially in Kazan and Crimea where some time elapsed before they could be entirely shaken off. In the west, Poland, gradually controlling and absorbing Lithuania, was looming as a dangerous foe. What was now needed was a ruler who could put an end to the continual quarrels among the princes for supreme control so that outside foes might be met with united resistance. A strong leader was needed, who was more autocratic, more cruel, more merciless than any of the others, and such a person appeared in Ivan IV, or Ivan the Terrible, grandson of Ivan III.

3

Ivan Grozny[1] (Ivan IV) the First Tsar

1530-1584

IVAN IV was but three years of age when his father, Vasily III, died in 1533, and his mother, Elena Glinskaya, assumed the regency. The country was in a state of great confusion. Not only were the princes constantly quarreling, but the *boyars* had taken a hand in the struggle for power. After the death of Vasily, the government fell into the hands of these *boyars* and passed from one prominent family to another, the exchange of authority being accompanied by atrocities and executions. Thus Ivan grew up in an atmosphere of dissension, cruelty, and murder, which in addition to his negative and unsystematic education predisposed him to his later abnormal brutality, especially toward the *boyars,* whom he hated with particular bitterness, deeming them responsible for the disrupted state of the country. In estimating his character and policies, it must be borne in mind also that he was a true child of his generation, a product of the Mongol period when self-interest, coupled with indifference to human suffering, had been the rule. Two hundred forty years of Tartar domination were necessary to produce a man like Ivan Grozny.[2] Yet strange as it may seem, he was the right man at the right time. He had sound judgment and vision and looked forward to a strong, united, mighty state under an autocratic monarchy, different from any that existed in Europe at that time.

---

[1] The customary English translation of *grozny* as "terrible" or "dreadful" is incorrect rendition of the Russian term, which in reality means "awe-inspiring," "great," "wonderful," or "dreadful" in a reverential sense.

[2] Ivan IV was married seven times but left only two young sons at his death. In 1580 in a fit of fury he killed his eldest son, which action lent confirmation to the general belief that he suffered from insanity. His wives were as follows: Anastasia Romanov, Maria (Circassian), Martha, Anna, Anna Vasiltchikuf, and Maria Nagaya.

In 1547 the Metropolitan Macarius, a scholar steeped in Byzantine philosophy and predisposed toward a strong monarchy, declared Ivan of age but placed him under the guardianship of the Church until 1553. Ivan married Anastasia Romanov and assumed the title of "tsar," which was to be borne by all future emperors.[1] At first, Ivan attempted to deal diplomatically with the *boyars,* who sought to wrest his authority from him. He tried to win their support by concessions, now to one group, now to another, but these efforts on his part were interpreted as weakness by his opponents.

In his efforts to establish the supreme authority of the monarchy, Ivan was encouraged and advised by Ivan Peresvetov, a man of Lithuanian-Russian extraction, who had chosen to serve the tsar. Peresvetov, an avowed enemy of the *boyars,* exalted monarchial power and urged Ivan to consolidate his position by seeking support from the lesser aristocracy and by leaning upon the army. The military monarchy he advocated was modeled upon that of the Sultan of Turkey, Mohammed II, who had seized Constantinople in 1453.

The reign of Ivan IV was marked by almost continuous warfare. In his early military campaigns, for which he made elaborate preparations in regard to men and matériel, the tsar met with marked success. In 1552, with an army of 150,000 men and, according to one of his generals, 150 pieces of cannon, he seized the stronghold of Kazan from the Tartars, thereby securing a gateway to further Russian expansion in Asia. Thereafter he subdued the Volga region, captured Astrakhan in 1556, and, having reached the Caucasus, constructed several fortresses on the River Terek. Ivan distributed the lands of Kazan among his supporters, built numerous fortresses, and manned them by Russian troops. To commemorate the great victory of Kazan he began the construction of the famous, if somewhat grotesque, Church of St. Basil in Moscow—a work which was not completed until 1679. This remarkable building, which stands at one end of the Red Square in Moscow, and which is sometimes misrepresented as "typical" Russian architecture, is in reality a collection of some twenty-one chapels, all differing in shape and color, and with no two domes alike, the over-all structure of which bears some resemblance to the old wooden architecture of Russia.

While his military prestige was still high, the tsar in 1558 began

---

[1] It is extremely doubtful whether the title "tsar" (also Zarr, Czar, Czarr, Ksar, Tsar) is derived from the Latin "Caesar," as is usually contended. The Tartar princes of Kazan were also called "tsars." See Graham, S., *Ivan the Terrible,* pp. 39, 125-126; and Wipper, R., *Ivan Grozny,* p. 70.

THE SIEGE OF KAZAN BY IVAN GROZNY (1552)

A scene from the Soviet film Ivan the Terrible

his campaign for the seizure of Livonia on the Baltic coast, which was destined to last some twenty-four years and to end in failure. For this task he undertook an extensive mobilization of man power, bringing cavalry from the Volga, the Nogai Steppes, and even from the Terek to the Baltic. The capture of Narva and Dorpat gave him an outlet to the Baltic, which he would fain have extended by the inclusion of the larger and wealthier ports of Riga and Reval. Unfortunately his Baltic campaign constituted a threat to the Poles and Lithuanians, who held Riga, and to the Swedes, who held Reval. In 1563, with the capture of Polotsk on the Dvina from the Lithuanians, he added one more triumph to an already imposing succession of military victories.

By 1563 Ivan Grozny had reached the apex of his power and prestige. Even his limited successes on the Baltic, and the effectiveness of his artillery, aroused great fear in the West, especially in Sweden, Poland, and among the Germans. In 1560 Albrecht of Mecklenburg whose lands were in danger due to the advance of the "Moscow tyrant" called upon Western European nations to stop providing arms and provisions to the Russians. The German Reichstag, apprehensive about the possibility of a Russian fleet appearing in the Baltic, took measures to prevent trade with Russia via Narva.

An event of prime importance in the reign of Ivan Grozny was the establishment of trade relations with England, first by way of the Arctic and later via Narva and the Baltic. In 1553 Richard Chancellor. a survivor of the ill-fated English expedition of Sir Hugh Willoughby, which was searching for a passage to the Orient, arrived at the mouth of the Dvina on the ship *Bonaventure* (160 tons). Chancellor was welcomed and feted in true Russian style in Moscow. Having promised to furnish cloth and military supplies to the Russians via the Dvina, the English secured many concessions from the tsar in the years that followed. In 1555, following the conclusion of an Anglo-Russian trade agreement, Queen Mary of England granted the "Russia Company" a complete monopoly of English trade with Muscovy. Ivan likewise granted the English an exclusive monopoly of the Northern Route, to the great distress of the Swedes, and after 1558 permitted them free entry by way of Narva. The English not only secured the right to trade, duty free, throughout the Moscow state, but acquired exclusive rights to trade with Kazan and Astrakhan, together with the right of free transit by way of the Volga to Persia and Central Asia. By the Charter of 1569 an English company was given the right to prospect for iron and to erect a smelter near the River Vychegda. The English were permitted to mint English money at Russian mints, to use Russian post horses and to hire Russian labor—all at a time when the tsar was seeking the favor of Russian merchants in opposition to the troublesome *boyars*. It is not surprising that Ivan Grozny was upon occasion called the "English Tsar." Ivan later appears to have proposed marriage to Queen Elizabeth and, when that failed to materialize, to Lady Mary Hastings. Although he displayed keen interest in English trade, the tsar consistently rejected English efforts to secure a monopoly of all the commerce of his realm.

Of the English adventurers who traveled to Russia in the time of Ivan Grozny, Richard Chancellor and Anthony Jenkinson have left accounts of their experiences. One of Chancellor's statements was almost prophetic in nature: "If they (the Russians) knew their strength, no man were able to make match with them, nor they that dwell near them should have rest of them." [1] Both men were impressed by the wealth and luxury of the tsar's court, by his military might, and his autocratic authority.

It was toward the end of 1564 that Ivan adopted a course of action which was to bring him absolute authority and make it possible for him to crush the *boyars*, who were still conspiring against him. He suddenly and secretly left Moscow and took up his residence in the village of Alexandrovskaya Sloboda, near Trinity monastery, from whence he announced his abdication owing to the treachery of the *boyars*. This "abdication" immediately evoked terrified entreaties from the civil and ecclesiastical population to the effect that he should not forsake them. Thereupon Ivan laid down the conditions of his return and forthwith instituted a regime marked by great cruelty and atrocities.

Since his prime purpose was the complete destruction of the hated *boyar* class, Ivan demanded absolute and unquestioned authority to deal with the "traitors" as he saw fit. He further demanded that he be allowed to create a private guard for himself, which came to be known as the *Oprichnina*. The term, which was coined in the time of Ivan IV, means a "separate" or "private" household or court. The members of the *Oprichnina* were men who, regardless of rank and station, abandoned everything in order to devote themselves exclusively to the service of the tsar. They numbered about 6000, held the rank of monks, and wore a special uniform consisting of "black cassocks over sable necklets and cloth of gold." They became Ivan's most powerful agent in his purge of treason from within. He gave the *Oprich-*

---

[1] See Hakluyt's *Voyages*, N. Y., 1903, Vol. II, p. 232.

nina license to slay and drive out the *boyars,* whose lands they secured eventually for themselves. There followed an "open season" for *boyars,* who had lost all protection of life and property.

One method of execution, much in favor with Ivan, consisted in inviting to dinner a group of *boyars* who were hostile to him. When they had been reduced to a semi-comatose state by gluttony and drunkenness, the waiting *Oprichnina* would fall upon them and indulge in wholesale decapitation. The country at large, although not exactly approving of Ivan's course of procedure, regarded it with more or less indifference, since the policies of the *boyars* had brought extreme hardships to the people. Ivan, himself, who was firmly convinced that Russia's future demanded the destruction of this class, continued his ruthlessness until he had attained his objective. The *boyars* who managed to remain alive either fled from the country or were rendered impotent by being stripped of all wealth and position. In this fashion Ivan strengthened the monarchy by a policy of terrorism. Like Ivan III before him, he broke up the strongholds of untrustworthy *boyars,* disbanded their private armies, confiscated their property, and substituted a service class, composed of new men of obscure lineage who were dependent on him alone. These he settled on lands beyond Moscow, and they proved to be an important factor in the maintenance of the tsar's authority in the long years of warfare and defeat that followed. Ivan's new group of courtiers later became known as the *dvorianie.* From the *Oprichnina* there gradually developed a new landowning, politically powerful class, known as the *pomiestchiki,* who earned their wealth and preferment by service for the tsar. This group continued to be a factor to be reckoned with as late as the middle of the nineteenth century.

Shortly after the establishment of the *Oprichnina,* Ivan, in order to win public backing for a renewal of the war for the possession of Livonia, summoned in 1566 what is ordinarily termed the first genuine *Zemsky Sobor*—an assembly of representatives of the clergy, the princes, the government bureaucracy, as well as the merchants and traders. The merchants and traders were invited for the first time, and this step affords one more indication of Ivan's efforts to win the support of other classes against the hated *boyars.* Ivan's calling of the *Zemsky Sobor* recalls the comparable action in England of Simon de Montfort in 1265 and Edward I in 1295.

The second half of Ivan's reign, especially the years from 1571 to 1583, was marked by constant warfare, in which Russia was under attack from the Crimean Tartars in the south and from the Poles and

Swedes in the west. Although Russia had virtually thrown off Tartar control, the khans were still powerful enough to threaten seriously the peace and security of the country. In 1571 Devlet Girei, Khan of Crimea, conducted a raid into the interior of Russia, sacking and burning Moscow. The following year he made another raid, and only the united forces of all Russia were able to drive him off. In the west, where Ivan failed to secure election to the vacant Polish throne in 1573 and 1575, he was soon involved by his successful rival, Stephen Bathory (1576-1586), a Magyar nobleman of great military ability, in a renewal of the struggle for Livonia. Bathory, who had been in the service of the Sultan of Turkey before he acquired the Polish throne, did not hesitate to ally himself with the Crimean Tartars against his Russian adversary. Poland and Lithuania having been united since 1569, Bathory conceived the idea of an even greater union by the ultimate inclusion of Russia and its conversion to Roman Catholicism. He captured Polotsk and the important Russian fortress of Velikie Luki, but the heroic defense of the city of Pskov stopped his advance. By the peace that followed in 1582 Ivan Grozny renounced his claims to Livonia and abandoned his previous Lithuanian conquests, in return for which Poland recognized his title as "Tsar." In the following year Ivan was forced to surrender Esthonia to the Swedes. Thus ended, for the time being, Ivan's persistent effort to secure access to the Baltic and thereby to the West. The long war, which had begun in 1558, had strained the resources of the country to the limit.

It was in Ivan's reign that the foundation was laid for the institution of serfdom. No matter who the various landowners in Russia had been, the peasants were the people who lived on the land and cultivated the soil. They had been free to move from one estate to another in accordance with their economic needs and desires. In 1497, however, Ivan III had restricted their freedom of movement to St. George's Day, in the late autumn. The *pomiestchiki* found even this migration distinctly disadvantageous to them and, as the long period of warfare drew to a close, they secured further legislation for its limitation. Beginning in 1581, certain years were designated as "prohibited," and the peasant had to remain on a given estate during such a year. It was but a step, then, to make all years "prohibited," and the peasant became "attached" to the soil without freedom to leave. Thus the formerly free peasants were reduced to the status of serfs.

A census begun by Ivan in 1581 and completed after his death in 1592 afforded further evidence that by this time serfdom had become

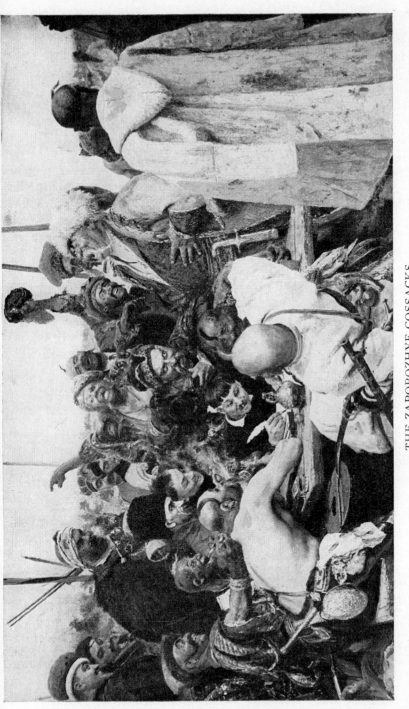

THE ZAPOROZHYE COSSACKS

The Cossacks are composing a provocative letter to Sultan Mahomet IV of Turkey. The painting is by the Russian artist Ilya Repin.

well established. In addition to the legislation against migration, the peasants had fallen into debt to the landowners and were prevented from leaving the land. The peasants, therefore, were registered as belonging to the land. They were not slaves in the sense that they were personal property of the landowner, for when the land was sold they were transferred with it. In addition to the serfs there were. however, house servants, or *kholopy,* who belonged to the owner and hence were true slaves.

Ivan's policy of ferocity did much to hasten the formation of the Cossack states, if it did not actually create them. These states first came into existence in this wise. In the fourteenth century, the Ukraine was conquered by the Lithuanian forces under Prince Gedimin and became entirely separated from the North and from Tartar jurisdiction. By the middle of the fifteenth century Russians and even Tartars, who found Tartar or Lithuanian control entirely unbearable, would seek homes in border territories by the southern steppes where they enjoyed a high degree of independence. One of their most profitable occupations consisted in robbing caravans. These freebooters were called *Cossacks* by Turks and Tartars alike. The Turkish word for robber is *Kazak.* The same word is found in the Tartar language, but means a "light-armed warrior."

When the oppression of Ivan Grozny became excessive, many persons, especially of the lower classes, fled to this Cossack "land of the free and the home of the brave." In time this heterogeneous population established two states: the Host of the Don in southeastern Russia and the Zaporog Host in southwestern Russia.[1] The government of these states was quite democratic. All citizens were regarded as equal, and all property was held in common. At the head of the state was the Ataman or Hetman, elected by universal suffrage and in pos-

---

[1] The literal meaning of "Zaporog" is "beyond the Cataracts" and refers to those of the Dnieper River. It is interesting to note that the Soviet Government, as part of the Five-Year Plan, constructed in the neighborhood of these cataracts the modern Dnieprostroy, the largest hydroelectric plant in Europe. The following book gives a vivid portrayal of the Zaporog Cossacks: *Taras Bulba,* a short historical novel by Gogol. *The Cossacks* and *Hadji Murad* by Leo Tolstoy are interesting, fictional accounts of Cossack life in general. For a description of Cossack life before and during the Great War and the Civil War in Russia, see *The Silent Don,* by Sholokhov. See also, *The Cossacks* by Maurice Hindus (N. Y., 1945).

IVAN GROZNY RECEIVES THE ENVOYS OF YERMAK

The envoys have come to offer Siberia to Ivan in return for a pardon for Yermak and his followers.

session of strictly limited authority. Judicial power resided in the popular council or the "Circle." Serious offenses were punished by drowning. A peculiar feature of the government was the imposition of celibacy upon members of the ruling class. The states were completely indifferent in their allegiance to their "Mother" land, fighting either for or against Russia as it suited their humor and interests. Their service to Christian civilization was rendered unconsciously but was none the less effective. It consisted in their acting as buffer states to check further Mohammedan encroachment. These rude Cossacks of mixed antecedents were fully as fierce as the Asiatic invaders and kept the latter from completely overrunning Europe.

Since fighting and depredation occupied most of their time, as a matter of course the Cossacks developed a system of military training and became adept in a kind of brutal warfare. Compulsory military service began when a youth reached the age of eighteen and entered the *stanitsa*. It continued for seventeen years, twelve of which were spent in active service. In addition to active service, there were two other types or classes of service, that is, on furlough with arms and horses and on furlough with arms but not with horses. The soldiers were equipped and clothed by the army or "host" from revenue granted by the government. At the beginning of World War I their forces numbered about 3,000,000 with 300,000 ready for immediate active service. They were divided into eleven hosts or corps, namely, Don, Kuban, Terek, Astrakhan, Orenburg, Ural, Siberian, Semiryetchensk, Transbaikal, Amur, and Ussuri.

The Cossacks were instrumental in adding the realm of Siberia, then dominated by Kuchum Khan, to the expanding empire of Ivan Grozny. As early as 1555 Ivan had secured Siberian recognition of the supremacy of Moscow and exacted an annual tribute of furs. When this was ignored by Kuchum Khan, Ivan IV in 1571 bestowed upon the powerful feudal family of the Stroganovs, located west of the Urals, a huge tract of territory east of that range in the control of the khan. The Stroganovs made use of a strong and troublesome band of Cossacks under the leadership of Yermak to enforce the tsar's edict east of the Urals. In 1580 Yermak and some 1600 of his warriors crossed the Urals to Siberia. Few in numbers though they were, their firearms and cannon proved too much for the khan's troops, who were armed only with bows and arrows, and Yermak captured Iskar on the Irtysh, the capital of Siberia. Siberia was annexed in 1584. Ivan

Grozny had greatly expanded Russia's possessions and, in spite of his defeats on the Baltic, had built up one of the largest kingdoms in the world.

Perhaps the greatest achievement of Ivan IV was his victory over the Mohammedan world which, at the time of his accession, extended as far west as the gates of Vienna. By his conquest of Kazan and Astrakhan he not only stemmed the tide of Mohammedan conquest but reversed the trend. Not only did Russian expansion in Asia date from his reign, but Russia broke the ground for other European nations in this respect. A recent Soviet biography has depicted Ivan Grozny as "one of the great political and military leaders of Europe of the sixteenth century." [1]

---

[1] Wipper, R., *Ivan Grozny*, Moscow, 1947, p. 231.

4

The End of the Rurik Dynasty
1598

A T HIS death in 1584 (March, Kyril's Day), Ivan Grozny left
two sons, Fyodor (1584-1598), who became the second tsar
of Russia, and Tsarevitch Dimitri, who was mysteriously
murdered in 1591.[1] Indeed the entire reign of Tsar Fyodor is
shrouded in deep mystery, and no one knows for certain what dark
deeds marked the closing years of the Rurik dynasty. Tsar Fyodor
Ivanovitch was weak of will, fearful and lacking in initiative, the complete opposite of his father. Consequently it was easy for his brother-
in-law, Boris Godunov, to direct the policy of the government.

Concerning the personality and character of this man, Boris Godunov, historians have come to no agreement. Some declare that he was
a true patriot, who endeavored to render his country real service.
Others maintain that he was influenced solely by motives of self-
interest, his main purpose being to usurp the throne. It must be said
that there is evidence to justify either opinion. There can be no doubt
that as the person who virtually ruled Russia during the last years of
the reign of Ivan Grozny and throughout the reign of Fyodor, he was
responsible for many a cruel edict, including the *ukaz* of 1581 by which
serfdom was instituted. On the other hand, he exhibited ability as a
statesman and not a few of his acts bear the stamp of true patriotism
as it was understood in his time. In any event when Tsar Fyodor died
childless on the eighth of January, 1598, thus bringing to an end the
Rurik dynasty, Boris Godunov was elected tsar by the *Zemsky Sobor*,
a popular assembly organized by Ivan IV in 1566. Since he was re-

---

[1] Early historians accused Boris Godunov of instigating this murder in order to
remove a troublesome obstacle to his usurpation of the throne. For a different point
of view consult *Boris Godunov* by S. F. Platonov, Petrograd, 1921; *Pushkin* by Prince
D. S. Mirsky, 1926, pp. 156-157; and *Boris Godunof* by Stephen Graham, Yale, 1933.
For literature dealing with this event see: Pushkin, *Boris Godunov*; also Count A. K.
Tolstoy's trilogy: *Ivan the Terrible, Tsar Fyodor Ivanovitch*, and *Boris Godunov*.

sponsible for raising the metropolitan of Moscow to the rank of patriarch (1588-1589), it is not surprising that his election received the backing of the Church. Like Ivan IV, Boris Godunov (1598-1605) recognized the importance of a strong middle class and tried to advance its interests. This policy, however, merely served to alienate the *boyars* and rich, untitled nobility, whereas the middle class had not yet sufficient strength to take advantage of its opportunities and counteract the dissatisfaction not only of the upper classes but also that of the other extreme of society, namely, the lower classes. Boris Godunov's policy in this respect and its results call to mind similar efforts and similar results on the part of Stolypin in the reign of Nicholas II, 1906-1911. While the upper classes were enraged because of curtailment of their political power, the lower classes were suffering dire want, especially during the years of famine in 1601, 1602, and 1603. Hence the ruler had two problems to handle, one political, and the other, economic. Boris Godunov did his best to solve both and made concessions and advances to all classes of society, without, however, gaining any support. This was not due solely to the fact that in endeavoring to satisfy one group, he estranged the others, but chiefly because he did not belong to the Rurik royal line. The people would tolerate a weak or cruel legitimate ruler, but when it came to enduring oppression and suffering from an elected tsar of Tartar extraction, that was an entirely different matter.

The dissatisfied *boyars* finally declared void the election of the *Zemsky Sobor* by which Boris Godunov had become tsar. They announced that the real ruler was in Poland, thus again bringing foreign influence to bear upon Russian affairs. In the Pretender, they claimed to have discovered the Prince Dimitri who, they said, had not been murdered in 1591 after all but had found refuge in Poland.

Under Sigismund III (1587-1632), a Swedish prince who was elected to the throne of Poland following the death of Stephen Bathory, the Polish Empire was one of the largest in Europe. The successful Polonization of the Lithuanian upper classes after the dynastic union of 1569 encouraged the Poles and the Jesuits, who were active in Poland after 1565, to believe that a larger union and the conversion of the Russians to the Roman Catholic faith were both possible and desirable. The religious controversy between the Poles and the Russians, especially during the era of the Counter-Reformation, assumed a bitterness not unlike that engendered by the ideological struggle between the USSR and the West in later years. Sigismund of Poland and the Jesuits therefore viewed the appearance of the "False Dimitri" with delight, for they saw an opportunity to widen the sphere of both Polish and Catholic influence.

Encouraged by the promise of support both within and outside Russia, the Pretender appeared in Moscow in 1605. Immediately insurrection broke out, and still another "Tsarevitch Dimitri" appeared, this time the candidate of the lower classes, who had risen under the leadership of an escaped serf, Ivan Bolotnikov. Hardly had this revolt been put down when the Cossacks led another uprising. In a short time Russia was embroiled in the most bitter civil war and anarchy, and hence an easy prey to external foes, especially the Poles and Swedes, who made haste to occupy Russian territory. The Swedes occupied Novgorod, while the Poles seized Smolensk and entered Moscow in 1610. Vladislav, the son of Sigismund III, was installed as tsar in Moscow from 1610 to 1612.

The invaders, however, pressed their advantage too far and brought about a reaction which led to their expulsion. During the Polish occupation of Moscow, the patriarch of that city, Hermogen, refused to recognize foreign domination, and in punishment he was starved to death by the enraged Poles. This, together with other atrocities, aroused a religious and nationalistic feeling among the Russians. A middle-class meat merchant of Nizhni-Novgorod, K. Minin by name, took the initiative [1] in arousing his own class and bringing about a union with the nobility, led by Prince Dimitri Pozharsky, against the foreign encroachments. Aided by the more moderate of the Cossacks, they succeeded in driving out the Poles and in taking possession of Moscow in 1612. The Poles nevertheless retained Smolensk and it was five years before the Russians recovered Novgorod from the Swedes. A few sporadic and minor uprisings still called for suppression, but in the course of another year these were checked and the country gradually returned to more normal conditions. In 1613 the *Zemsky Sobor* elected as tsar of Russia a young *boyar*, Michael Romanov, with whom the Romanov dynasty began. The "Time of Trouble," as the years 1605 to 1613 were called, had come to an end. Although the Poles thereafter abandoned their efforts to win Russia for Roman Catholicism, the Russians did not soon forget the part played by the Poles in Moscow during the "Time of Trouble" and it served to accentuate the bitterness between the two peoples.

---

[1] This indicates that in recognizing the important potentialities of the middle class both Ivan IV and Boris Godunov exhibited sound judgment.

II

RUSSIA from 862 to 1917

The Romanov Dynasty
1613-1917

5

From Tsar to Emperor
(Michael to Peter I)
1613-1682

REIGN OF TSAR MICHAEL FYODOROVITCH (1613-1645)

THE *Zemsky Sobor* elected the new tsar without a dissenting vote, despite the fact that he was very young and not in particularly robust health. The problem which confronted him was difficult indeed and would have tested the powers of a mature man; nevertheless, Tsar Michael approached his task with praiseworthy energy and good judgment. The insurrectionists of the "Time of Trouble"—Cossacks, peasants, and others—had produced a condition of chaotic confusion in the state and had been guilty of atrocities which caused the deeds of Ivan Grozny to pale into insignificance. The tsar's first efforts, therefore, were directed toward the suppression of the activities of various brigands and outlaws. Scarcely had he succeeded in producing a degree of order in his distracted country when he had to cope with a yet more difficult problem; the *boyars* resumed their old tactics of exploitation of the country for their private ends. Stooping to any despicable means of attaining their purpose, they were able to secure the most desirable "pork barrel" appointments, and the treasury became a prey to their systematic plundering. One of their most dastardly practices was their custom of demanding of the tsarina that she use her influence to further their nefarious schemes. Failure on her part to comply endangered her career and even her life. Thus they secured by false charges the expulsion from the palace of Michael's first bride, whereas her successor was poisoned. It was the general knowledge of this atrocious procedure which caused the King of Denmark to refuse to permit his niece to become Michael's wife.

Fortunately an able adviser came to Michael's assistance in this crisis. In 1619 his father, Philaret Romanov, was returned as an exchange prisoner after nine years of captivity in Poland. He was immediately consecrated patriarch as successor to the martyred Hermogen, the office having remained vacant up to this time in anticipation of his return. His ecclesiastical duties, which he performed with great efficiency, did not prevent him from aiding his son in the most effectual manner. In fact, although Michael retained the title of tsar, it was his father who, to all intents and purposes, was the real ruler. The country benefited enormously under the direction of this able statesman, who was well versed in all worldly, as well as clerical matters, and whose impelling and brilliant oratory swayed the people to his will. Under his guidance, Michael checked the depredations of the *boyars,* established internal order, and set about adjusting Russian foreign relations.

The Swedes and the Poles constituted the most serious menace to the national integrity of the country, the latter even laying claim to the throne of Moscow. Russia was not yet strong enough to force her assailants to make a satisfactory peace. Thus the Treaty of Stolbovo which Michael was able to secure from the Swedes in 1617 was far from favorable to his country. Although the Russians recovered Novgorod and Pskov, they were still cut off entirely from the Baltic Sea, with Archangel as the sole port for direct water communication with the rest of Europe.

Although Poland, like other states adjacent to Russia, had become distinctly uneasy about the spread of anarchy during the "Time of Trouble," no agreement between the Poles and the Russians was immediately forthcoming. After a new Polish invasion led by Prince Vladislav was repulsed at Moscow, the tide began to turn in favor of the Russians. Other European governments, including that of Sultan Osman of Turkey, which were more than a little relieved by the restoration of order in Russia, offered their assistance in checking Polish pretensions. In the war against Poland (1632-1634), the Russians tried unsuccessfully to recover Smolensk. The "perpetual" peace of Polyanovka in 1634 proved indecisive, although the Poles finally recognized Michael as tsar.

One of the most beneficial results of Russia's relations with the Western powers was the importation of foreign goods and the influx of a large number of foreigners. Although James I of England loaned Russia 20,000 rubles—a loan which was promptly repaid—Moscow refused to grant England the exclusive use of two trade routes, one by way of the Volga to Persia and the other through Siberia to Hindustan. The tsar did afford, nevertheless, wide facilities to English and Dutch merchants for trade inside Russia. He encouraged foreign merchants and craftsmen, military officers, scientists, and physicians of various nationalities to take up residence in the country and did his best to stimulate foreign trade. Thus Western influence was considerably extended during his reign, and his subjects began to adopt some of the customs of their European neighbors and hence had more in common with them. Not all European customs, however, met with equal favor. Thus the people were commanded to abstain from the use of tobacco, while snuff addicts were discouraged to the extent of having their noses cut off.

It will be remembered that during the reign of Ivan Grozny the peasants lost their freedom and became "attached" to the soil, the length of time which they were obliged to spend upon a given estate being gradually lengthened. Nevertheless, the landowners were not satisfied but were continually clamoring for legislation to deprive the wretched peasants of the modicum of liberty left to them and to "attach" them permanently to the estates. The peasants, for their part, were immeasurably discontented with their hard lot and were constantly seeking some alleviation of their misery. In consequence, there was much ill-will and strife between them and the landowners, and fugitives from the estates increased in number. In order to relieve the situation, laws were passed during Michael's reign which, however, were entirely in favor of the owners of the estates, and which established serfdom even more firmly than before. The term of "fixation" to the soil was extended from the five-year period instituted by Boris Godunov to ten and even fifteen years and landowners were given the right to reclaim fugitive peasants.

To sum up, Michael, during his reign, restored internal peace and established important foreign relations. He maintained an "open door" policy toward foreign trade and foreign tradesmen. He rescued Russia from a state of anarchy and secured for her the recognition of Europe as a power which must be respected. He developed a national feeling so that the people no longer regarded themselves as members of various principalities but as Russians, natives of a united state with a central authority emanating from Moscow. It was Ivan Grozny who from the principalities forged the state of Moscow and placed the tsar above all princes, who had a claim to the throne or any connection with the royal line. Michael, for his part, made the Moscow tsardom the

entity which later developed into the Russian Empire. His most negative policy was the strengthening of serfdom which rendered the peasant problem still more acute, and which was to become an increasing
source of difficulty to the country. Some historians are wont to compare Michael's reign with the reign of Henry IV of France. There
were many similarities in the problems and difficulties, both domestic
and foreign, which confronted the two monarchs.

REIGN OF TSAR ALEXEI MIKHAILOVITCH (1645-1676)

Michael was succeeded by his sixteen-year-old son, Alexei. The
most important event of the latter's reign was the *Raskol,* or Schism,
which resulted from the development of two opposing groups in the
Church. Of these, the Old Believers, or fundamentalists, vigorously
opposed any changes in the existing creed and liturgy, whereas the
Reformers, or modernists, advocated certain ritualistic modifications.
Heretofore Russians had been little concerned with religious controversy. Isolated even from Byzantine religious influences from the
twelfth to the fifteenth centuries, the Russian Church had tenaciously
clung to the ritual and customs established in the Kievan era. To be
sure, some faint echoes of the Protestant Reformation reached the
country. Even Ivan Grozny had been sufficiently interested to make
investigations concerning the new faith. The terrific altercations, however, which were rocking all other European nations, did not affect
Russia to any marked extent. The problems which arose as an aftermath of the Mongol period, together with the serious disorders of the
"Time of Trouble," had so occupied all classes of society that they had
little time or inclination to engage in doctrinal disputes. In the seventeenth century, however, increased contacts via Kiev with the Orthodox centers of Constantinople, Antioch, and Jerusalem, and the trek
of Greek, Arab, and Slavonic pilgrims to Moscow to enlist Russian
aid against the Turks, produced an awareness on the part of certain
Church leaders of the discrepancies between Greek and Russian ritualistic observances. Stephen Vonifatiev, chaplain to Alexei, inaugurated
a movement to raise the standards of the Russian clergy, to improve
their education, and to encourage a return to the purer traditions of
the Church.

On July 23, 1652, Nikon, an able and ambitious Churchman of
distinctly modernist tendencies, became patriarch in Moscow. He at
once set to work to introduce the ritualistic changes and reforms he
regarded as essential. In a Pastoral Letter of 1653 he directed the

Russians to follow the Greek practice of joining three fingers in making the sign of the cross, thus symbolizing the Trinity. The Russians had been accustomed to join two fingers to denote the dual nature of Jesus Christ. Nikon met with no little opposition on the part of both clergy and laity, who bitterly resented any innovations, particularly if these seemed to indicate an imitation of Western practices. In their opinion, Moscow was the "Third Rome" and the Russian Church alone had retained Christianity in its original purity, even the Greek Church having deteriorated to a lamentable extent. Any changes, therefore, assumed in their eyes the aspect of a disastrous retrogression. To understand why such an issue was made of Nikon's program, it is necessary to realize the vital importance the Russians attached to ritualistic observances and their deep-seated distrust of the Greeks, whom they suspected of subservience to Roman Catholicism.

Nikon pursued his headstrong course, brought scholars from Kiev to Moscow to support his cause, and appealed to Greek spiritual leaders for a decision. He was so successful that in 1654, 1655, and 1656 his reforms were approved by Church Councils and incorporated in canons and rituals. In the beginning the nonconformists were given an opportunity to present their case, which, under the leadership of the Archpriest Avvakum,[1] they did effectively and produced a valuable literature on the subject. Nevertheless, under pressure from the Eastern patriarchs, the Old Believers were excommunicated by a Church Council in 1667. Moreover, the state, with a view to assuming the role of protector of all Orthodox Christians persecuted abroad, and incited by Nikon, took a hand in the matter and began to persecute dissenters by torture, imprisonment, and death at the stake.

Even these measures failed to bring conformity. For the Old Believers, the changes in the Church bore all the marks of a world catastrophe, and they subbornly refused to relinquish their principles. Persecution made fanatics of the dissenters, whose ranks originally included many progressive priests and reformers. It is recorded that more than 20,000 of them voluntarily sought death at the stake rather than accept the new forms of worship. Others buried themselves alive. Being unwilling to participate in services following the new order, they either dispensed with priests entirely or chose from among themselves men to act as their leaders, who unfortunately were often ignorant and untrained. Sometimes they availed themselves of

---

[1] *The Life of the Archpriest Avvakum Written by Himself* has been translated by Jane Harrison and Hope Mirlees (London, 1924).

the services of priests, who came from southwestern Russia. These priests, by reason of their frequent contact with Roman Catholic Poles, had become very argumentative. They, as well as their untrained brethren, brought distinctly undesirable elements into the Russian priesthood. A detailed description of the life of the Old Believers can be found in the two novels of Andrei Petchersky (P. I. Melnikov), *In the Forests* and *On the Mountains*.

The persecution of the Old Believers proved to be an important factor in Russian colonization and expansion. Many were exiled or fled to the vast open spaces of the north and Siberia, to the Volga, the Don, the Urals, the Kuban, and the Caucasus, where they established new settlements. Avvakum and his wife were exiled first to Tobolsk and Yeniseisk in Siberia, later to the White Sea, and finally to Pustozersk on the Petchora in the Arctic, where he spent fourteen years and was burned at the stake in 1681. Dispersed in this fashion the Old Believers were unable to offer effective opposition to the govern-- ment, although in their new localities they sometimes supplied a nucleus for dissident elements of the population. Others fled abroad as refugees to Poland, Prussia, Rumania, Turkey, and even to China. There are no reliable statistics as to the numbers of the Old Believers. Nevertheless their views persisted, and it is estimated that at the time of the Revolution their ranks included from twenty to twenty-five million persons in Russia.

Having secured official adoption and governmental support of his reforms, Nikon could afford to disregard the ineffective resistance of the dissenters, and he turned his energies in another direction. Following the precedent set by Philaret Romanov, he reached out for temporal power, dreaming of a future in which the head of the Church should stand above the tsar, in spiritual matters at least. His efforts to bring this about led to the first serious clash between Church and state in Russia and caused his own downfall. In 1666 he was deposed from his patriarchate and exiled. He died in 1681. Within forty years of his death the Russian patriarchate itself was abolished by Peter the Great.

The religious controversy gave rise to discussions, which embraced social issues, as well as purely religious interests. In a sense they constituted a manifestation of social opposition to the growing centralization of power in both Church and state. Eventually two rather sharply opposed groups made their appearance. One was intensely national in outlook. Its supporters had much in common with the Old Believers, inasmuch as they also maintained that pure Christianity was to

be found in Russia alone and that Moscow was the "Third Rome."
Further they maintained that the Russian people constituted a "New
Israel," over which the tsar reigned as the sovereign of all Orthodoxy. As a matter of course, they did not favor innovations or foreign
"isms" but sought rather to develop and intensify that which was
national and innate, either in spiritual or material concerns.

Those who favored a Western orientation, on the other hand, welcomed foreign ideas much as their predecessors of the Mongol period
had welcomed foreign armies. They believed that Russia was behind
other European countries, both in the field of thought and in material
progress, and that, in consequence, the West had much to give her
that was beneficial. Hence they favored the adoption and incorpora-
tion into the national life of any elements which would contribute to
the national welfare and progress. They sedulously cultivated, therefore, all foreign contacts and endeavored to govern their lives in accordance with Western ideals.

One potent source of Western influence much utilized by them was
to be found in the colonies of foreigners established within the country.
While, during the reign of Alexei, tradesmen of foreign extraction
were compelled to confine their activities to the neighborhood of Archangel, the same restrictions were not imposed upon foreign intelligentsia. Many of the latter of German or Anglo-Saxon antecedents
settled more or less permanently in Russia, particularly in the neighborhood of Moscow, from whence they contributed to the dissemination
of reforms in line with Western concepts.

These exponents of the two opposing ideals for national betterment
continued to advocate their principles with the utmost energy. The
respective movements gained such momentum that by the nineteenth
century, when they came to be known as Westernizers and Slavophiles,
they occupied a disproportionate amount of public thought and discussion, as is so ably revealed in the writings of Turgenev and
Dostoyevsky.

In Alexei's reign a committee headed by Odoyevsky achieved further progress in the codification of Muscovite law. The *Ulozhenie* of
1649, some 2000 copies of which were printed in 1650 and distributed
throughout the country, continued to serve as a landmark in Russian
jurisprudence until the reforms of Speransky in 1833. The new code
included provisions which forbade the clergy to acquire more land,
restricted foreigners to Archangel for trade, and bound the peasants
more closely to the soil.

While the various religionists and national idealists were consuming their energies in what were often mere hairsplitting controversies, the mass of the population was in dire need of a practical handling of serious economic and social problems. Unemployment had increased alarmingly, and the discontent engendered thereby constituted a serious menace to national peace and welfare. The bondage of the serfs had become so increasingly oppressive that they were raging in impotent misery. Among all orders of society, intense and dangerous class hatred prevailed. A contributory cause of this class feeling was the legislation which Alexei, in imitation of his predecessors of the Rurik dynasty, had enacted with the intent of advancing the interests of the slowly developing middle class, or minor nobility. As a result both the upper nobility and the lower were equally enraged by discriminating laws, while the middle class was neither of sufficient size nor strength to take advantage of its privileges and assume a position of leadership.

The general and widespread dissatisfaction found an outlet among the lower classes in the years 1667 to 1671 in an uprising headed by Stepan (Stenka) Razin, the Russian Robin Hood. This man, who proclaimed himself an enemy of the rich *boyars* and merchants and a brother of the poor, had none of the qualities of an able leader, who could inaugurate beneficial social reforms. He was merely a bandit at the head of a motley crew of robbers and murderers. He drew his first followers from the most indigent Cossacks, the "Naked," as they were called. With a force augmented by recruits from the dissatisfied villagers, he quickly overran a great expanse of territory, plundering wherever the opportunity offered and murdering *boyars,* public officials, and even members of the clergy. Alternately appeased and threatened by Moscow, he not only subdued the Lower Volga and invaded Persian territory along the Caspian, but he seized the Volga river posts of Tsaritsyn (Stalingrad), Samara (Kuibyshev), and Saratov, and established himself at Astrakhan. Finally his own Cossacks turned against him and betrayed him to the authorities. After being put to torture, he was executed in Moscow in 1671, and the uprising came to an end.

The following song is attributed to Razin, who is said to have left it as a "bequest" to his followers:

> Bury me, brothers, between three roads,
> The Kiev, and the Moscow, and the Murom, famed in story.
> At my feet fasten my horse;
> At my head set a life-bestowing cross; .

In my right arm place my keen sabre.
Whoever passes by will stop;
Before my life-bestowing cross will he utter a prayer;
At the sight of my black steed will he be startled;
At the sight of my keen sword will he be terrified.
"Surely, this is a brigand who is buried here!
A son of a brigand, the bold Stenka Razin." [1]

The internal disorders of Alexei's reign were paralleled by external troubles. Extended and bitter wars with Poland and Lithuania over the possession of Little Russia, or the Ukraine, occupied many years. Heretofore the Western powers had always been the aggressors, and Russia had not been strong enough to check their encroachment effectively. This time, however, she took the offensive and succeeded in acquiring control of much territory, which had been wrested from her in former years. Faced with rebellion at home, trouble with the Cossacks on the Dnieper (1648-1657), under the leadership of the Ukrainian Cossack, Bogdan Khmelnitsky, and foreign intervention, the Poles were engulfed in their own "Time of Trouble," ordinarily referred to as "the deluge" (1654-1667). By the Treaty of Andrusovo in 1667 they were forced to cede to the Russians Smolensk, Sieversk, Kiev, and that part of the Ukraine located on the left bank of the Dnieper. Although the cession was for two years, Moscow retained these territories, which never again reverted to the Poles. Kiev was ceded permanently to the Russians in 1686. Out of the conflict with Poland there developed struggles with Sweden and Turkey, which were, however, of little significance. The combatants withdrew from the Swedish War (1656-1659) without gain or loss of territory on either side. A few skirmishes on the banks of the Dnieper constituted the whole of the war with the Turks. In Siberia, the Russians continued their expansion toward the Pacific, and entered into diplomatic negotiations with the Manchus at Peking.

REIGN OF TSAR FYODOR ALEXEYEVITCH (1676-1682)

Tsar Alexei left three sons and a daughter, Fyodor, Ivan, and Sophia, children of his first wife, Maria Miloslavskaya, and Peter, son of his second wife, Natalia Narishkina. Fyodor succeeded his father to the throne. He was a man lacking in ability and ambition, and of so feeble a constitution that he survived Alexei by only six years, dying in 1682. After his death a bitter feud broke out between two

---

[1] Ralston, Sh., *Songs of the Russian People,* p. 46.

opposing court parties. One of these supported Ivan's claim to the throne, calling themselves Miloslavskys in honor of his mother. The other party, known as the Narishkins, demanded the accession of Peter on the ground that Ivan was incapacitated. Supported by the patriarch, the *boyars* and a considerable number of the citizens, the Narishkins succeeded in gaining their point temporarily. The Miloslavskys, however, stirred up the *Streltsy*,[1] who demanded that Ivan be given his rightful place in the succession and instituted a period of such confusion and bloodshed that a compromise became necessary. It was decided that the throne should be held jointly by Ivan and Peter, with their elder sister, Sophia, as regent. Thus governmental control was in reality in the hands of the Miloslavskys.

Although Tsarevna Sophia (1682-1689) was a woman of much intelligence and ability, she was not a successful ruler; especially was her foreign policy disapproved by her subjects, despite the fact that in 1686 she succeeded in making a treaty of "perpetual" peace with Poland, thereby securing an alliance with the Poles against the Turks. It was by this treaty that the Polish ruler, Jan Sobieski, recognized as permanent the cession of Kiev to Russia.

The last official act of the regency of Sophia—the signing of the Treaty of Nertchinsk on August 26, 1689—was of considerable consequence for Russian expansion in the Far East. In the middle of the seventeenth century Russian traders and adventurers had reached the Amur River, where they soon clashed with the Manchu-led Chinese army and with the Buryat Mongols. In a manner reminiscent of French and English expansion in North America, the Russians constructed a line of forts (*ostrogs*) from Lake Baikal to the left bank of the Amur. In their efforts to oust the Russians from the Amur basin, the Chinese conducted a successful offensive against the Russian fortress of Albazin, following which peace negotiations were held at Nertchinsk, with Count F. A. Golovin representing the Russians and a Jesuit missionary serving as intermediary for the Chinese.

The Treaty of Nertchinsk, which delimited the frontiers between China and Russia and made provision for a Russian mission at Peking, was the first that China signed with any Western power. By excluding Russia from the Amur, this treaty served to stem the tide of Rus-

---

[1] As a protection for Moscow, Ivan Grozny had organized several regiments of infantry, known as the *Streltsy*. This body became very powerful by reason of its good military organization and the special privileges granted to it. It eventually became so independent and arrogant that it was able to enforce its will upon the government, which did not dare to check its activities.

sian expansion to the Pacific until the nineteenth century. Since Peter the Great was primarily concerned about an outlet on the Baltic, the Treaty of Nertchinsk proved to be of mutual advantage to the Chinese and the Russians. The discrepancies in the Manchu, Chinese, Mongol, Russian, and official Latin versions provided the Russians, some 150 years later, with a pretext for further claims against the Chinese.

Meanwhile Sophia, who hated and feared her half-brother, Peter, recognized in him a dangerous menace to the continuation of her authority and considered ways and means for his removal. He was not unaware of her animosity, and discovering that she was plotting against his life, he took measures to secure her overthrow. With the support of one faction of the *Streltsy,* he brought about a *coup d'état* in 1689, which wrested the government from Sophia's hands. She was sent to a convent, where she was virtually a prisoner, and Peter assumed absolute control, although his brother, Ivan, lived until 1696.

6

From Reformer to Reformer (Peter I to Alexander II)

1682-1855

REIGN OF PETER I, THE GREAT, THE FIRST EMPEROR

(1682-1725)

PETER was only seventeen years of age when he made himself master of Russia, but he had already attained mental and physical maturity. His superior intelligence had been manifest at an early age when he had rapidly mastered the subjects which constituted a liberal education of his day. His interests and abilities were not exclusively academic, however, for ships and shipbuilding had a great fascination for him. He also had a strong militaristic bent, which led him as a very young boy to begin the organization of regiments among his youthful companions, which regiments later served him well.

Peter's formal instruction was interrupted by the hostilities following the death of his brother, Fyodor. When Sophia became regent, she selected tutors for him, but his mother so strongly disapproved of them that she withdrew with him to the village of Preobrazhenskoye. This village was near the German Suburb, the rendezvous of all sorts and conditions of foreigners. The German Suburb was originally founded by some adventurous Englishmen and a group of soldiers from the army of the Austrian general, Albrecht von Wallenstein, famous for his defeat of Gustavus Adolphus and the Swedish forces in the Thirty Years' War. Later some 3000 Scottish refugees, who fled from their homeland following the imprisonment of Charles I of England, joined the community. As time went on the population became exceedingly cosmopolitan. Since very few of the inhabitants could speak Russian,

RULERS OF RUSSIA
(A.D. 862-1917)

I. Rurik Dynasty (862-1598)

Princes

Rurik	862- 879
Oleg	879- 912
Igor	913- 945
Olga, his widow	945- 969
Svyatoslav	962- 972
Yaropolk	973- 980
Vladimir, the Saint	980-1015
Sviatopolk	1015-1019
Yaroslav, The Wise	1036-1054
Vladimir Monomakh	1113-1125

Grand Princes of Moscow

Ivan I, Kalita	1328-1341
Simeon, the Proud	1341-1359
Ivan II, the Red	1353-1359
Dimitry II	1359-1362
Dimitry III, Donskoi	1362-1389
Vasili Dimitrievitch I	1389-1425
Vasili Vasilievitch II	1425-1462
Ivan III, the Great	1462-1505
Vasili, Ivanovitch III	1505-1533

Tsars

Ivan IV, Grozny	1533-1584
Fyodor Ivanovitch	1584-1598

II. Romanov Dynasty (1613-1917)

Tsars

Michael Fyodorovitch	1613-1645
Alexei Mikhailovitch	1645-1676
Fyodor Alexeyevitch	1676-1682
Ivan V, and Peter I	1682-1689

Emperors and Empresses

Peter I, the Great	1682-1725
Catherine I	1725-1727
Peter II	1727-1730
Anna	1730-1740
Ivan VI	1740-1741
Elizabeth	1741-1762
Peter III	1762
Catherine II, the Great	1762-1796
Paul	1796-1801
Alexander I	1801-1825
Nicholas I	1825-1855
Alexander II	1855-1881
Alexander III	1881-1894
Nicholas II	1894-1917

Note: The period from 1598 to 1613 is called the "Time of Trouble." None of the rulers, including Boris Godunov

the Russians applied to all of them the name, *Nemetz* (German), from *Nemoi,* meaning speechless. The Church regarded the colony as a resort of heretics and an abode of evil and reluctantly tolerated its existence. Patriarch Joachim, who died in 1690, left as a bequest to Peter the injunction not to associate with Lutherans, Calvinists, Catholics, and like heretics, but rather to banish them from the country and raze their places of worship to the ground. The German Suburb was, nevertheless, much frequented by Russians who found stimulus in the varied intellectual contacts which it offered, or who sought relaxation from the restraints imposed by Russian conventions. An English historian, B. H. Sumner, has rather appropriately termed the colony "a little fragment of industrious, ingenius, Protestant Europe." [1]

Peter visited the German Suburb often and made numerous friends and acquaintances among its inhabitants. Through his association with philosophers, scholars, and technicians of various nationalities, and with Protestant missionaries of German and Dutch extraction, he became imbued with Western ideas and turned a critical eye upon conditions in his own country. From the Scottish members of the German Suburb—among them the Gordons, the Ogilvies, and the Carmichaels—he learned much of English naval and military techniques, and he planned to reorganize the armed forces of Russia in conformity with those of Western Europe. He began to study Russian history and became convinced that in pre-Mongol days Russia had possessed a degree of culture and had reached a stage of development which would have enabled her easily to keep abreast of, or even to outstrip, other European nations. He also saw that the Mongol invasion and the long period of foreign bondage, which completely severed Russia from cultural contacts with the West, had resulted in a fearful retardation of her civilization, so that she was centuries behind her neighbors. In order to bridge the gulf which separated Russia from Western culture, he determined to effect by force a complete change in the customs, ideas, and character of his people by the eradication of all relics of Mongolism and the substitution of European civilization. Whereas the Tartars had *trans*formed Russia, it was his purpose to *re*form her in accordance with Western ideals, toward which end he proceeded with relentless determination.

INTERNAL POLICY

In order to understand Peter's internal policy, we must bear in mind that his prime purpose was to make of Russia a European nation.

---

[1] Sumner, B. H., *A Short History of Russia* (New York, 1943), p. 319.

His program of Europeanization was modeled largely after the Protestant countries of northern Europe, and many of his reforms were accomplished at the expense of the Orthodox Church. As has been noted previously, during the Mongol period the Church incorporated within itself many Oriental features, the origin of which came to be forgotten in the course of centuries. Peter was keenly alive to this source of Oriental and, in his opinion, pernicious influence, and knew that it must be destroyed if his program of Europeanization was to succeed. Moreover, he resented the efforts of the Church to secure temporal power and resolved to crush such pretensions without delay. Thus, although he joined with the Church in its persecution of the Old Believers, whom he likewise regarded as a troublesome obstacle to progress, he omitted nothing which would serve to injure ecclesiastical power and prestige and render its influence ineffective. In consequence his procedure was bitterly resented by many Churchmen, who voiced their indignation so emphatically that for many years he was referred to as an infidel, the "Anti-Christ," whose rule had wrought incomparable harm to his country.

One of Peter's most effective blows against the Church was the abolition of the patriarchate upon the death of the Patriarch Adrian in 1700. There was no supreme ecclesiastical authority until 1721 when Peter instituted a Synod, or Committee of Bishops, in accordance with German Protestant practice; but as this body could act only at his direction, he himself became thereby the actual head of the Church. He also turned against Moscow—the "Third Rome," the "Second Jerusalem"—and robbed it of its glory by removing his capital to the new city of St. Petersburg, founded in 1703 at the marshy estuary of the Neva. To be sure, he had selected this site because he considered that the capital needed a more strategic location than Moscow afforded, but he also had in mind the entire separation of the government from any possibility of Church control or influence. So determined was he to stamp out this influence that when he learned that his son, Alexei, had promised the clergy to restore the capital and to reassert the authority of the Church upon his accession, he had the young man murdered (1718).

By this time monasticism had become a well-established institution in the Church and exerted no little influence along educational lines. Peter, however, made it the object of ridicule upon all occasions, passed laws to eradicate it, and deprived its members of any public offices that they had secured. For example, the Department of Education had been in charge of an Orthodox monk; Peter dismissed him and gave the office to a Protestant pastor.

As a further "Church reform," in 1721 he discarded the title of "Tsar" because of its Oriental and ecclesiastical implications and substituted for it the Western title of "Emperor." The people in general, however, continued to call their ruler the "Tsar." In order to give this change special significance, Peter selected as the day for announcing it, November 4, the anniversary of the freeing of Moscow from the Poles in 1612. As a matter of course, he also changed the name "Grand States of the Russian Tsardom," to the "Empire of all the Russias" to conform with European usage. Already, as early as 1708, he had reorganized the country into provinces in accordance with European principles of government.

Second only to the Church, Peter regarded the *boyars* as a reactionary and detrimental force. Although he did not seek to annihilate them as did Ivan Grozny, he effectively deprived them of all political and social power. Thus in 1711 he established the Administrative Senate, a body of officials who enjoyed Peter's confidence, and who soon began to exercise supervision over state finances, the judiciary, and the provincial governors, in practice superseding the Boyar's Duma. Peter further transformed the haphazard Muscovite bureaucracy in 1718 by reducing the number of government departments to eight "Colleges," each headed by a board, and by adding two new ones to handle commerce, and mines and manufactures. In January 1722 he published the well-known "Table of Ranks" which, in place of the old aristocracy by right of birth established a new aristocracy, the *dvorianstvo,* whose titles were bestowed because of service to the government. Military, civil, and court services were organized in an ascending series of ranks (*tchins*), fourteen for military and naval service, and parallel to them, another fourteen for civilian service. In practice the upper eight came to be identified with the nobility. Peter thus made possible a career open to talent, irrespective of birth and social origin. Several of his top administrators, including Alexander D. Menshikov (1670-1729), were of lowly origin. The "Table of Ranks" was abolished on December 10, 1917.

In accordance with the prevailing mercantile theories of his day, it was Peter's objective to develop Russian industry and make Russia economically independent of foreign lands. Peter's hostility to the Church and to the *boyars* rested, in part, on their uncompromising opposition to his program of Westernization and industrialization. Nevertheless he soon found himself handicapped by the lack of a

middle class capable of building up the Russian mining and manufacturing industries necessary to provide the nation with iron, steel, munitions, and textiles. Although state economic control was greatly
extended during his reign, Peter was forced to grant monopolies of
certain industries to members of the nobility and to attach villages of
serfs to their factories to provide the necessary labor, thereby initiat-
ing factory-serfdom. During Peter's reign more than two hundred
factories and mills were established in Russia, including important new
iron works and textile mills in the Urals. The abiding interest of the
state in the new enterprises was evinced by the establishment of a Ministry (College) of Mines and Manufactures in the government, and by
a policy of generous state subsidies for industry.

    In the field of education and science, Peter adopted a distinctly
constructive policy and was responsible for much valuable progress.
Among other things, his adoption of the Julian calendar on January
1, 1700, brought Russia into line with the majority of the countries of
Western Europe. The Academy of Science, organized in imitation of
a similar institution in Paris and the Royal Society in London, was
founded at the close of his reign. It speedily attracted scientists and
mathematicians in great numbers and contributed much to progress
along scientific and technical lines. Its most valuable accomplishments
were the geographical survey of Siberia and the great Siberian expedition of 1733 to 1743. To assist the work of the Academy, Peter
also had books on technical subjects translated from various European
languages. His instructions to the translators show that he had a true
comprehension of what constitutes the art of translation. He admon-
ished them to acquire a thorough understanding of the content and to
translate the thought rather than mere words. In regard to language,
Peter was likewise responsible for the simplification of the old Church
Slavonic script in order to facilitate the production of secular literature, including technical and historical works.

    With the capture of an outlet on the Baltic it became Peter's ambi-
tion to create a great occidental capital at Petersburg (now Leningrad), one that differed in every respect from Moscow. For this purpose he secured the services of European architects, engineers and artists, the most outstanding of whom were the Frenchman, A. Leblond,
and the Italian, Domenico Trezzini. The best-known work of the latter was the Church of Saint Peter and Saint Paul, which was far removed in design from the traditional Russian-Byzantine churches.
Leblond built the summer residence of the tsar, the palace of Peterhof,
in the Regency style, later altered by Rastrelli.

THE VICTORY AT POLTAVA (1709)

The Russian artist A. Kotsebu depicts Peter the Great on horseback.

Of the numerous Dutch, German, French and Italian architects and craftsmen employed by Peter, the majority were, unfortunately, second or third rate. Not infrequently a structure designed by an Italian, started by a German, was continued by a Frenchman or Dutchman, with the inevitable result that the new capital on the Neva lacked architectural unity. St. Petersburg became a hodgepodge of French, Dutch, German and Italian Baroque, and little or no attempt was made to assimilate the foreign styles with the Russian.[1] With the advent of Peter, Russian art, which had been essentially religious, became secular and was divorced from the art of the people. The new Western forms appealed only to the aristocracy. It remained for a later generation of Russian artists, trained abroad, to improve the architecture of St. Petersburg.

With his customary energy, the tsar took the initial steps to provide a modicum of secular education for children of the nobility and gentry. With very limited success, his schools attempted to promote the study of the three R's, mathematics, and science, as a minimum, in order to enable young Russians to qualify for service under the requirements of the new "Table of Ranks." With a view to furthering education of a more popular character, Peter established the first public newspaper, *Vedomosty,* in 1703, and in the same year authorized the erection of the first public theater, the Comedy House, at Red Square.[2] Thus the initiative in education, as in so many other fields, came from the state, and education was thereafter carefully controlled by the state.

In his zeal to reform his subjects, Peter did not forbear to interfere with the minor details of their daily lives. He commanded all of them to adopt European dress. He forced the men to shave their abundant beards and made the women abandon their Oriental seclusion. Although such regulations could not be enforced throughout the length and breadth of Peter's domains, his officials and those Russians within the reach of the long arm of the Government had to conform. Taxes were imposed on those who failed to do so. Despite Peter's harsh rule, he won popular respect by his unaffected, oft-times coarse behavior, and because he often conducted himself as if he were one of the "common people." His great height of six feet seven and his huge frame were also not without effect in arousing respect and inspiring fear.

---

[1] See Voyce, A., *Russian Architecture,* pp. 11-13.
[2] In 1672 the Comedy *Khoromina* was constructed near Moscow at the summer residence of Tsar Alexei Mikhailovitch. Nine plays were presented there, the majority on biblical themes. This was not, however, a public theater.

The clergy, the *boyars,* and those who opposed Western ideas in general, censured his methods, citing his private life, which was indeed far from immaculate, as an evidence of his depravity and characterizing him as the "Deformer" of Russia. He was, however, above all things, heart and soul a Russian, and the practices and customs which he opposed were for the most part outmoded or were relics of the Mongol period. The reforms which he forced upon his people contributed in general to their welfare and progress. His vision extended far beyond that of his Russian contemporaries. He had a great intellect and a great mission, and from this standpoint he was indeed the Reformer of Russia.

Unfortunately the institution of serfdom became more firmly established during his reign. His great building projects, for instance the construction of St. Petersburg and his initiation of a canal project to link the capital with the upper Volga, required much forced labor by the serfs, which caused control of them to become stricter and more harsh. To meet the increased burdens of government, Peter resorted to innumerable taxes on land, wearing apparel, implements, food, birth, and marriage, most of which weighed upon the peasants. His poll tax and his passport system, which made it illegal for peasants to move from a locality without the proper credentials, contributed still further to bind them to the soil. The only mitigation in the lot of the serf was the introduction of a law forbidding the sale of individuals among them; henceforward "the family must be disposed of as a unit."

Years later the opposition to Peter's reforms was still reflected in the works of the renowned Russian historian, N. M. Karamzin (1766-1826), who voiced the sentiment of the nineteenth century Slavophiles as follows: "We became citizens of the world, but ceased in some respects to be citizens of Russia." Under the Soviet regime, especially since the inauguration of the Five-Year Plans, new emphasis has been placed by Soviet writers on the constructive aspects of the policies of Peter the Great. They have found much to approve in Peter's program of industrialization, his attitude toward the *boyars* and the Church, his emphasis on the obligation of all individuals to serve the state, his tolerance of minorities, and his establishment of Russia's "window" on the Baltic. They have been inclined to see in Peter's program the beginnings of a planned society which is now a major aspect of Soviet policy. The historical novel, *Peter I,* by Alexei N. Tolstoy, and Sergei Eisenstein's film based upon it, have done much to rehabilitate and popularize Peter in the USSR.

EXTERNAL POLICY

At Peter's accession in 1682 Russia had already wrung from Poland at least nominal sovereignty over the Ukraine, although the Turks still barred the way to the Black Sea and the Swedes prevented access to the Baltic. Peter energetically addressed himself to the task of further Russian expansion at the expense of Turkey and especially of Sweden. During his long reign there were scarcely two years of peace. Nevertheless Peter established Russia as a first-rate military and naval power, with an ice-free port on the Baltic.

As the first step in his plan of expansion, he resolved to advance against the impregnable Turkish stronghold of Azov. A campaign of this nature necessitated an army drilled to the last degree of perfection in military tactics, and Peter had long been preparing such a force. The regiments which he had drilled as a boy in the village of Preobrazhenskoye were now seasoned, disciplined troops. Their long training produced valuable results, for in spite of initial setbacks the unconquerable Azov was surrendered to the Russians in 1696. During Michael's reign it had once been taken by the Cossacks, but they had been unable to hold it without assistance from Moscow. Turkey was to regain the fortress by the Treaty of Pruth in 1711, but the Russians recovered it in 1736. The effect of Peter's victory upon Russia and all Europe can hardly be overestimated. At one stroke, he made of Russia a power which could no longer be ignored in European politics. It became clear that Russian armies, organized and armed in accordance with Western techniques, were once again, as in the days of Ivan Grozny, assuming the offensive. Peter promptly fortified the Azov area and established a fleet of some eighty vessels there in 1699. In the same year the appearance of his fleet at Kertch constituted a demonstration of Russian naval power in the Black Sea, and a challenge to exclusive Turkish domination of that area, which prompted the Sultan to conclude a thirty-year truce with Russia. At home Peter took care to ascribe his success to his European reforms and gained thereby much support for his policy of Europeanization.

After the success at Azov, Peter resolved to attempt a peaceful penetration of the West before following up his plans against Sweden. He hoped to bring about an alliance of all Christian European nations, with Russia as the leader, against the Turks and Mohammedans in general. If this plan succeeded, he believed that he would be able to deal with Sweden and to acquire the territory he sought without war. He therefore began to organize a suite which should accompany him on a tour of the principal countries of Europe, for the purpose of observing and studying all phases of the life of the people. This suite was known as "The Great Ambassadors of the Tsar" and consisted of some 270 persons selected with the greatest care by Peter himself. Although their mission was unofficial and Peter traveled incognito as Peter Mikhailovitch, its prime purpose and his great ambition was to secure for Russia a place of dominance among the nations.

The "ambassadors" left Russia in March 1697 and visited many of the chief cities of Europe, such as Riga, Königsberg, Amsterdam, London, Leipzig, Dresden, Prague, and Vienna, gaining much valuable information thereby, but Peter's plan for a great European alliance did not materialize. The time was not propitious. Europe was torn by the conflicts of the Hapsburgs and the Bourbons, and although there had been general satisfaction over the fall of Azov, the great powers had no intention of looking to Russia for future leadership. Realizing that he could not secure the alliance, Peter abandoned his efforts and returned to Moscow in August 1698.

In this connection it is important to note that the group of carefully selected young men who accompanied Peter abroad and who were expected thereafter to play a leading role in the Europeanization of Russia, also imbibed the advanced political theories current in Britain and other parts of Western Europe. No sooner was Peter dead than they demanded a constitutional government for Russia. They may, in fact, be regarded as the progenitors of the Decembrists of 1825 and of subsequent agitators for political reform.

Immediately after his first European tour Peter began preparations for a campaign against the Swedes, whose military prestige, under the brilliant leadership of Charles XII (1682-1718), was soon to startle the world. In order that he might not be harassed by attacks from other sources, he sought and secured treaties with King Augustus II of Poland and King Christian of Denmark. By the summer of 1700 he had also negotiated a treaty of peace with Turkey. Thus assured, he began the campaign against Sweden, which developed into the Great Northern War (1700-1721). In his initial efforts Peter met with constant reverses. The battle of Narva ended in a disastrous defeat for the Russian forces, and it required four years of dogged persistence and stubborn fighting on his part before he was able to conquer the desired Swedish territory of Ingria. Finally he became master of the site which he had long had in mind as a desirable "window to Europe," and in May 1703, he was at last able to found his new capital of St. Petersburg and make arrangements for the creation of a

PETER THE GREAT

Baltic fleet. The campaign and the building of the city caused so much suffering and cost so many lives that discontent and rebellion became general. Peter was nevertheless able to put down all revolts effectively. Then came the overwhelming defeat of the Swedes in the great battle of Poltava in 1709 in the Ukraine. Peter was once more the national idol, and popular discontent was stilled.

Peter's initial reverses in his conflict with the Swedes led to the introduction of important military reforms in Russia. To secure a larger professional army he instituted a kind of compulsory universal service, by which all single men from fifteen to twenty, and all married men from twenty to thirty, were liable for service and received a modicum of training to prepare them for the regular army, into which they were drafted as needed. From 1705 to 1709 Peter resorted to annual conscription to raise an army of around 300,000 men, with which he was able to rout the Swedish forces at Poltava.

Although Sweden's power was broken and she was henceforth forced to assume the defensive, Charles XII escaped to Turkey. There he had little difficulty in inciting the Turks, never very friendly to Russia, to declare war late in 1710. The struggle which followed was nothing but a series of defeats for the Russian forces. The situation seemed so hopeless that Peter was ready to sue for peace when overtures for a cessation of hostilities came from Turkey. By the Treaty of Pruth in 1711, Russia lost Azov, but was not compelled to pay any more severely for her sorry showing throughout the war. This fortunate turn of affairs for Russia has been credited to efforts put forth by Peter's second wife, Catherine.

In 1716, five years after the Russo-Turkish War (1710-1711), Peter the Great made a second European tour. His first visit, nineteen years earlier in 1697, had been chiefly for the purpose of collecting information and establishing diplomatic relations. Upon this occasion, however, he was concerned mainly with scientific matters. At a very early age he had evinced a deep interest in science, and during his reign he had lent encouragement and assistance to scientific enterprise. Thus, immediately upon his accession to the throne, he had taken cognizance of the efforts of his energetic Cossacks, who were blazing new trails in Siberia, and had sent to their aid certain Swedish prisoners of war, who gave them intelligent guidance and taught them "to build sea-going vessels, to use nautical instruments and to construct modern maps." Peter was likewise instrumental in bringing about the discovery and exploration of Kamtchatka and the Kurile Islands, which took place between 1700 and 1715. When reports of these accomplishments reached the scientific world, the scholars of Western Europe began to pay homage to Peter and to the achievements of Russian men of science. Oxford University conferred upon him an honorary doctor's degree, and the Paris Academy made him one of its members. Therefore when he came among European scientists in 1716-1717, he was cordially received and urged to make explorations for the purpose of determining once and for all whether Asia and America were united.

Upon his return to Russia in 1718, Peter therefore ordered two of his officers, Fyodor Luzhin and Ivan Yevreinov, "to go to Kamtchatka and farther . . . , and determine whether Asia and America are united; and go not only north and south but east and west, and put on a chart all that you see." Although this expedition (1719-1722) failed to establish the fact in question, it was not entirely without results.[1] Peter's interest did not flag and on December 23, 1724, shortly before his death, he drew up orders for further explorations, thereby paving the way for the famous Bering[2] expeditions (1725-1730; 1733-1742), the Gvozdev[3] expedition (1731-1733), and the Baranov[4] explorations (1790-1818).

---

[1] The question whether Asia and America were united was not answered until the coming of another Russian, Baron Ferdinand Wrangel, who, during the winters of 1821 and 1823, walked along the Arctic coast from the Kolyma to Kolyutchin Island.

[2] Vitus Bering, born in 1681 at Horsens, Denmark; died in 1741 on Bering Island. In 1704 he joined the Russian navy with the rank of sublieutenant. By 1724 he was promoted to captain of the first rank and was put in charge of the expedition. See Lauridsen, Peter, *Vitus Bering,* translated by Olson, Chicago, 1889; Golder, F. A., *Bering's Voyages,* Vol. I, 1922, p. 8. See also Berg, L. S., "The Three-Hundredth Anniversary of the Discovery of Bering Strait by Semyon Dezhnev (1648-1948)," *Soviet Press Translations,* Vol. IV, March 15, 1949, pp. 178-184.

[3] Michael Spiridonovitch Gvozdev, a Russian officer, is believed to be the first of his nationality to sight America, although he was not aware of the fact. He saw the American coast on September 1, 1732, but thought, however, that he had discovered an "island."

[4] Alexander Andreyevitch Baranov (1746-1819), head of the Russian American Company for nearly twenty-eight years and first governor of Russian America, rendered valuable service in the North Pacific. Under his direction the Russian possessions in the New World attained their widest extent. In 1796 he established a colony on Bering Strait. In 1799 he took possession of the largest of the Sitka Islands (now Baranov Islands), began trade with the natives, and subsequently extended his operations to Canton, the Hawaiian Islands, Boston, New York and other distant regions. He also founded a small colony in California, near the present site of San Francisco. See Andrews, C. L., "Baranof the Builder," *The Washington Historical Quarterly,* Vol. VII, No. 3, pp. 215-216; and Kiril Khlebnikov's *Zhizneopisanie Alexandra Andreyevitcha Baranova (The Life of A. A. Baranov),* St. Petersburg (Russia), 1835. Consult also Golder, F. A., *Guide to Materials for American History in Russian Archives,* Washington, D. C., 1917; Golder, F. A., *Russian Expansion on the Pacific. 1641-1850.* Cleveland, 1914.

"When Bering's second expedition came to an end in 1749," says F. A. Golder,[1] "Bering Strait had been discovered, the Arctic coast of Asia from the White Sea to the Kolyma River had been charted, and the North Pacific coast of America from Cape Addington to Bering Island had been placed on the map. This was Russia's share in the work of discovery and exploration, and a very important contribution to geographical knowledge it was."

Thus it was that, stimulated by Peter's energy and encouragement, explorations were made which opened a window to America and eventually solved the problem as to "whether Asia and America are united." Although Russia's territorial expansion elsewhere was distinctly imperialistic, the explorations in America were motivated chiefly by scientific interest, albeit "for the benefit and glory of Russia" (Russian Senate).

Despite the loss of prestige which the clash with Turkey had cost him, Peter did not relinquish his efforts to force from the Swedes the Baltic territory he desired. In 1721 his persistence finally triumphed, when Sweden by the terms of the Treaty of Nystadt ceded to Russia the entire Baltic coast from the strategic port of Viborg (Viipuri) to Riga, thus bringing to an end several centuries of conflict. Finland proper was to remain in Swedish possession until 1809. Russia, having eclipsed Sweden, now loomed as one of the major powers, a fitting rival of France, Prussia, and England. Peter's window on the Baltic was to have important economic and cultural effects upon Russia. In recognition of his conquests the grateful Senate bestowed upon him the titles, "Father of his Country," "Emperor," and "The Great" (Pater Patriae, Imperator Maximus). In order to strengthen his hold upon the Baltic region, Peter sought to win foreign support by means of diplomatic marriages. His daughter, Anna, was married to the Duke of Holstein; his niece, Catherine, to the Duke of Mecklenburg, whereas another niece became the wife of the Duke of Courland. These marriages for the sake of diplomacy were productive later of much misfortune to Russia. With his window on the Baltic secure, Peter in 1722 turned to the southeast to the Caspian Sea, where in the course of the following year he was able to win an important cession of territory, including Baku, from the Shah of Persia.

Peter's success in the Baltic may be said to have marked the culmination and well nigh the end of his career. Despite his robust constitution, he was not destined to reach extreme old age. Early in No-

---

[1] *Bering's Voyages*, p. 5.

vember 1724, he happened to see a boat in distress. Always courageous, he plunged into the icy water to go to its assistance. He was seized with an illness as a result of this exposure from which he never recovered. He died on February 5, 1725, at the age of fifty-three.

THE SUCCESSORS OF PETER THE GREAT, 1725-1762

Peter's heir apparent, his son Alexei by his first wife, Eudokia Lopukhina, whom he put away in 1698, had been murdered by Peter's own orders in 1718. Another son, Alexander, died at an early age. Although Peter in 1722 had issued a law enabling the tsar to select his own successor, he died without expressing a decision in this respect. Because of the influence of Menshikov and his lieutenants, Peter's second wife succeeded to the throne as Empress Catherine I (1725-1727), the first of a series of women to become autocrat of all the Russias. Her accession, which was an unheard-of innovation, far greater than the regency of Sophia, aroused the bitterest opposition, and many adherents of the Orthodox Church submitted to torture rather than take an oath of allegiance to her. They objected to her not only because she was a woman and not of royal descent, but also because she had been a captive and, although legally the second wife of Peter, her repute was scarcely more than that of his mistress.[1] Nevertheless, despite all opposition she was crowned Empress in May 1724 and succeeded him to the throne on February 19, 1725. Her short reign was marked by no significant event and was in reality merely a sequel to the reign of Peter. Shortly before her death (May 17), she named as her successor Peter's grandson, Peter, son of the murdered Alexei by his first wife, Sophia Charlotte of Wolfenbüttel. Next in the line of succession she named her daughters, Anna of Holstein and Elizabeth.

Peter II was twelve years old at the time of his accession and lived only three years longer, dying of smallpox on the eve of his marriage. Considering his extreme youth and short reign, we would not look for any startling changes or spectacular events during this period. As

---

[1] She was of obscure origin, possibly Lithuanian, and a Lutheran. Her parents died when she was very young and a preacher's family, Glück by name, took her into their home as a servant. In 1701 she married a soldier in the Swedish army, but, only two days after the marriage, she was taken prisoner by Russian soldiers and separated forever from her husband. Because of her beauty, Field Marshall Boris Petrovitch Sheremetiev made her his mistress. Later General Menshikov took her into his house. Here Peter I saw her and fell in love with her, made her his mistress, and three years later, his wife. She was only twenty years old at the time of her marriage to Peter.

a matter of fact, however, his reign was marked by certain significant occurrences, which seemed to give confirmation to the fears of Peter I that his reactionary offspring would utterly destroy everything that he (Peter) had accomplished with so much difficulty. In any event, the Church and the *boyars* again became active participants in public affairs and the Imperial Court was transferred from St. Petersburg to Moscow, although the former city still remained the capital.

When Peter II died the Supreme Secret Council took up the matter of succession, and passing over the daughters of Peter the Great, offered the throne to Anna of Courland (1730-1740), allegedly the daughter of Ivan, who had shared the throne with Peter I until 1696. Before her coronation, a movement was set on foot to transform the government from an absolute to a limited monarchy, in accordance with the English example of 1688. The sponsors of this change were not able to rally enough adherents to their support and the attempt failed.

Anna's reign was a period of debauchery and foreign influence. Governmental and court positions were in the hands of Germans from the Baltic area. These officials, who knew nothing and cared less about Russian ideals and temperament, and who could not even speak the language, rode roughshod over the people's rights and outraged every national feeling. Chief among them was Anna's favorite, Count Johann Ernst Biron, Duke of Courland (1690-1772), who enjoys the unenviable reputation of being the most unpopular German in Russian history, and who, to all intents and purposes, became the real ruler of Russia. Under his direction the foreign policy of the country was characterized by disgraceful retrogression. Russia's meddling in Polish affairs brought her little credit. In a war with Turkey (1733-1739), General Münnich won brilliant victories, but since no advantage was taken of them, Russia failed to secure access to the Black Sea. Even the Persian conquests of Peter the Great were lost, when in 1732 Russia voluntarily relinquished to Persia certain cities on the Caspian Sea. Although Russia participated in an alliance with Austria and England against France and Prussia in the War of the Austrian Succession (1740-1748), she was snubbed by both sides and peace was made at Aix-la-Chapelle without her.

Anna led so corrupt a life that it shattered her health and caused her death. She had named as her successor her young grandnephew, Ivan VI, but had appointed Biron as regent. The country, however, had had more than enough of Biron. As has been indicated elsewhere, the Russian people would tolerate debauchery and misrule in the case of a legitimate ruler but absolutely refused to endure the same things from a foreigner. Biron was speedily removed from power and sent to Siberia, where he remained for twenty years. Anna's choice of a successor was disregarded, and the crown was offered to Elizabeth, daughter of Peter the Great. She became Empress on November 25, 1741, and early the following year the boy, Ivan, was put under arrest in order to avoid complications and plots.

During the years 1725 to 1741, Russia was almost constantly subject to foreign influence. One foreign party or another at court was usually able to control the governmental policy and the distribution of official positions. By reason of their family connection with the royal line, the Germans were the most numerous and powerful among the foreign favorites. The period came to be known as the "period of favorites."

The Empress Elizabeth (1741-1762) began her reign auspiciously by removing Germans from office and appointing Russians in their places. This produced universal satisfaction among all classes, which welcomed the end of the "German yoke." The rejoicing was somewhat premature, for although the period of favorites had come to an end, foreign influence was by no means eliminated. In Elizabeth's reign French influence came into prominence, especially along cultural lines, where it contended for supremacy with German and English influence until the middle of the nineteenth century. Russia stood on the threshold of the Age of Enlightenment which reached its zenith under Catherine II.

In establishing intellectual contacts with France, Elizabeth was inspired by a sincere desire to contribute to the cultural advance of her country. Her ideas of progress were in accord with those of her father and she directed her efforts toward the education and improvement of her subjects. With this in mind and realizing that the theater was an educational force of tremendous power, she established the Russian Theatre by the *ukaz* of August 30, 1756, and provided for a theatrical staff. Elizabeth was determined that her subjects should have the benefits of the theater whether they wished it or not. Therefore, when performances were scheduled, she sent her servants into the streets with directions to secure an audience by force if necessary. Likewise when she discovered that the clergy had become deplorably lax, both morally and intellectually, she made a determined effort to raise ecclesiastical standards.

Stimulated by her encouragement, the progress made in arts and letters was noteworthy. The year 1755 (January 25) marked the founding of the University of Moscow, which soon attained academic prestige and contributed greatly to the·development of Russian scholarship. Among the leading scholars of the time we find the famous physicist, poet, and artist, Mikhail V. Lomonosov (1711-1765), son of a lowly fisherman from the White Sea region, and the historian. V. N. Tatishtchev (1686-1750), who began writing his *History of Russia from the Most Ancient Times,* which appeared during the reign of Catherine II. Several other writers, who were to become prominent during the latter's reign, began their work under Elizabeth. Among them was the great artist and playwright, A. P. Sumarokov (1718-1777), director of the first St. Petersburg theater, who has been called the "Russian Racine."

Elizabeth shared Peter's zeal for new construction. The chief architect of her reign, Rastrelli the Younger, trained in France, built the Winter Palace, an outstanding example of Russian Baroque, and also Tsarskoe Selo, the Russian "Windsor Castle," the interior of which was noted for its lavish rococo decoration. In 1758 Elizabeth founded the Academy of Fine Arts, which she staffed with French artists from the Académie Française, and which in the course of time produced a new generation of Russian architects, such as Starov. Bazhenov, Kazakov, Veronikhin, and Zakharov.

Elizabeth's government also took steps to stimulate agriculture and industry. Banks were established, from which landowners could borrow money for the improvement of their estates. Promising sons of merchants were sent to Holland at government expense in order to become acquainted with the latest methods of business procedure. The mining industry was encouraged, and commerce with the East increased enormously in volume.

Despite her subservience to French intellectual influence, Elizabeth was intensely patriotic and won the good will of her subjects thereby. She intended to treat them kindly but often failed, either through the influence of bad advisers or through a mistaken conception of justice. For example, she was of a very liberal turn of mind and left to herself would have been very tolerant, no doubt, in her dealings with the various religious minorities in her realm. Members of the clergy, however, brought pressure upon her, and at their instigation she closed Roman Catholic churches and Mohammedan mosques and forced many Jews to leave the country. When there was a rebellion to be put down or a vice to be checked, she shrank from exacting a death penalty, resorting instead to banishment and flogging as punishment for crimes. However, the floggings were so severe that they usually caused the victim's death!

Elizabeth's reign was marked by several events of importance in foreign relations. In 1743, Sweden ceded to Russia the territory of the Finns east of the Kuno River. In the Seven Years' War (1756-1763), Russia joined with Austria and France against Frederick the Great of Prussia. In conjunction with the Austrians, Russian forces under General Saltykov defeated Frederick in battle at Kunersdorf in 1759. In 1760 Russian troops temporarily took possession of the city of Berlin but reaped no benefits therefrom, for Elizabeth died and her successor, a fanatical admirer of Frederick the Great, brought the campaign to an abrupt termination.

Immediately after her ascent to the throne, Elizabeth had named as her successor, her nephew, Karl Peter Ulrich, Duke of Holstein, son of her sister Anna. In 1742 he came to St. Petersburg, where he adopted the Greek Orthodox faith and was baptized as Grand Duke Peter Fyodorovitch. He was then proclaimed the heir apparent. Elizabeth selected as his wife Sophia Augusta, daughter of the Prince of Anhalt-Zerbst. She likewise accepted the Greek Orthodox faith, being baptized as Catherine. This princess later became Catherine II, known as Catherine the Great.

Peter's sympathies had always been intensely pro-German, and upon Elizabeth's death he speedily restored the German influence which she had been at such pains to eradicate. "Bironism" returned once more to plague the country. The new emperor's first step was to make a peace with Prussia on April 22, 1762, by the terms of which Russia lost every shred of the advantage which her victories should have brought her. Nevertheless the presence of large numbers of Russian troops in Prussia made a lasting impression upon Western Europe and may well have served to prevent the further expansion of Prussia at the expense of Russia. Peter would have been glad to ally himself with Frederick the Great of Prussia against Austria and France, but popular feeling ran too high to make it expedient for him to go so far. As it was, his complete about-face in foreign policy estranged Russia's former allies in Western Europe.

In order to detract attention from his unpopular foreign policy, Peter followed the suggestion of certain of his German advisers and on March 2, 1762, issued a manifesto with the intent of disarming the hostility of the nobles. This manifesto freed them from compulsory service to the state, and while it did, in a measure, do away with their opposition, it stirred up discontent in another quarter, which was productive of nearly a century of seething ill-will. The peasants, whose lot was still immeasurably wretched, had their hopes raised by the manifesto and eagerly awaited a second manifesto which would alleviate their predicament. With perfect logic they reasoned as follows. The nobility had held their lands contingent upon service to the state, that is, they were required to furnish revenue and, in time of war, men. The peasants, who were attached to the land, served the nobles and hence indirectly the state. Since the nobles were now freed from compulsory state service, they could no longer demand service from the peasants. However justified their expectations were, the unfortunate peasants were doomed to disappointment, for the manifesto freeing them did not appear until March 3, 1861.

Peter alienated and disgusted his subjects by his vulgar and ridiculous behavior, not less than by his unpatriotic foreign policies and sympathies. When under the influence of drink, he would rail against everything Russian and heap abuse upon the clergy and the Orthodox Church. Toward his wife, he was brutal, not forbearing to insult her publicly. With great astuteness, she never permitted him to shake her self-control. She was ever on the alert, however, to seize any opportunity of ridding herself and the country of a creature who had none of the qualities of a sovereign. When Peter had finally tried the patience of Russia beyond endurance, she took an active part in stirring up the revolt which deprived him of his throne. She was aided and abetted in this by certain officers of the Guard, some of whom later became her favorites.

On July 12, 1762, less than a year after his accession, Peter was forced to abdicate. His death followed shortly afterwards. It was officially announced that he died of colic, but a current rumor attributed his demise to a wound given him in the course of a drunken brawl by one of Catherine's favorites. Catherine had already been proclaimed Empress and absolute monarch. Her son, Grand Duke Paul, was named as her successor.

REIGN OF EMPRESS CATHERINE II, THE GREAT
(1762-1796)

INTERNAL POLICY

The internal reforms and foreign policies of Catherine the Great, the outstanding representative of enlightened despotism in Russia, were in many respects an extension of those instituted by Peter I, while in Russian annals her reign stands second in importance to his alone. An indefatigable worker and the possessor of a fine intellect, she spared no pains to increase her own intellectual equipment or to promote the interests of her country as she saw them. Perhaps her most short-sighted policy was her intensification of the bondage of the serfs and her continual support of the upper classes at their expense. Although she was keen enough to realize, as later events have borne out, that an autocracy which has the support of the powerful upper classes need not trouble itself about the discontent of the impotent submerged groups, she failed to comprehend that the peasant problem was a kind of social volcano, upon which the superstructure of society rested precariously. One of the most significant occurrences of her reign, although not the first in chronological order, was the peasant revolt, which arose from her failure to ameliorate the lot of these people.

It will be remembered that the peasant population eagerly hoped for a manifesto in their favor, following the nobles' manifesto of 1762. Time went on, however, and nothing was done to improve their condition, which, on the contrary, rapidly became more wretched. To be sure, Catherine passed a law to prevent free men and freed peasants from being reduced to the status of serfs and likewise forbade the selling of peasants during times of military conscription. The serfs on Church lands also benefited by her legislation, but in general she showed an absolute lack of comprehension of the plight of the peasants and the serious problem created thereby. By her legislation, they lost the small remnant of liberty still left them and became actual slaves, the personal property of their respective owners. She even instituted laws which forbade them to complain of the treatment they received from their masters!

The nobles, on the other hand, were granted an increasing number of privileges, among which were exemption from taxation and military service. They even gained the right in 1765 to banish rebellious serfs to Siberia and, in general, disregarded all claims of humanity in dealing with them. In addition Catherine constantly favored the upper classes with a view to strengthening her numerous favorites, who enjoyed unusual benefits.[1] Consequently revolts of the lower classes, espe-

---

[1] Catherine's favorites, while numerous, were often men of ability, who gave her efficient service in furthering her policies of internal reform and foreign expansion. Among these favorites were the Orlov brothers, Gregory and Alexei. Above all others, however, stood Gregory Potemkin (1739-1791) who enjoyed Catherine's favor to an extent without precedent. She esteemed him for his loyalty and intelligence, showered great wealth upon him and made him governor of "New Russia," as the southern territory was called. Much of this was conquered by him. See Kyzevetter, A., *Istoritcheskie Siluety*, Berlin, 1931, pp. 7-123.

cially the Cossacks, became frequent, and in 1773 the matter came to a head.

In that year there appeared in the Urals a Cossack by the name of Emelian Pugatchev (1726-1775), who proclaimed that he was the Emperor Peter III. The death of the latter had been so sudden, and the circumstances surrounding it so clothed in secrecy, that several persons had already claimed to be the deposed ruler. Although Peter had had neither the respect nor the liking of his subjects, the oppressed classes merely sought an excuse for an uprising, and his reinstatement furnished as good a pretext as any. In addition to announcing a program for the extermination of the hated nobility, Pugatchev also injected into his revolt a religious element. He was one of the Old Believers, who had suffered more than a little through the Church reforms. Indeed the peasants had become convinced that they owed their wretchedness in great part to these reforms which had seemed to advance merely the interests of the upper classes while their lot became continually worse. Moreover the country had just been ravaged by an epidemic of cholera which appeared to indicate the aroused wrath of an outraged deity. Hence Pugatchev had little difficulty in giving his revolt religious significance. In addition Russia's war with Turkey and Poland made the moment for revolt most propitious. He announced his purpose as follows: "We shall behead every noble in the land. We shall make the true faith prevail and take over the land for ourselves." In a brief space of time, he collected a large number of followers with whom he instituted one of the most ghastly periods of bloodshed in the history of Russia. As in the case of Razin, he was betrayed by his own followers and was executed in 1775. His uprising, however, was not without results. Since it coincided with the American Revolution, it aroused serious concern in Russia. The more thoughtful among the upper classes began to feel that something must be done to improve the condition of the serfs and keep the system from spreading. This popular demand for a more even-handed justice to all classes of society did, after many years, produce some readjustments.[1] For the time being, however, the government was content to take measures to strengthen the landowners against any possible repetition of the revolt.

Fifteen years later the plight of the serfs was boldly described in the guise of a dream by a nobleman, Alexander N. Radishchev (1749-1802), in *A Journey from St. Petersburg to Moscow*

---

[1] See *The Evil Empress* by Grand Duke Alexander of Russia. Philadelphia, 1934.

(1790).[1] Radishchev, who had been sent abroad to study at the University of Leipzig, was imbued with the ideas of the French philosophers of the Age of Enlightenment, including those of Voltaire, Montesquieu, Mably, and Rousseau. Upon his return he served in the Senate and in the "College" of Commerce, where he became head of the St. Petersburg Customs House. His *Journey,* printed by his own private press, was the first Russian book to attack the institutions of serfdom and autocracy, thereby antedating Turgenev's famous *Memoirs of a Sportsman* (1847-1852) by half a century. "Tremble, hard-hearted landlord," said Radishchev, "for on the brow of each of your peasants I read your condemnation." The Pugatchev revolt and the French Revolution having cooled Catherine's ardor for reform, she denounced Radishchev as a worse rebel than Pugatchev. He was condemned to death, but the sentence was commuted to exile in Siberia, where Radishchev remained until after Catherine's death.

Whereas Catherine's policy in regard to the serfs was narrow and short-sighted,[2] in other respects she was very liberal. In imitation of Peter the Great, she was careful to limit the powers of the Church and kept it strictly subordinate to the state; however, she engaged in no religious persecutions. On the contrary, she offered a refuge to all who suffered such persecution in other lands. In 1771 as many as 26,000 refugees came to Russia. In 1785 she followed the example of Emperor Joseph II (1741-1790) of Austria and issued an "Edict of Toleration," which permitted freedom of worship to all creeds. She even gave official support to Mohammedanism, which flourished especially in the middle eastern part of Russia. Pursuant to her policy of toleration, she at first befriended and protected the organization of Free Masons, which began to spread throughout Russia at this time. Later, however, the mystery with which they surrounded their rites aroused her suspicions, and, fearing that they were engaging in political intrigues, she enacted laws against the organization and imprisoned its leaders.

---

[1] As recently as 1948 only one excerpt from *A Journey from St. Petersburg to Moscow* was available in English. See Hecht, David, "Alexander Radishchev; Pioneer Russian Abolitionist," *The American Review on the Soviet Union,* Vol. VII, August 1946, pp. 45-50.

[2] Recognizing that nothing was to be hoped for from Catherine in this matter, those who wished to bring about an amelioration of the lot of the serfs and at the same time a limitation of the powers of the nobles, sought the support of Catherine's son, Paul. He feared for himself the fate of Tsarevitch Alexei, son of Peter I. Indeed at the time of her death in 1796, Catherine actually had in preparation a manifesto which was to deprive Paul of his right of succession and give the throne to her grandson, Alexander.

In matters of education Catherine was unusually progressive, so that her reign was a period of unparalleled intellectual activity, although French influence was measurably increased. During the first part of her reign she took great delight in French ideas and did much to disseminate them throughout the country. She admired Voltaire greatly and corresponded with him from 1763 until his death in 1778. She likewise carried on a correspondence with Diderot, D'Alembert, Grimm, and other leading representatives of the Age of Enlightenment. Under her influence, French, the international language of Europe in the eighteenth century, became the language of the Russian court; and Russian writers began to translate the works of Molière, Racine, Corneille, LaFontaine, Montesquieu, and, above all, Voltaire, and to compose works of their own in imitation. Indeed French became the chief medium through which the ancient classics of Greece and Rome, as well as those of English and German origin, reached Russia. The Russian aristocracy was thus subjected to an infusion of Western culture, and its members hired French tutors for their children.

Like the enlightened despots of her time, and like her immediate predecessors in Russia, Catherine had a passion for building. Already throughout Europe the ornate baroque style was giving way to Roman classicism. Catherine II, who shared the revived European interest in the classical monuments of ancient Rome, with characteristic energy devoted her attention to the construction of palaces, public buildings, villas, and private residences. The Russian architect, Starov (1743-1808), the first of the Classic School to graduate from Elizabeth's Academy of Fine Arts, built the Tauride Palace of Prince Potemkin, which in later years housed the Russian Duma. Catherine showered her favorites with villas and residences. Other structures of note in the classic style include Quarenghi's Theater of the Hermitage, Cameron's addition to Tsarskoe Selo, and his restoration of the fifteenth century Palace of the Khans in the Crimea. Such classical models were copied throughout Russia by members of the Russian aristocracy. Catherine's grandson, Alexander I, carried on the classical tradition, although his predilection was for Greek rather than Roman models.

Catherine was much in advance of her contemporaries in realizing the value of popular education and its importance with regard to character and training for citizenship. In order, therefore, to make education more general, she appointed in 1782 a "Committee for the Establishment of Public Schools." Although she did not believe universal education to be feasible for a country the size of Russia, she did give

CATHERINE THE GREAT

additional stimulus to the schools for children of the nobility, which she had founded as early as 1764.

Following in the footsteps of Peter the Great, Catherine established a Russian Academy in 1783. She encouraged the study of medicine, sending for foreign physicians, who could bring new knowledge and practices to her countrymen. At that time smallpox was widespread and usually fatal. Louis XV of France and the children of the King of Spain were among the royal victims of the dread disease. Inoculation was just coming into use and to introduce it into her country, Catherine took the decisive step of being the first to submit to the process. This took no little courage, considering the superstition of the day and her own age of 40 years. The people soon followed her example and inoculation became general. The Senate bestowed upon her twelve gold medals and put up the following inscription in the Senate House: "She saved others to the danger of herself." It was due to her efforts that a Department of the College of Pharmacy was founded at Moscow. Always a patron of arts and artists of whatever nationality, she set aside in one year 1,000,000 rubles for the purchase of valuable works of art. She also gave to the new Russian theater the benefit of her patronage.

Catherine's personal accomplishments along intellectual lines are little short of amazing. She read widely, studied constantly, and became exceedingly well versed in European literature and philosophy. She neither inaugurated any new policy nor instituted any reform without having made it the subject of painstaking study and investigation. Her intellectual accomplishments were not merely the passive results of scholarship, for she wrote extensively on subjects which ranged from fairy tales and satires on manners to erudite treatises on pedagogy and the science of government. Thus for her grandsons, Alexander and Constantine, she compiled the first children's textbook in Russia. It was known as the "Grandmother's A B C Book" and consisted of tales of history. One of her most scholarly accomplishments was the compilation of "Complementary Notes" for the first volume of the first dictionary of the Russian language, which was issued in six volumes, during the years 1789 to 1799 and contained 43,257 words. The work was re-edited from 1840 to 1850.

Under the influence of her example and the encouragement of her patronage, it is not surprising that able men of letters made their appearance and that there was an unprecedented increase in literary productivity. The period boasts such great men as G. R. Derzhavin (1743-1816) and Denis Ivanovitch Fonvisin (1745-1792), together with a host of lesser literary lights. In addition, following Catherine's example, approximately seventy other women took to writing during her reign and made valuable contributions to Russian letters. As a result of their beginning the nineteenth century produced some 1200 emulators among Russian women in the field of Russian literature. Outstanding among them were U. V. Zhadovskaya, Marko Vovtchok, and Gan. Activity was likewise manifested in journalism, and several periodicals made their appearance. In short, Catherine's broad culture and intelligent patronage of the arts, sciences, and letters gave Russia much intellectual prestige throughout Europe.

It was while Catherine was still under the influence of Montesquieu and Beccaria that in 1767 she summoned a Legislative Commission of 564 delegates, representative of all parts of the country and of all classes, except the serfs and the clergy. Her immediate objective was the formulation of a new code of laws. Catherine's *Instructions* (*Nakaz*)[1] to the deputies, according to the Russian historian, V. O. Kliutchevsky, constitute her "political confession," and Voltaire lauded them as the finest monument of the eighteenth century. The *Instructions* were, within a few years, translated into practically every language in Europe, with the result that Catherine became, for a time, the cynosure of all reformers.

In the *Instructions* Catherine expressed herself unqualifiedly in favor of religious toleration and in opposition to the use of torture and capital punishment. She called for a Code of Laws, written in the vernacular and available to all at no greater cost than the Catechism. On the subject of slavery, Catherine's conclusions were even at this time largely negative. She urged the deputies to shun all occasions for the further reduction of people to slavery, except in cases of dire necessity, but opposed any general measure of emancipation. Other sections of the *Instructions* bearing upon economic conditions called for a more judicious method of taxing the peasants, encouragement of agriculture, greater freedom of commerce with all peoples, and other progressive ideas. In view of the fact that England was at this time on the eve of the Industrial Revolution, it is of interest to note Catherine's skepticism about the use of machines in manufacturing, except in the case of goods for export. As regards education, her advice was chiefly directed toward parents, who were enjoined to imbue their children with fear of God and love of country.

---

[1] See Reddaway, W. A. (ed.), *Documents of Catherine the Great* (Cambridge, England, 1931), pp. 215-309.

These and other recommendations indicate that Catherine covered a wide range of subjects, and that, although she took pains to justify her own absolute authority, she was sincerely convinced that even an absolute ruler should govern in the interests of the people. The members of the Legislative Commission, who were required to re-read her *Instructions* monthly, worked diligently for seventeen months, but with the outbreak of the Turkish War in 1768 their sessions were suspended. There seems little doubt, however, that Catherine had implanted in the minds of many people the idea that the best government was the one that shackled freedom the least. The precepts to which she committed herself in writing, although soon violated and never incorporated in the projected code, could scarcely be eradicated.

It is not without interest that the Russian dramatist, Fonvisin, in his play, *The Minor,* was able even as late as 1782 to make guarded references as to how a monarch should conduct himself. In the words of Fonvisin:

The most stupid peasant in the village is usually chosen to pasture the herd, because it does not require much wit to tend cattle. A Tsar who is worthy of his crown endeavors to elevate the souls of his subjects. This we see with our own eyes. . . .[1]

The final statement is, of course, a direct reference to Catherine.

As indicated by the *Instructions,* Catherine gave serious thought to the economic problems of the country. To improve the credit system, she abolished the banks that Elizabeth had established for the benefit of the landowners and opened in their place a "State Loan Bank" with a capital of 1,000,000 rubles, which lent money to all classes at an established interest rate of 5 percent. It was also empowered to issue bank notes. Soon paper currency likewise came into general use. With the improvement of credit, factories began to spring up. More than 2000 were built, which employed a steadily increasing number of workmen. Under Catherine's encouragement and protection, foreign colonists began to enter the country. The population increased from 13,000,000 at the end of the reign of Peter I to 40,000,000, which led to the founding of nearly 200 towns. This, together with the new territory acquired by expansion, led to a re-division of the empire in 1775 on the basis of the census, whereby the twenty provinces of Peter I were increased to fifty.

---

[1] See Noyes, G. R., *Masterpieces of the Russian Drama* (1933), pp. 76 ff.

FOREIGN AFFAIRS

The period under consideration was marked by the acquisition of much territory by Russia. The possibility of expansion in the Far East began to arouse considerable interest, but the central government was too much occupied with foreign affairs nearer at hand to give the matter much attention. Therefore such progress as was made in that direction was the work for the most part of adventurous traders, who penetrated into the most remote regions. It must not be overlooked, however, that Catherine's policy of religious toleration to all creeds contributed not a little to this program of expansion, inasmuch as the population of the eastern territories was largely Mohammedan. In the course of time, settlements were planted as far east as Alaska and the neighboring islands. This advance, however, was not adequately followed up until a later day.

In the West the problem of foreign expansion was much more immediate. Catherine was determined to regain the considerable Russian territory which had come under Polish control and to wrest from the Turks that region extending to the natural frontier of Russia on the shores of the Black Sea. The Turks, alarmed at the prospects of further Russian expansion at their expense, precipitated a conflict in 1768 by invading the Crimea. In the course of the first Turkish War General Peter Rumyantsev (1725-1796) was able to defeat the Turks and cross the Danube. This war was likewise notable, in that it marked the first appearance of the Russian Baltic fleet in the Mediterranean, with the subsequent annihilation of the Turkish Navy in the Aegean (1770).

The Treaty of Küchük Kainarji in 1774, concluded largely as a result of the Pugatchev revolt, is a landmark in Russian diplomacy. By this treaty Russia became a Black Sea power, her right to free navigation of its waters being duly recognized, as was her control of its northern shores from the Bug to the Dnieper. With a Turkish pledge to permit freedom of religion in the provinces of Moldavia and Wallachia, Russia emerged as the champion of Orthodoxy in the Balkans. Although the treaty merely stipulated the "independence" of the Crimea, this region was annexed by Catherine within a decade (1783). The treaty of 1774 was of great significance in all future international settlements with reference to the Black Sea and the question of the Dardanelles, as well as in regard to the protection of Orthodox Christians under the Ottoman Empire. The stage was set for the role of Turkey as the "sick man of Europe" in the nineteenth century. One of Catherine's favorites, Gregory Potemkin, was placed in charge of the newly acquired territory and he lost no time in promoting its development.

It is sometimes customary to divide Catherine's foreign policy in the West into two periods, with the year 1780 as the line of demarcation. The so-called first period, prior to 1780, witnessed the establishment of the "Northern Accord," an alliance of Russia, Prussia, Poland, Sweden, Denmark, and England against Austria and France. The fact that Poland was a member of the "Accord" did not prevent Catherine from taking steps to secure the coveted Polish territory, with the result that Poland was arbitrarily partitioned three times in the course of her reign in 1773, 1793, and 1795.

With regard to Poland, Catherine as early as 1763 had intrigued to place her own candidate, Stanislas Poniatovski, on the Polish throne. Using the religious issue—a cardinal feature of her policy toward both Turkey and Poland—Catherine joined forces with Frederick the Great of Prussia and Maria Theresa of Austria to effect the first partition in 1773. Poland helped to precipitate her own downfall by her internal dissensions, her failure to respect treaties, and her persecution of various religious sects, particularly Orthodox worshippers.[1] Nor was the entire population of Poland hostile to the advent of Russian control. Many of the nobility and the Catholic priests, as well as the Jewish population [2] of the Polish Ukraine, had suffered horribly at the hands of the Ukrainian Cossacks, the "Haidamaki." From time to time these "Haidamaki" would rise in retaliation for the persecution of Orthodox believers and leave a trail of massacre and devastation in the regions inhabited by the aforementioned classes of citizens. Those who believed that Russia would put an end to this reign of terror were not averse to partiton, and there was always a small faction—in contem-

---

[1] As early as 1591, certain Orthodox bishops, residing in territory taken by Poland from Russia, were advised to approach King Sigismund III with suggestions of the desirability of a union between the Orthodox and Catholic Churches. As a result, in 1595, a petition was presented to the Pope, asking him to take over the control of the West Russian Church and a council was called for the following year to consummate the union. The deliberation of the council resulted in a disagreement between the Uniates and their opponents. Naturally the king supported the Uniates and maintained that a union of the Churches had been effected. Orthodox believers who refused to conform were deprived of the right to hold public office of any kind and were heavily taxed for the benefit of the Catholics. Their religious books were subject to Catholic censorship, and they were not permitted to repair, much less build, churches.

[2] The Jews, because of their business ability and knowledge of languages, were extensively employed by the Polish government to collect taxes and enforce certain unpopular measures. Acting under instructions, they were often compelled to resort to drastic methods, which aroused great hostility against them.

porary terminology, a fifth column—that actively supported it. Of course the masses of the people bitterly resented foreign dominance, as their frequent revolts have testified.

Russian acquisitions by the first partition were confined to territory in northeastern Poland, occupied mainly by White Russians. In the years that followed the Poles proved unsuccessful in reorganizing their government to resist outside pressures, although the interlude between the first and second partitions was one of marked progress in the intellectual and financial spheres. Even the new Polish Constitution of 1791 —which provided for a hereditary instead of an elective monarchy, abolished the notorious *liberum veto,* and introduced a bicameral legislature—promoted internal dissension. The French Revolution and the preoccupation of Austria with French affairs made it possible for Prussia and Russia to carry off a second and more drastic partition in 1793. Indeed Catherine discreetly let it be known abroad that she was curbing Jacobinism in Warsaw while her allies sought to do the same in Paris. The heroic efforts of the renowned Polish patriot, Thaddeus Kosciuszko, failed to offset the losses Poland had suffered or to prevent the final partition of that unhappy land among the Russians, Austrians, and Prussians in 1795.

By the three partitions Russia secured Eastern Poland, including the old Grand Duchy of Lithuania and large areas occupied mainly by White Russians and Ukrainians (Little Russians). It was only in the final partition that the Russians acquired large numbers of Polish subjects. The new Russian frontier, except for eastern Galicia, was not unlike that re-established by the Soviet Government in the fall of 1939, after the outbreak of World War II.

The transition to the second period of Catherine's foreign policy was marked by the proclamation of the "Act of Armed Neutrality" (1780). This measure affirmed the right of neutral ships to trade with belligerent nations in all commodities save war supplies. It was a product of the American War of Independence and was designed to obstruct the English in their efforts to subdue the rebellious colonies. It should not be assumed, however, that Catherine, already embittered by the Pugatchev revolt, looked with favor on American revolutionaries. Although the United States, as early as 1781, sent Francis Dana to St. Petersburg to obtain recognition of the young republic, he accomplished nothing. Indeed, Catherine viewed the American "rebels" in much the same light as many Americans have regarded Russian Communists in our own day. Thirty-three years elapsed before Russia finally recognized the American Government in 1809.

Catherine was more concerned, during these years, with the implementation of her famous "Greek Project" (1782), which was announced during the celebration of the birth of her grandson, who was appropriately enough named Constantine. Voltaire was responsible for giving Catherine the idea of the "Greek Project," which he discussed in detail with her. This project had as its objective the banishment of Turkey from Europe, the establishment of a Greek Empire under an Orthodox monarch at Constantinople, and the division of the remaining Turkish possessions among European nations. As a first step in this direction Catherine established an alliance with Austria. Of course the immediate result was a conflict with Turkey, which was further complicated by a struggle with Sweden, not to mention the usual Polish problem. Although the "Greek Project" failed to materialize, Russia consolidated her territorial gains and put an end to the Tartar menace. Turkey continued to resent Catherine's imperialistic designs, and in 1787, partly as a result of English pressure, hostilities began on a large scale. Under the leadership of the brilliant Russian general, Alexander Suvorov (1730-1800), who stormed the great fortress of Ismail, Russia again emerged triumphant, and by the Treaty of Yassy in 1791 acquired additional territory on the Black Sea between the Bug and the Dniester and on the Sea of Azov, including the fortress of Otchakov. The entire north shore of the Black Sea fell into Russian hands.

Sweden had taken advantage of the Turkish war to attack Russia in 1788. Two years later, however, the Peace of Verela left the boundaries of the two countries as they were before hostilities began. Thus, under Catherine, Russia regained all the "Western Lands" lost in previous centuries, with the exception of Galicia, and extended her boundaries to the Black and Azov Seas. By way of analogy it may be said that both Peter and Catherine strove to increase Russia's prestige among the powers. But whereas Peter's methods were autocratic and based on the use of force, Catherine, as in the case of the Polish partitions, made effective use of diplomacy.

As elsewhere in Europe, the outbreak of the French Revolution in 1789 at first evoked great enthusiasm in Russia among the nobility and intellectuals—even those as high in station as the grandsons of the empress, Alexander and Constantine.[1] In Paris a prominent representative of the Russian colony, Count Paul Stroganov, even joined the Jacobin Club and expressed a desire to witness a similar cataclysm in

---

[1] See Lobanov-Rostovsky, Andrei, *Russia and Europe, 1789-1825*, Chap. I, pp. 3-30.

Russia. The excesses of the revolutionaries soon dampened the enthusiasm of the proponents of the revolution in Russia, and Catherine,
who had never shared it, severed diplomatic relations with France in
October 1789. Although she confined herself to promises of aid for
her Austrian ally, granted subsidies to needy French *émigrés,* and
signed a treaty of "friendship" with England in 1793, by which, among
other things, she agreed to close Russian ports to French ships, Catherine bluntly rejected a British request that she send an expeditionary
force to the Rhine. In spite of her opposition to the French Revolution,
Catherine continued to pursue measures short of war until her death
in 1796.

That Catherine was able to reign over Russia for thirty-four years,
without an altogether legitimate claim to the throne, is a real tribute
to her political genius. There can be no doubt but that her initial role
as the patron of liberal and progressive ideas, regardless of the fact that
she failed in large measure to put them into practice, contributed to
her popularity, not only in Europe, but in Russia, especially among the
upper classes. Thus her reputation was that of an "enlightened" despot.
Moreover, her consistent support of the upper classes, often at the expense of the masses, helped to establish the security of her position.
Revolt, as in the case of the Pugatchev uprising, came mainly from
the lower classes, and, without leadership and organization from above,
it was suppressed. Chiefly, however, Russian military victories and
territorial acquisitions from Turkey and Poland contributed greatly
to Catherine's prestige and served, as such expansion has always served
under a despotic regime, to quell discontent at home.

REIGN OF EMPEROR PAUL (1796-1801)

INTERNAL POLICY

Paul was in many respects the direct opposite of his mother, Catherine II. At an early age he had been taken by the Empress Elizabeth
and reared under her supervision. As a result he was scarcely acquainted with his parents and early developed a great antagonism toward his mother, which increased with the years. He held her
responsible for the death of his father and disapproved of her private
life and governmental policies, including the partition of Poland. Upon
his ascent to the throne he was forty-two years of age, but so physically
and mentally broken that many of his contemporaries, as well as later
historians, believed him to be insane. Despite this, and his short reign

of five years, he was responsible for some very important innovations in the laws and customs of the land, not all of which were detrimental. Intent upon reversing, or at least mitigating, the results of some of Catherine's policies, Paul hastened to release all Polish prisoners in St. Petersburg, including Kosciuszko, who received a grant of 60,000 rubles and permission to set out for the United States.

Paul had long been of the opinion that, with the exception of the peasants, all classes of society had been granted too many concessions by his predecessors, with the result that the monarch had lost much of his autocratic power. He began his reign, therefore, with a reassertion of the principle of absolute autocracy, plus a strengthening in every possible way of his own personal authority. That all classes of society might feel the weight of his authority, he issued statements and promulgated legislation which established him as the supreme head of all institions, both civil and ecclesiastical.

It will be recalled that by the reforms of Peter I the Church became distinctly subordinate to the state, and was placed under the control of a specialized department of the government, the Synod. At this time, as far as the government and the upper classes were concerned, it lost its worth as a source of spiritual influence. It was tolerated solely as an institution, which dispensed a necessary moral "opiate" to the lower classes and thus reconciled them to their miserable condition. Paul revived the power of the Church as a moral influence but, at the same time, made it completely subject to his authority. He was the first to give precise expression to the doctrine, "The Tsar is the head of the Church." This doctrine was definitely incorporated into the laws of the empire under Nicholas I (1825-1855). In this way he made Church control synonymous with autocratic control and despotism, for which reason the Church never gained the support of the upper classes of society and the intelligentsia. From the reign of Paul almost up to 1917, the more thoughtful classes of society recognized that the revival of Church authority meant the institution of reactionary policies and despotic rule.

In order to compel general recognition of his supreme authority, Paul demanded that his subjects pay him the most servile homage upon all occasions. When he appeared in public all persons were required to fall upon their knees in token of their submission, irrespective of the condition of the streets at the time. Anything which savored of democracy and equality was anathema to him; hence he was extremely hostile to such tendencies as were manifested in France. He even forbade the wearing of certain articles of apparel which were in vogue among the

French Jacobins, while he eliminated from court language some of their favorite words, such as "citizen." Moreover no Frenchman was allowed to enter Russia unless he had a passport bearing the signature of the Bourbon princes, thus proving that he would not be a source of revolutionary propaganda.

In order to isolate his subjects from the slightest taint of foreign revolutionary influence, Paul no longer permitted foreign books, or even music, to be imported. Permission was also refused to any who sought to leave the country for travel or study and those who had already done so received peremptory orders to return. As a matter of course, the theater and press were subjected to the most rigid censorship.

In contrast to his dislike and suspicion of everything which emanated from democratic France, Paul had a considerable predilection for anything of Prussian origin. For instance he abolished the army uniform so admirably adapted to Russian needs and substituted in its place Prussian military dress, which was characterized by powdered wigs, buckled shoes, and similar unsuitable articles of attire. General Suvorov regarded the new uniforms as objectionable in the extreme and is reported to have said: "Wig powder is not gun powder; curls are not cannons; a pigtail is not a sabre; I am not a Prussian, but a Russian." He paid for this expression of opinion by being exiled to his village.

As the culmination of his efforts to re-establish an absolute autocracy, Paul issued on April 5, 1797, the "Law of Succession to the Throne." This law established the principle of primogeniture in Russia.

In the measures considered thus far, the policy of the emperor was reactionary. On the other hand, his attitude toward the serfs revealed him to be far more progressive than any of his immediate predecessors; the *ukaz* which he promulgated in their behalf was of the greatest importance and subsequent influence. As will be remembered, serfdom had its beginnings in 1581 during the reign of Ivan Grozny, when the peasants became "fixed' to the soil for a limited term of years. From that time forth, the period of fixation was continuously lengthened, and the liberties of the peasants were increasingly curtailed until they virtually became slaves through the legislation of Catherine II. Not the least of Paul's objections to what he deemed the injudicious concessions of his mother to the upper classes originated from his conviction that these concessions were made at the expense of the peasants, who were existing under oppression well-nigh unendurable. It had also been pointed out to him that in time of war the serfs constituted a most serious problem. He was therefore the first ruler for many generations to enact legislation in their favor. While he was not able to institute so revolutionary a measure as a complete emancipation of the serfs, he issued an *ukaz* limiting their compulsory service to three days a week. Although this law was not strictly enforced, it became a guiding principle for succeeding monarchs. Whereas all rulers before Paul aided in intensifying the bondage of the serfs, each one thereafter made serious efforts to improve their condition until they finally attained their freedom under Alexander II.

FOREIGN POLICY

Despite the stigma of insanity attached to him, Paul did manifest some good judgment in his foreign policies. As a gesture of peace, he recalled Russian forces stationed in Persia and relinquished suzerainty over the state of Georgia. He also sought and secured a friendly understanding with Turkey, hoping by this means, rather than by force of arms, to extend the scope of Russian influence to include the regions bordering on the Mediterranean and Adriatic Seas.

Affairs in Europe were destined to assist him in his ambitions in this direction. The chief European powers had become exceedingly alarmed by the aggression of France and her steady expansion. Already she had brought under her control all of Switzerland, northern Italy, and the Ionian Islands, where Orthodox Greeks made up the bulk of the population. Although under Catherine Russia had played no more than a nominal role in the First Coalition against France, and Paul at first abandoned all idea of sending an expeditionary force to the Rhine, he was gradually converted to the need for concerted European action to forestall further pretensions on the part of the French. Paradoxically enough, Paul, who entered into negotiations with the Knights of St. John over their property rights in Poland, was persuaded to assume the position of Grand Master of this Catholic Order, when in 1798 Napoleon occupied their headquarters at Malta. Paul seems to have dreamed of the possibility of a crusade against France. Concerned about the French threat in the eastern Mediterranean following Napoleon's occupation of Egypt, Paul was persuaded in December 1798 by William Pitt the Younger to join the Second Coalition, which ultimately included Austria, England, the Kingdom of Naples, Russia, and her ally, Turkey.

Meanwhile, in collaboration with Turkey, he undertook to liberate the Ionian Islands from French "tyranny." A Black Sea squadron under the command of Admiral Ushakov was ordered to proceed to the

Adriatic where, with the backing of a few Turkish warships, the public support of the Greek patriarch at Constantinople, and the favorable disposition of the local population, the French were expelled from the Islands. A republic was established in the Ionian Islands, nominally under Turkish control, but in reality a dependency of Russia. Thus Paul's ambition approached realization, since a Russian base had been secured in the Adriatic, from which he could exercise control over the Orthodox and Slavonic population of the Balkan regions. In 1799 the Prince-Bishop of Montenegro, a country which had maintained relations with Russia since the reign of Peter the Great, voluntarily sought an alliance with the Russian emperor, thereby promoting still further his designs in the Adriatic.

In accordance with the terms of his alliance with Austria, Paul dispatched a Russian expeditionary force to Italy under the leadership of the brilliant General Suvorov, who had been designated commander-in-chief of the Austro-Russian armies in that part of Europe, which included some 52,000 men. Suvorov's spectacular offensive drove the French from Italy, and the elderly Russian general became a popular idol in Western Europe. Suvorov medals, hats, feathers, portraits, etc., became the fashion of the day. Suvorov, himself, when directed to evict the French from Switzerland, performed the well-nigh impossible task of crossing the Alps late in the season via the St. Gothard Pass. Unfortunately friction had developed between Suvorov and the Austrians, who were none too enthusiastic about the whirlwind Russian campaign which they were unable to control, and they withdrew from Switzerland, leaving Suvorov to face French armies that were greatly superior in numbers. As a result the Russian losses were heavy.

Another expeditionary force of 12,000 men, which Paul had dispatched by sea to effect a joint landing with the English in Holland, met with disaster, allegedly because of the military inefficiency of the Duke of York. Convinced that both his Austrian and English allies had failed to co-operate, and incensed by the English occupation of Malta in 1800, Paul abruptly recalled his armies and withdrew from the Second Coalition. Making a complete about-face in policy he revived Catherine's League of Armed Neutrality against England and entered into peace negotiations with Napoleon. The two erstwhile enemies planned a joint expedition against the English possessions in India. On January 12, 1801, Paul actually ordered the dispatch of 22,000 Cossacks by the overland route to India. He pictured in the most glowing terms the glory, wealth, and imperial favor these Cossacks would gain and the service they would render their country.

No adequate preparations had been made, however, for the long and arduous march they were to undertake. In consequence, although eleven regiments actually set out, half of their horses were lost in the desert, the forces became utterly demoralized, and the campaign dwindled to a miserable conclusion.

The break with England had disastrous consequences for Paul. His autocratic and violent rule had aroused much hostility against him in Russia, especially in military circles, where his wrath found vent in wholesale banishments. The English, who were aware of this, proceeded to make use of it to their own advantage. An English fleet under Nelson was dispatched to the Baltic, where it completely destroyed the Danish fleet at Copenhagen. English agents began to foment opposition against Paul, who was assassinated on March 24, 1801. He was succeeded by his son, Alexander I.

REIGN OF EMPEROR ALEXANDER I (1801-1825)

Like his father, Alexander was brought up apart from his parents, for the Empress Catherine II had taken him at an early age and had trained him as her own son. The tutors she selected were instructed to educate him "in accordance with the laws of reason and the principles of virtue." One of these men was Frederick Caesar Laharpe (1754-1838), a native of Switzerland and a devotee of liberalism and republicanism. A great friendship grew up between teacher and pupil, and Alexander became so imbued with the principles he was taught that he believed to the end of his life that he was a republican. Shortly before his death, Alexander said: "They may say of me what they will; but I have lived and shall die a republican." Although the republicanism which he championed bore little resemblance to present-day conceptions, nevertheless his policies and government were regarded by his subjects as such an improvement over those of his father that they referred to him as the "angel." Many of them, however, especially those closely associated with him, were not unaware of his subtle and devious diplomacy. Possessed of a pleasing personality and a persuasive tongue, he was able to win people to his way of thinking and then, by skillful flattery, he led them to believe that the ideas in question had originated with them. In this way he gained support and avoided opposition. He also accomplished much by winning the favor of women, with whom he was very popular because of his personal charm. These practices caused certain of his contemporaries to characterize him as being "as sharp as a pin, as fine as a razor, and as false as seafoam."

In conformity with his republican leanings, Alexander began his reign with very liberal ideas. The censorship was relaxed, foreign books were once again imported, and the ban on foreign travel was withdrawn. Alexander commissioned a group of his progressive friends, including Count Paul Stroganov, Prince Adam Czartoryski, Nicholas Novosiltsev, and Count Victor Kochubey, to serve as a Committee of Public Welfare with the object of drafting a program of reform for Russia. Laharpe was called back to St. Petersburg to advise them. However, the opposition of the conservative nobility and the course of European events outside Russia were destined to cool Alexander's ardor for reform. His "splendid beginnings" gave way to a regime of reaction and autocracy. Inasmuch as outside influences were so potent in altering internal policies, it seems appropriate to turn first to the foreign policy of Alexander I.

FOREIGN AFFAIRS

With respect to foreign affairs, the reign of Alexander tends to divide itself naturally into two periods. The first period extended from 1801 to 1815 and was occupied chiefly by the struggle with Napoleon. The second period embraced the years 1815 to 1825 and witnessed the concerted efforts of the powers, under the aegis of the Holy Alliance, to maintain the *status quo* in Europe against the resurgent forces of revolution.

Although Alexander's initial move, upon his accession to the throne, was to recall Paul's India expediton, thereby preventing a possible war with England, his relations with France remained for the time being outwardly friendly. The murder of the Duke d'Enghien at the instigation of the French Government in 1804 led to a breach of relations with France and to Russian participation in the Third Coalition (1804-1807) of Russia, Austria, England, and Sweden against Napoleon. There followed a series of setbacks for the Russian forces at Austerlitz (1805), Eylau (1807), and Friedland (1807) which, after the brilliant victories of Rumyantsev and Suvorov in the preceding reigns of Catherine and Paul, Alexander found particularly humiliating, especially since he had disregarded the advice of his commanding general, Mikhail Kutuzov (1745-1813), a former pupil of Surorov. The Russian emperor was equally bitter over lack of support from his Austrian and Prussian allies, the latter having met with complete disaster at Jena (1806), and at the failure of England to furnish a promised detachment of 10,000 to 15,000 troops. He thereupon performed an about-face in foreign policy, as startling as that executed by the Emperor Paul before him, when, on June 25, 1807, he came to terms with Napoleon at Tilsit on the Niemen River in East Prussia, and the two leaders prepared to divide the world between them.

By the terms of the Treaty of Tilsit Alexander was given a free hand against Sweden, including the right to annex Finland and thereby remove a threat to the near-by capital of St. Petersburg. In return he agreed to adhere to Napoleon's Continental System, which prohibited all trade with England, and, should the English refuse to make peace, even to enter the conflict against her as an ally of the French. The alliance envisaged the eventual partition of the Ottoman Empire, provided that the Turks failed to come to terms with Russia. Thus Alexander, the former leader of the anti-French bloc on the continent, became the ally of Napoleon and his partner in the struggle for world domination. This reversal in foreign policy was extremely unpopular among the Russian nobility in general, but it did provide the Russian armies with a breathing spell, which was used by Alexander to secure possession of Finland (1809) in a war against Sweden, to bring about the termination of hostilities with Turkey, which had dragged on from 1806 to 1812, as a result of which the Russians acquired Bessarabia, and to reorganize the Russian forces for a renewal of the struggle with Napoleon.[1]

The Franco-Russian alliance did not put an end to the mutual distrust of Napoleon and Alexander. The involvement of Napoleon in the uprising in Spain after 1809 led the Russians to encourage Austrian and Prussian opposition to Napoleonic domination, and Alexander became more evasive in his dealings with the French emperor. In 1810 a revised Russian tariff, designed to offset some of the detrimental effects of the Continental System in Russia, placed heavy duties on wines and luxuries, most of which were imported from France. Both sides violated the terms of the Treaty of Tilsit, the French by annexing the Grand Duchy of Oldenberg, whose ruler was an uncle of the tsar, and the Russians by failing to live up to the letter of the Continental System. By 1811 it became apparent that the renewal of hostilities between France and Russia was just a matter of time.

---

[1] For an opinion to the effect that Alexander never considered the agreement at Tilsit as other than a truce in his struggle against Napoleon, see Strakhovsky, Leonid I., *Alexander I of Russia*, N. Y., Norton, 1947, pp. 71-108.

Both Napoleon and Alexander began to prepare feverishly for the approaching struggle. Napoleon assembled some 600,000 men (the Grand Army), and was in a position to array all of Europe, with the possible exception of Sweden and Turkey, against Russia. In spite of the timely warning of General Armand de Caulaincourt (1772-1827), French Ambassador in St. Petersburg, to the effect that Napoleon would encounter stiff resistance from a united Russian nation, the Grand Army crossed the Russian frontier at the Niemen River near Kovno in June 1812.

It is inevitable, as a result of World War II, that the invasion of Russia in June 1812 by Napoleon should recall the invasion in June 1941 by Nazi Germany. Like Hitler, Napoleon seems to have expected that *Blitzkrieg* tactics and one resounding victory like Austerlitz or Friedland would bring Alexander quickly to terms. After all, he had an army of 600,000 at his disposal as compared with fewer than 200,000 for the Russians. But the Russian armies retreated before him, avoiding battle wherever possible, and carrying out a scorched earth policy. After the French capture of Smolensk, popular outcry resulted in the recall of Kutuzov to command the Russian forces. Kutuzov faced the French army at Borodino, about seventy-five miles west of Moscow. In one of the bloodiest battles of the war, the French lost 30,000 men, together with 49 generals, and the Russians, 18 generals, 1732 other officers, and 35,000 men. The Russian retreat nevertheless continued, even Moscow being evacuated and abandoned to the enemy.

The burning of Moscow has been termed the turning point of the war.[1] Napoleon was confronted with the prospect of spending the winter in a devastated and looted city, without adequate supplies of food and clothing, in the midst of a hostile population. Any expectations he may have had of arousing the peasants against the tsar had failed to materialize. Any hopes that he may have entertained of dictating peace in Moscow were likewise doomed to disappointment. For the Russians this had become a war for national survival.

When, on October 20, Napoleon undertook his now famous retreat from Moscow, over the same route by which he invaded Russia, Cossack cavalry harried his rear, Russian partisans prevented his army from acquiring the necessary supplies, and Kutuzov's armies virtually destroyed his forces. When the French crossed the Russian frontier into Prussia early in December, the Grand Army had been reduced to a

---

[1] See Lobanov-Rostovsky, *op. cit.*, p. 228.

NAPOLEON'S RETREAT FROM MOSCOW

bare 30,000 of the 600,000 troops that had entered Russia just six months before.

Many reasons have been assigned for the defeat of the Napoleonic forces in the campaign of 1812. It has been ascribed to the weather, to the vast open spaces of Russia, to the polyglot composition of Napoleon's armies, to the Russian tactics of retreat, to the fact that Napoleon extended his lines too far, to the resistance of the Russian people, and to other reasons. In this connection, the well-known historian, Lobanov-Rostovsky, gives the following estimate:

> No war has been more generally misinterpreted in history than Napoleon's campaign in Russia. Too readily it has been dismissed with the statement that Napoleon was driven out by the cold. In saying this, historians forget that they thereby merely endorse Napoleon's "war propaganda"— the official explanation which Napoleon gave Europe to account for his defeat and make it appear an "act of God" for which he could not be responsible. Thus accepted, the legend of the defeat of the Grand Army by the cold in Russia has crept into history, and this superficial view has been repeated glibly ever since.[1]

He goes on to point out that the French defeat was due to a combination of military, national, and geographical factors. The contemporary Soviet historian, Eugene Tarle, interprets the campaign of 1812 as a people's war and suggests an interesting parallel between the Russian and Spanish campaigns:

> Not the cold and not Russia's vast expanses conquered Napoleon, but the resistance of the Russian people.
>
> The Russian people asserted their right to an independent national existence; they asserted it with an indomitable will to victory, with the true heroism that despises all phrases, with a surge of spirit unequalled by any other nation save the Spanish.
>
> The Russians revealed greater physical strength and material potentialities than Spain. Within six months Napoleon's hordes were dispersed and destroyed in Russia, while the Spaniards, despite their equally indisputable heroism, took five years, even with the immense help given them by England, to get rid of Napoleon—and ultimately succeeded in 1813 in direct consequence of Napoleon's defeat in Russia.[2]

With the liberation of Russian territory from the invader, Alexander was at once faced with the decision as to whether to carry the conflict

---

[1] Lobanov-Rostovsky, *op. cit.,* p. 212.

[2] Tarle, Eugene, *Napoleon's Invasion of Russia—1812,* N. Y., Oxford, 1942, pp. 408-409.

to foreign soil or to make peace with Napoleon. Contrary to the advice of the ailing Kutuzov, the tsar decided to continue the conflict until Napoleon's downfall was assured. The war lasted another two years, during which time Russian losses in man power were greater than those of any other nation which joined the Fourth and Fifth Coalitions. Napoleon's retreat was marked by the great Battle of Leipzig, September 16-19, 1813, commemorated as the Battle of the Nations. In January-February 1814 the allied armies crossed the Rhine into France. Although England and Austria were at first disposed to make peace with France without further delay—a development which evoked profound discord among the allies—Alexander, with the support of Prussia, insisted on the continuation of the conflict until Napoleon was overthrown. At Chaumont the four great powers, upon British initiative, signed a twenty-year alliance by which they agreed to continue the war and to make no separate peace. On March 31, 1814, the allied troops entered Paris. Shortly thereafter Napoleon abdicated, and on May 30, 1814, the First Treaty of Paris was signed, leaving France with the boundaries of 1792.

No sooner was victory in sight than the deep-rooted divergences of opinion among the great powers came to the fore. Alexander had entered Paris in triumph as the liberator and "savior" of Europe. The unprecedented display of power by the Russian army, and Russian pressure in favor of moderate terms for defeated France, aroused the fear and jealousy of England and Austria, whose representatives, Metternich and Castlereagh, began to suspect that they had destroyed one colossus only to be confronted with another, and that Alexander's expansionist program constituted a threat second only to that of Napoleon.

This rift among the allies reached its climax at the Congress of Vienna, which began in October 1814. Here Alexander's program for a united Poland, with himself as monarch, and with compensation elsewhere in Europe for Prussia and Austria, almost broke up the Conference. The efforts of Castlereagh and Metternich to line up all the powers, including France, in opposition to Russia failed when Prussia, in the expectation of compensation in Saxony, continued to support Alexander. The deadlock over the Polish-Saxon issue was broken by the sudden return of Napoleon from Elba, which rendered compromise imperative and Russian military participation indispensable. In the compromise that ensued it was agreed that the greater part of Poland should be established as a constitutional monarchy under Alexander, with Prussia receiving two-fifths of Saxony. Russian expansion on the continent proved to be moderate, as compared with the acquisitions of Prussia and Austria, as well as the colonial acquisitions of Britain.[1] Following the defeat of Napoleon at Waterloo and the conclusion of the Second Treaty of Paris on November 20, 1815, the Russians for several years maintained an army of occupation of 27,000 men in France.

It was at Paris, in September 1815 that Alexander proclaimed his celebrated Holy Alliance of European powers pledged to conduct their relations in accordance with the "precepts of justice, Christianity, charity, and peace." During the closing stages of the Napoleonic conflict Alexander had come under the influence of the Baroness Julia von Krüdener, an exponent of the mysticism and pietism then spreading rapidly throughout Europe in the wake of the war. He became convinced that the principles of Christianity, if applied to international policies, would lead to an exalted conception of international relations and thus prevent wars in the future.

The Holy Alliance was signed by all European nations with the exception of England, the Papal State, and Turkey. Its "Covenant" stated that the "supreme truths dictated by the eternal law of God the Saviour" should be the basis of the government of the league and that international questions should be decided "by no other rules but the commandments of this sacred faith, the commandments of love, truth, and peace." However, there was a further stipulation in the pact which was extremely significant. The members of the Alliance were to govern their various subjects "as fathers of their families," and each was pledged to go to the assistance of any other if need arose. Although the Holy Alliance was generally regarded as too vague and mystical to be practical, the renewal by the Second Treaty of Paris of the twenty-year alliance of the four great powers (Quadruple Alliance) provided the machinery for the implementation of these precepts.

After the European settlement of 1815 the power and prestige of Russia remained undeniably great in Western Europe. Through the French foreign minister, the Duke de Richelieu, who had spent many years in the service of Russia, Alexander for some time exercised a preponderant influence over the affairs of France. That influence was exerted in 1818 at the Congress of Aix-la-Chapelle, to secure the withdrawal of the allied occupation forces from France and the admission

---

[1] Russia obtained 2100 square miles of territory with a population of more than 3,000,000; Austria received 2300 square miles and a population of 10,000,000; and Prussia got 2217 square miles, with a population of 5,360,000. (See Lobanov-Rostovsky, *op. cit.,* p. 352.) England obtained from France the islands of Malta, St. Lucia, Tobago, Mauritius, and the Ionian Islands; from the Netherlands, Ceylon, part of Dutch Guiana, and South Africa; and from Denmark she took Heligoland.

of that country to the Concert of Europe. Although Alexander at first supported the establishment of liberal constitutions in the German states of Saxe-Weimar, Württemberg, and Baden, with the resurgence of revolution and violence in Europe, he became increasingly alarmed. Beginning with the Conferences of Troppau (1820) and Verona (1822), which were concerned respectively with revolution in Naples and Spain, Russia lined up with Metternich on the side of legitimacy and the *status quo*. Henceforth the Holy Alliance began to serve in practice to make the world safe for autocracy. Thus in 1821, when the Greek Christians rebelled against Turkish despotism, they met with no sympathy at first on account of their disobedience to a lawful ruler.

The United States was invited to become a member of the Holy Alliance, a league which at first Americans regarded sympathetically. When it became apparent that the Alliance served as a tool of despotism and reaction in Europe, however, American sympathy was alienated. While the Alliance curbed the expansionist ambitions of its members in Europe, including those of Russia, it may have served to direct Alexander's attention to the Pacific Northwest. In 1821, in what amounted to unilateral action, he issued an official *ukaz* which closed the entire North Pacific from the Bering Straits to the fifty-first parallel to the trade and navigation of any foreign power. Only Russian ships were to be permitted to approach within 100 Italian miles (115 English miles) of the territory of the tsar in this region. Needless to say, this *ukaz* aroused the antagonism of all Americans, especially the commercial and fur-trading interests of New England, who were concerned about the future of the Pacific Coast. In 1822, when Russia and France, as members of the Holy Alliance, expressed their readiness to lend military support to Spain in her efforts to recover Spanish America, the United States was still more alarmed by the extent of European encroachments, which by now amounted to a pincer movement. The immediate result was the proclamation of the Monroe Doctrine on December 2, 1823, which warned Russia and all other powers against intervention in the American hemisphere. On April 17, 1824, the United States and Russia reached an accord with regard to the Northwest which removed the danger of a future clash between these two countries in the Pacific.

As a result of World War II and the obvious parallels afforded by the Nazi and Napoleonic invasions of Russia, there has been in the Soviet Union a great revival of interest in, and a general reinterpretation of, the age of Alexander I.

INTERNAL POLICY

As previously stated, Alexander began his rule with liberal ideas. Two serious problems confronted him, both of which he endeavored to solve in accordance with humanitarian and progressive ideals. The first had to do with the institution of serfdom. Alexander would have been glad to free the serfs outright but was unable to take so decisive a step for fear of antagonizing the landowners. He did set aside 1,000,000 rubles per year with which to redeem for the state land held in private ownership. Since the peasants were attached to the land, they, of course, went with it. Thus they came directly under state control, and fully 50,000 were redeemed in this way during his reign. Although they were still serfs, their lot was immeasurably improved. There were other measures designed to alleviate the condition of the serfs. As early as 1802 landlords were forbidden to exile their serfs to hard labor. A few years later, in 1808, the public sale of serfs in the market place was banned. The liberation of Polish serfs in the Duchy of Warsaw in 1807 (by the French), and their emancipation in the Baltic Province, 1816-1819, served as a clear indication of the trend of the times. Nevertheless these steps involved only a fraction of the serfs in the Russian Empire, and as Alexander succumbed more and more to conservative pressures the prospects for any general settlement of the problem receded.

The other major problem that confronted Alexander was the reorganization of the government along republican ideas of popular representation as they had found expression in France or in regions under Anglo-American control. Upon his accession, as previously noted, he had established a commission to handle this problem. As the first step toward governmental reform he limited the functions of the Senate chiefly to judicial questions. This was followed in 1802 by a continuation of a policy already begun by Paul, namely, the creation of eight administrative departments of government, or ministries. These were the departments of foreign affairs, war, navy, justice, interior, finance, commerce, and education.

In his investigation of Anglo-American and French republicanism, Alexander enlisted the services of able statesmen, two of whom brought considerable distinction to themselves. One of these, Michael Speransky (1772-1839),[1] favored a centralized state in accordance with the French form of government. The other, Nicholas Novosiltsev (1761-1836), inclined to the United States conception and urged a federal state within the boundaries of the Russian Empire.

---

[1] See Raeff, Marc, "The Political Philosophy of Speransky," *The American Slavic and East European Review,* February 1953, pp. 1-21.

In 1806 Alexander began a correspondence with President Jefferson relative to the governmental organization of the United States. This correspondence, however, was productive of no results in Russia. Although the time was ripe for the development of a republican, or at least of some form of constitutional government in Russia, the war and the conservative nobility, who fiercely opposed such a change, prevented further political reform in Russia proper. The projects of Speransky and Novosiltsev were rejected. The temper of the reactionaries perhaps was best illustrated by the memorandum of the renowned historian, Nicholas Karamzin, to Alexander I in 1812, entitled *Old and New Russia*. Karamzin scoffed at the reforms proposed by Speransky and called in no uncertain terms for the maintenance of the *status quo*, with a strong monarchial government, free from such trimmings as a Senate, a State Council, or any representative institutions. Paradoxically enough, Alexander had granted a constitution to Finland, following its conquest from Sweden in 1809. With the reconstitution of the Kingdom of Poland under Alexander in 1815, that country secured, for a time, one of the most liberal constitutions in Europe. Thus Alexander, still an autocrat in St. Petersburg, was a constitutional monarch in Warsaw and Helsinki, an anomaly which many of his subjects found it increasingly difficult to understand.

In the period of political reaction which followed the Napoleonic Wars, Alexander employed ultra-conservative ministers like Count Alexander Araktcheyev (1769-1834) and Prince A. Golitsyn, head of the Holy Synod and subsequently of the Ministry of Education, to conduct a campaign against subversive, un-Russian ideas, which savored of Jacobinism, "false reasoning," "free thinking," and "atheism." The five Russian universities were among the first to suffer from the repression of free thought, and many professors were expelled because of their predilections for a constitutional form of government. In 1823 Russian students were forbidden to attend German universities. Drastic censorship was likewise imposed upon the press, which was forbidden to discuss the problem of serfdom or constitutional questions. Schiller's *Jeanne D'Arc* and Zhukovsky's translation of Sir Walter Scott's ballad *The Eve of St. John* were banned as immoral by the literary censor. One of the most unpopular measures of this era of reaction was the revival of an earlier project for the establishment of military colonies in such places as St. Petersburg, Novgorod, Mogilev, Ekaterinoslav (Dnepropetrovsk), and Kherson, under the direction of the iron disciplinarian, Araktcheyev.

Such persecution led to the organization of secret societies and sub-sequently to the Decembrist uprising of 1825, which has been called the First Russian Revolution.[1] Many Russians representative of the liberal nobility, the Guards, and younger officers who were veterans of the Napoleonic campaigns, were bitterly disillusioned with the failure of the government to achieve basic political and social reforms over a period of many years—in fact, since the days of Catherine the Great. Some had been exhorted to fight Napoleonic despotism abroad and had returned to find even worse political and economic conditions. Nearly all of these discontented and conscience-stricken noblemen later acknowledged that they had derived their liberal convictions from foreign literature and from exposure to the revolutionary movements abroad. They were unanimous in their opposition to the institution of serfdom and in their demand for some form of constitutional government.

Two secret organizations were established. The Northern Society, with its headquarters at St. Petersburg, had for its leaders the Muraviev brothers, Nikita and Alexander, the poet Ryleyev (1795-1826), and Prince Sergei Trubetskoy. The leader of the Southern Society was Colonel Paul Pestel, a veteran of the Battle of Borodino. Although the Northern Society aimed at the establishment of a limited monarchy, and its southern counterpart favored a republic after the model of the United States, both came eventually to have one chief purpose, namely, the precipitation of a revolution. Colonel Pestel, one of the most radical leaders, has been called a Russian Jacobin. The two societies kept in constant communication and only awaited a favorable opportunity to test their strength. This opportunity did not arise in Alexander's lifetime, but at his death in 1825 a misunderstanding in regard to the succession provided an opportunity for the revolutionaries.

According to the "Law of Succession" promulgated by Paul in 1797, Alexander should have been succeeded by his brother Constantine. But Constantine, who was stationed in Warsaw as commander-in-chief, had never been enthusiastic about the succession, being well aware of the revolutionary trend of the times. In 1823 Alexander therefore appointed his third brother, Nicholas, as his successor, but failed to make this momentous decision public. When Alexander died Constantine promptly swore allegiance to Nicholas, who, either in real or feigned ignorance, swore allegiance to Constantine. By reason of the poor means of communication, much time elapsed before it became known that Nicholas was the rightful ruler.

---

[1] See Mazour, Anatole, *The First Russian Revolution, 1825,* Berkeley, 1937, for an interesting study of this revolt, its background, leaders, and results.

Nicholas was known to be a reactionary with a predilection for Prussianism, hence the revolutionaries and others of liberal leanings were very much disturbed. The former decided not to delay action any longer and chose as the day for instituting their revolt December 26 (hence the term, Decembrists), on which day the oath of loyalty to the new emperor was to be taken. The uprising was poorly organized and consisted of little more than demonstrations of disapproval. Certain revolutionaries among the army officers induced two regiments of soldiers to refuse to take the oath, telling them that Nicholas was a usurper. They instructed the soldiers to proceed to a given point and cheer for Constantine and the Constitution. The soldiers were so densely ignorant that they thought that "Constitution" was Constantine's wife. Nicholas had no trouble in putting down the uprising. He executed five of the ringleaders, sent more than one hundred to Siberia, and granted a conditional pardon to the less active.

Although the Decembrist revolt was of short duration and without immediate results, it was, nevertheless, of profound significance, partly because the center of the revolt was the capital, St. Petersburg, and its leaders, far from being counterparts of Pugatchev and Razin, represented in many instances the flower of the Russian nobility and some of the most powerful families in Russia. They came to be regarded as martyrs to the constitutional cause, and were celebrated as such by the writer, Alexander Herzen, from his refuge in London. Although the suppression of the uprising amounted to a serious setback for the Russian constitutional movement, it did serve, as we shall see, to focus the government's attention on domestic conditions, with a view to preventing a repetition of the revolt. Those Decembrists who were exiled to Siberia formed the nucleus of an intelligentsia there, and in spite of the restrictions imposed upon them, they contributed greatly to the development of education, better agricultural methods, medical knowledge, improved administrative methods, and to the scientific study of the region in general. The Decembrist uprising has been called "the logical prologue to the drama which found its apotheosis in 1917." [1]

The reign of Alexander witnessed the increase and spread of sectarianism. The Old Believers, who opposed Nikon, had been the object of governmental persecution almost constantly since 1653. In the course of time, these original dissenters became divided into various denominations or sects. Toward the close of the seventeenth century, there appeared a mystic sect, the *Khlysty* (flagellants), which was second only to the Old Believers in numbers and importance. The *Khlysty* held that

1 Mazour, *op. cit.*, p. xvii.

God could become incarnate in a human being and sought to produce this incarnation by means of ecstatic dancing. Their gyrations often terminated in sexual orgies, which brought them ill repute.[1]

Some members of the sect, to whom certain of its practices became repugnant, withdrew about the middle of the eighteenth century and formed another group which rapidly gained followers. The sect took the name *Dukhobors* and was made up largely of peasants, who had communistic leanings and objected to war. Because of the latter principle, they suffered much persecution from the government. In southern Russia a number of their leaders were condemned to death at the stake in 1792, but Catherine II commuted the sentence to exile. Under Nicholas II, members of the Society of Friends in England and America, hearing of their sufferings, raised funds to assist the Dukhobors. The Emperor's consent to their departure from Russia was obtained. In 1898, 1150 refugees came to Cyprus. In the following year an asylum was offered them in Canada, and 4000 availed themselves of the offer. Their numbers were soon increased by the arrival of those who had originally gone to Cyprus, together with 2000 additional refugees. Leo Tolstoy gave to them all the money which he realized from his novel, *Resurrection.*

The late eighteenth century witnessed the development of yet another sect, an offshoot of the Dukhobors, the Molokane, who rejected many rituals of the Orthodox Church. Although all of the sects drew their numbers at first almost exclusively from the peasant and small trader classes, in the reign of Alexander I they began to win many adherents in the upper orders of society. This was especially true in St. Petersburg.

While the present reign was not so distinguished along intellectual lines as certain other periods in Russian history, it was not without its great names. Alexander Pushkin, the poet, who became famous during the succeeding reign, began to attract attention at this time. The ripest accomplishment within the compass of the reign was the work of the historian Nicholas Karamzin (1766-1826), whose eleven-volume *History of the Russian State* (1818) represents the first attempt to treat the history of Russia from a scientific standpoint.

REIGN OF EMPEROR NICHOLAS I (1825-1855)

INTERNAL AFFAIRS

Nicholas I was born in 1796 and hence was almost twenty years Alexander's junior. He was the exponent of absolutism and reactionary

---

[1] Gregory Rasputin was a member of the *Khlysty.*

aristocracy. As Nicholas informed the Marquis de Custine, during his sojourn in St. Petersburg in 1839: "I can understand the republic—it is an open and sincere government, or at least it can be; I can under-

Courtesy Sovfoto

DECEMBRIST REVOLT, December 14, 1825

stand the absolute monarchy, since I am the head of such a government; but I cannot comprehend the representative monarchy—it is a government of lies, of fraud and corruption, and I would withdraw as far as China rather than ever adopt it." [1]

---

[1] Kohler, P. P. (ed. & tr.), *Journey for Our Time: The Journals of the Marquis de Custine*, New York, 1951, pp. 124-125.

Since Nicholas was not expected to succeed to the throne, he had not been educated in politics and diplomacy. Strongly militaristic, he was a great admirer of Prussianism in all its phases and his contacts therewith were greatly increased by his marriage with Alexandra, daughter of King Frederick William III of Prussia. The main objective of his reign was the development of a strong, well-disciplined army, modeled after Prussian standards. With such an army he thought to police all Europe and thereby bring about an immense expansion of Russian territory and influence. At the same time, through the process of building up his army, he planned to weld the heterogeneous elements of his nation into a homogeneous whole.

Despite his determination to militarize Russia, and the fact that he had put down the Decembrist movement with a firm hand, he, nevertheless, gave consideration to the causes and grievances responsible for the movement before devoting himself exclusively to his main purpose. The chief complaints of the Decembrists were as follows: (1) The legal machinery of the country was antiquated, unsystematic, and inefficient; (2) finances were in a lamentable tangle due to over-issuance of currency and consequent depreciation; (3) opportunities for education were so limited that the majority of the populace was condemned to dense ignorance; and (4) the institution of serfdom was a constantly increasing source of danger to national peace and security. This last point was the one which caused the Decembrists the most concern and the one upon which they were the most insistent.

While Nicholas I disapproved of an extension of educational opportunities, in other respects he recognized the justice of the criticism of the Decembrists and proceeded to institute certain reforms. In 1826 he appointed the statesman, Speransky, to examine the Russian legal code with the intent of bringing order and system out of the existing confusion. Speransky fulfilled his commission in a most able manner. His "Complete Collection of Russian Laws" consisted of forty-five volumes, in which the laws of the empire were arranged in chronological order from 1649 to 1825. The value and importance of this codification to the Russian courts cannot be overestimated. This code became the basis for a "Systematic Code of Laws of the Russian Empire," compiled in 1832.

Nicholas, with the help of Count P. D. Kiselev (1788-1872), an early exponent of emancipation, gave some attention to ameliorating the lot of the serfs. In 1826 slavery was officially prohibited in Siberia. He passed a law in 1827 which forbade the purchase of peasants unless they could be supplied with sufficient land to eke out an existence. This was followed by a law in 1833 which made it illegal to separate families by sale. In 1842, shortly after the publication of Nikolai Gogol's *Dead Souls,* provision was made whereby serfs could be emancipated by their landlords but remained "bound" by the terms imposed. So far as Russian landlords were concerned, this law remained a dead letter. Kiselev devoted his efforts mainly to the Crown peasants, seeking to introduce better agricultural methods, to supply grain in the event of crop failure, and to lay the foundations for self-government among them. However, the condition of the peasants at large was not greatly improved. The landowners, the *pomiestchiki,* were firmly entrenched in their prerogatives and did not permit themselves to be hampered too much by legislation in favor of the peasants. They had become increasingly arrogant and independent in proportion to their privileges and exemptions. Up to the time of Catherine II, land had been granted only in return for service—no service, no land! Catherine desired to advance the interests of certain of her favorites, and in her *nakaz* of 1776 did away with the requirements for land grants. In consequence the owners began to regard their estates strictly in the light of private property and governed themselves accordingly. It is interesting to note that before the time of Catherine II. Russian law did not contain a term which meant "property" in the English sense of the word. During her reign however the word *sobstvennost,* or private property, as we understand it, came into use. Like Catherine, Nicholas was inclined to regard the landlords as the bulwark of the Crown and the "watch-dog" of the state. He believed that emancipation was premature.

As indicated earlier, Nicholas I had no sympathy with the idea of education for the masses. He foresaw that an educated citizenry might put obstacles in the way of his complete militarization of the country and in other ways become difficult to handle. When he turned his attention, therefore, toward public education, he made at first some concessions, by establishing technical schools, teachers' colleges and even several women's institutes, but soon reversed his procedure and tried to limit it even more than heretofore. The dictum went forth from the office of the Minister of Public Instruction, Count S. S. Uvarov (1786-1855), that the gymnasiums were in general to be closed to all save the children of nobles and state officials. Count Uvarov's predecessor had stated that knowledge to be useful should be used sparingly like salt in proportion to the people's circumstances and needs. He maintained further that it would be actually harmful to teach the masses to read. The children of merchants and mechanics were given limited instruction in special secondary schools, but were discouraged from seeking a higher education.

The emperor also regarded the universities with a certain suspicion as institutions for fomenting radicalism. Once he remarked while passing the University of Moscow, "There is the wolf's den." The universities, together with the gymnasiums, were reorganized upon strict military lines and placed under the supervision of pronounced reactionaries. The maximum number of students at a given university was not permitted to exceed 300, and the curriculum was curtailed, philosophy being one of the subjects eliminated. Although foreign languages and literatures were likewise curtailed, greater emphasis was placed upon the study of the Russian language, literature, and history. Study abroad by professors or students was emphatically discouraged. This type of "higher" education was designed to turn out a number of standardized individuals of safe mediocrity who could be relied upon not to engage in too much thinking. Very often it attained its purpose, but not infrequently it also produced a rebel who dared to think for himself, and whose thoughts were often radical and anarchistic.

Before 1825 the intelligentsia,[1] or intellectual class, was made up entirely of nobles. By reason of their position and training, these intellectuals tended to be conservatives, who accepted the established order without much desire for change. This is the reason that the Decembrist movement was such an innovation and made so great an impression upon all classes, since heretofore, with the exception of a feeble effort in 1730, no such revolutionary tendencies had been observable among the nobles. The early concessions of Nicholas I in the matter of popular education, inaugurated with a view to satisfying these Decembrists, put education within the reach of an entirely new class, the *raznotchintsy* (plebeian, commoner), who eagerly and enthusiastically embraced the opportunities offered. When the emperor, alarmed by this zeal for education, repented of his liberality and imposed restrictions, it was too late. The young people of the *raznotchintsy* had had a taste of knowledge and were not to be restrained. If they were forbidden to attend the higher institutions of learning, they studied either privately or with the aid of tutors. This encouraged the practice of studying privately for an examination covering several grades of a government gymnasium. Passing such an examination entitled the student to a certificate or diploma, the latter of which admitted him to the university. The student was said to *externitchat;* he himself was called an *extern*. The new intellectual class had had experiences very different from those of the nobles. Its mem-

---

1 See pp. 255-256.

bers had been hampered by discriminatory laws and had even suffered oppression. In consequence they were much more susceptible to radical and advanced ideas than the earlier intelligentsia. The influence of these newcomers was such as to change entirely the face of the Russian intelligentsia, so that through succeeding generations this order of society manifested more and more revolutionary tendencies.

For the purpose of preventing a recurrence of the Decembrist uprising, Nicholas I organized in 1826 a police division, which was designated as the Third Division, or *Gendarmerie*. This body had instructions to crush without mercy any demonstrations of dissatisfaction or revolt. In order that its members might not be troubled by any conscientious scruples, they were selected for their brutality and lack of education. As a result, police standards, which had risen considerably under Catherine II, sank to a very low level. Under its control, freedom of speech and freedom of the press almost vanished from the land. No group or individual was safe from its high-handed repression and abuse. Even conservatives, such as Yuri Samarin (1819-1876) and Fyodor Dostoyevsky (1822-1881), fell victims to its suspicions. The establishment of the "police state" drove radicals underground, and Russian writers resorted to fiction as the only available medium for the expression of social and political thought. The *Gendarmerie* retained its power until 1917 and was responsible for much suffering and loss of life.

The Jewish population in Russia had grown considerably despite manifestations of ill will and governmental restrictions. The restrictions imposed upon them were of two kinds, namely, religious and economic. The Orthodox clergy, who acted as tutors for the future rulers of Russia and the nobility, had been in the habit of instilling in them the most bitter hatred against Protestants, Roman Catholics, and most of all against the Jews.[1] This method of instruction, from a modern standpoint, vicious in the extreme, had the result of breeding great intolerance, which found vent in discriminatory religious laws from which the Jews as a minority group suffered especially.

As has been mentioned before, Catherine II did not indulge in religious persecutions and even offered an asylum to the persecuted of other lands; nevertheless, she placed restrictions upon the Jews. She was constrained to do this both by the clergy and by certain business people, who were finding it increasingly difficult to compete successfully with the Jews. Catherine, therefore, in 1791 established a Pale of Settlement, or

[1] This practice continued to 1917. See Alexander, Grand Duke of Russia, *Once a Grand Duke*, pp. 91-93; Graham, Stephen, *Tsar of Freedom: Alexander II* (1935), pp. 72, 237.

segregated district, in which the Jews were compelled to live. In these districts, or Ghettos, they came in contact with few Russians other than uneducated peasants, together with a few unfriendly and prejudiced members of the clergy and public officials. These latter oppressed and bled the Jews whenever the occasion offered. Educational opportunities being as limited as they were, Jews had not the least chance of entering Russian schools. Consequently they remained entirely ignorant of the Russian language and Russian life. They lived to themselves and used the Talmud as their sole spiritual and cultural guide. It is not surprising, therefore, that by reason of association with the most ignorant and oppressive among the Gentiles, they began to regard all of them with detestation and distrust. On the other hand, any members of the upper classes, who occasionally came in contact with the Jews, considered them uncultured and often lacking in cleanliness. Thus there existed mutual misunderstanding and hostility. Despite this, however, the Jews were very loyal to the emperors and built up industry greatly in their districts.

This, then, was the situation at the accession of Nicholas I, who had his own ideas concerning the handling of the Jewish problem in his territories. Under his personal supervision, almost 600 laws were promulgated concerning the Jews, most of which were in line with his general policy of militarizing and amalgamating the diverse elements of his empire. In 1827, for the first time, Jews were required to render active service in the army. Heretofore it was generally accepted that, if conscripted, they could pay a specified sum for exemption. Nicholas, however, looked upon this service as an effective method of solving the Jewish problem. Recruits were taken from the ages of twelve to twenty-five for a compulsory military service of twenty-five years. The emperor foresaw that during this long period, far from their homes, they would not only become superlatively well-trained soldiers, but they would also forget their early religious teaching and accept the Orthodox faith. This amounted to compulsory conversion.

In order to encourage still further the acceptance of the Orthodox faith, the government resorted to various expedients, not the least of which was the offer of all the rights and privileges of Christians to baptized Jews. Two measures in their favor also met with response and approbation from some of the more far-sighted among them. One opened Russian schools to the Jews, the other made it possible for them to enter into agricultural pursuits. However, because in the past they had frequently been the victims of tricks and deception, the majority of them looked with suspicion upon any overtures of good will on the part of the government, sensing therein a subtle attack which would rob them of their Judaism. It is unfortunate in the extreme that there was not a more general response among them to the agricultural program. Had they left the congested cities and settled upon the land they would have escaped much persecution, and the country would not have been disgraced by pogroms. There were, to be sure, many Jewish colonies established in the provinces of Ekaterinoslav (now Dnepropetrovsk) and Kherson, while by the time of the Revolution of 1917, some 100,000 Jews were engaged in tilling the soil. These Jewish farmers had not suffered nearly so much persecution during the years as had their coreligionists in the cities.

It will be recalled that during the reign of Alexei there were two movements representing opposing theories as to how Russia could best fulfill her destiny. Under the impetus of the Decembrist uprising, these movements became well-organized groups, possessed of well-defined ideology. At this time they came to be known as Slavophiles and Westernizers.[1] The leaders of the former, in theory at least, were A. S. Khomyakov, the Kireyevsky brothers, Yuri Samarin, and the Aksakov brothers. They held that if Russia would assert herself and follow her own natural lines of development, she would attain results beneficial to herself and to all humanity. Never would she realize her true destiny by imitation or adaptation of Western ideas, for every nation as well as every individual was possessed of a unique personality, and only by full development of this true personality could success be attained. Furthermore they believed that in the Orthodox faith Russia had preserved the purest form of Christianity, far superior to anything which the West had to offer. Thus when Peter the Great had weakened the influence of the Orthodox faith and had forcibly introduced Western innovations, he had torn the land asunder, wresting from it its true tradition, and doing incomparable harm thereby. The only salvation lay in a return to former beliefs, ideals, and modes of life. It occasions no surprise that Nicholas I was in reality a Slavophile in outlook, since for him Orthodoxy and autocracy were the inviolable principles of government.

In contrast to all of this, the Westernizers, whose leaders were V. G. Belinsky, T. N. Granovsky, A. I. Herzen, I. S. Turgenev, and others, advocated following the course of European progress. They opposed the reactionary clergy and favored liberalism or socialism in politics. For them a return to the old order of the days preceding Peter I was equivalent to a return to the dark ages. They approved of Peter's reforms and held that he had rendered an inestimable service by his program of Europeanization. Both Slavophiles and Westernizers

---

See pp. 200-202.

consulted German philosophy, as expressed by Schelling and Hegel, in an effort to find support for their theories.

The most important internal improvements of the reign of Nicholas I were in the field of transportation and communications. In 1838 a private company undertook the construction of Russia's first railroad, which was completed between St. Petersburg and Tsarskoye Selo, a distance of sixteen miles. By 1842 another railroad was begun between St. Petersburg and Moscow, this time at state expense. The completion of this road took eight years and cost 100,000,000 rubles, even with the employment of slave labor. By 1875 there had been constructed in Russia 17,000 *versts* [1] of railroad, or nearly 13,000 miles. In 1851 St. Petersburg and Moscow were also connected by telegraph. The general backwardness of transportation and communications facilities was to prove a serious handicap during the Crimean War.

FOREIGN AFFAIRS

Nicholas I did not favor revolution abroad any more than at home and was ever ready to throw the weight of his influence against it. He never permitted himself to forget that the Decembrists had acquired their revolutionary ideas from the West. The chief object of his foreign policy, as far as Western Europe was concerned, was the maintenance of the settlement reached at the Congress of Vienna. For example, when the Bourbons in France were overthrown by the July Revolution of 1830, Nicholas prepared to intervene in their favor and was only prevented from so doing by the outbreak of a revolution in Poland.[2] At Munchengratz in 1833 Nicholas and Metternich reached an understanding which virtually amounted to a revival of the principles and policies of the Holy Alliance. For the next fifteen years Nicholas remained in fact the foremost leader of reaction in Europe, in opposition to the dangerous doctrines of liberalism, socialism, and nationalism. In 1848-1849, when most of Europe, including Belgium, France, Italy, Germany and Austria, was swept by revolt, Nicholas made one last attempt to save the European system established at Vienna. In response to the request of Emperor Francis Joseph of Austria in 1849 he dispatched

---

[1] A *verst* is equal to 0.6629 miles.

[2] Toward the close of the year 1830, the Poles, encouraged by the French and Belgian revolutions, raised an army of 80,000 men and staged a revolt of their own. They took possession of Warsaw, forcing the troops of Grand Duke Constantine to evacuate the city. They then demanded their independence, together with the surrender of Lithuania and Western Russia. The emperor's answer was to send a strong force against Poland under General Diebitsch. The revolt was crushed, and Poland was made part of the empire and divided into provinces like the rest of Russia.

General Ivan Paskevitch (1782-1856) and 100,000 troops to put down the Hungarian revolt led by the man who had become Europe's number one revolutionary, Louis Kossuth. The fact that Kossuth's forces included more than a thousand Polish refugees may well have contributed to the emperor's zeal, but his action served immeasurably to foster the development of anti-Russian sentiment in Hungary. His service to Austria at this time earned him the title of "the policeman of Europe."

Wars in the Near and Middle East broke out shortly after the accession of Nicholas I. The first of these was with Persia, where English officers had entered the service of the shah, and the mullahs preached a holy war against Russia. The Persian forces, which initiated the conflict, retreated before the army of General Paskevitch, who crossed the Araxes, seized the important stronghold of Yerevan, and proceeded to march on Teheran. In alarm the shah, who failed to receive the expected aid from England, hastened to conclude the Treaty of Turkmantchay in 1828, by which the Russians acquired the left bank of the Araxes, and a large part of Armenia, including Yerevan. In addition Persia paid a huge indemnity of 36,000,000 rubles and abandoned her claim to the Caucasus. Almost immediately, however, the Muridist revolution, a religious movement, broke out among the Moslem mountaineers in the Caucasus. Under the leadership of able *imams* and sheikhs, the best known of whom were Kazi-Mullah, who was killed in 1831, and Shamyl (1797-1871), who was captured by the Russians in 1859, the revolutionaries maintained a long and stubborn resistance and were not fully subdued until the reign of Alexander II. The conquest of the Caucasus took in all 137 years, from 1722 to 1859.

Scarcely had peace been concluded with Persia, when Russia was again involved in war, this time with Turkey. This conflict grew out of the Greek struggle for independence (1821-1829). For some time, in conformity with the sentiment of the Holy Alliance, Europe rendered no formal military assistance to the Greek rebels. In Russia, Alexander's opposition to revolution was somewhat compromised by the fact that the *Hetairia Philike,* a leading Greek revolutionary society, had been founded in Odessa in 1814 and many wealthy Greek merchants of that city extended very considerable financial aid to their rebel kinsmen. Although the possibility of supporting Orthodox Christians against the Turks was an idea that traditionally appealed to Russians, Alexander nevertheless promptly disavowed Prince Ypsilanti, pro-Russian leader of the Greek revolt and, until his death in 1825, refused to intervene actively on the side of the Greeks. However, his more militaristic brother, Nicholas I, who stood for the *status quo* in Western Europe, by no means applied the same principle to Turkey and the Balkans. The ruthless campaign of the sultan's vassal, Ibrahim Pasha of Egypt, against the Greeks had aroused popular opinion throughout Europe. This led to joint intervention on the part of England, France, and Russia to enforce a diplomatic settlement, and when that failed their combined fleets destroyed a Turko-Egyptian squadron in the Battle of Navarino in 1827. In the following year Nicholas, acting unilaterally, declared war on Turkey, and the Russian army, supported by the Serbs, almost reached Constantinople. The Treaty of Adrianople, which brought the war to a close in September 1829, was highly favorable to Russia and marked an important stage in the dismemberment of the Ottoman Empire. By its terms Russia gained possession of the mouth of the Danube and the coast of the Black Sea to Poti. Turkey also acceded to Russia's demand for a protectorate over Orthodox peoples living in Turkish territories and granted commercial privileges to Russian subjects in the same regions. In addition to her concessions to Russia, Turkey agreed to recognize the independence of the Greeks (1830) and to open the Bosporus and Dardanelles to friendly nations. Moreover certain dependencies of Turkey, namely, Moldavia, Wallachia, Serbia, and the principalities of the Danube, were granted autonomy under Turkish suzerainty.

Nicholas might have exacted far more by the Treaty of Adrianople, but he preferred to moderate his demands and pursue a policy of expansion by peaceful penetration, in conformity with the tactics of Catherine II in the Middle and Far East and those of Paul in the Near East. Therefore, when Mehemet Ali, the Pasha of Egypt, began hostilities against the sultan in 1833, Nicholas sent a force to Asia Minor to protect the Bosporus. This resulted in the Treaty of Unkiar-Skelessi in August 1833, by which the emperor's diplomacy scored a great victory, since Turkey agreed to close the Bosporus and the Dardanelles to the warships of all foreign powers, with the exception of Russia. With this treaty Russian influence at Constantinople reached its zenith. The implementation of its terms would have made a Russian satellite of the Ottoman Empire.

The unilateral policy of Nicholas in regard to Turkey in 1828 and 1833 aroused the fear of Austria and the antagonism of England and France. In spite of the Holy Alliance, Austria found herself increasingly at odds with Russia over the Christian principalities in the Balkans as a result of the Treaty of Adrianople. Since the reign of Catherine II England had watched, with increasing concern, the expansion of Russia at the expense of Turkey, Persia, and Afghanistan. With the appointment of Viscount Palmerston as foreign secretary in 1830, Anglo-Russian relations began to deteriorate rapidly. France, as the ally of Mehemet Ali, had her own reasons for discomfiture with regard to Russian policy toward Turkey. The groundwork was being laid for the formation of an anti-Russian bloc, which was before long to challenge Russia in the Crimean War.

In 1839 Nicholas, envisaging an opportunity to collaborate with England in the solution of the Turkish problem, agreed to let the Treaty of Unkiar-Skelessi lapse. In 1840, in a move to isolate France, the four great powers—Russia, Prussia, England, and Austria—signed the London Convention, which defined the position of Mehemet Ali in the Ottoman Empire and closed the Straits of the Bosporus and Dardanelles to the warships of all foreign powers in time of peace. These terms were confirmed by the Treaty of London in 1841, which included France. Still seeking English collaboration, Nicholas visited London in 1844, in order to obtain some assurance of English neutrality in the event of another Russian war against Turkey, or English participation in the dismemberment of Turkey, which he labeled "the Sick Man of Europe." His visit did little to allay English suspicions of Russian designs on the Ottoman Empire.

The foreign policy of Nicholas I during the breathing spell of the 1840's was characterized by two fixed ideas: (1) a firm determination to stop the spread of democracy and liberalism in Europe; and (2) the acquisition of the Dardanelles and Constantinople. In reality Nicholas achieved neither of his objectives. Not only did he fail to call a halt to democratic and liberal trends in Europe, but that continent became a hotbed of revolution in 1848, the year which marked the appearance of Karl Marx's *Communist Manifesto*. By using Russian troops for the suppression of revolt abroad, Nicholas brought Russia into still further disrepute among Western liberals as a reactionary and autocratic country. In the second place Nicholas's bid for Constantinople and the Dardanelles led directly to the Crimean War (1853-1856).

The immediate cause of the Crimean War, however, grew out of the efforts of Napoleon III of France to strengthen French influence and prestige in the Near East, particularly in the Holy Land. He demanded and obtained from Turkey concessions for Roman Catholics living in the Holy Land. He obtained for them also possession of the keys of the Church of Bethlehem, which by the Treaty of Küchük Kainarji (1774) had been assigned to the keeping of the Orthodox Church. Nicholas promptly demanded of the Turks that the treaty be respected and Orthodox rights restored. When Turkey temporized, Nicholas countered with a demand for the recognition of Russian claims for protection over Orthodox Christians throughout the Ottoman Empire, and Russian troops invaded the Turkish provinces of Moldavia and Wallachia to enforce these demands. The sultan, encouraged by Lord Stratford (Stratford Canning), the English ambassador in Constantinople, to believe that English and French aid would be forthcoming, declared war on Russia on October 1, 1853.

Russia's first move was to dispatch Russian warships to Sinope, where a Turkish squadron was destroyed. Anglo-French naval forces entered the Black Sea, and, after a futile effort to achieve a diplomatic settlement at Vienna, England and France declared war on Russia on March 27, 1854. They were later joined by the ambitious King of Sardinia. Austria and Prussia, from whom Nicholas expected a display of friendship, preserved a hostile neutrality. Russia was thus left alone to face an enemy alignment of the chief powers of Western Europe. In September 1854 the allied forces landed in Crimea near Eupatoria and laid siege to Sevastopol. The city surrendered after a siege which lacked only fifteen days of lasting a year. Nicholas did not live to see its downfall, for he died on March 2, 1855. It was rumored that he committed suicide by taking poison because he was unable to outlive the defeat of all his plans and the collapse of Russian military power. Peace was concluded in 1856 by his son, Alexander II, under the terms of the Treaty of Paris.

The Crimean War revealed the backwardness of tsarist military and naval equipment and Russia's lack of adequate transportation and communications facilities. Russian generals even lacked good maps of the Crimean peninsula. Whereas the Russian fleet was still predominately a sailing fleet, the ironclad British and French warships were run by steam, and their guns had a range double that of the Russian shore batteries. It must not be forgotten, however, that the Russians not only fought in the Crimea, but had to maintain fronts in the Caucasus and the Baltic, while large forces were immobilized throughout the war on the Austrian frontier. Even in the Pacific, units of the Anglo-French fleets attacked the port of Petropavlovsk on the Kamchatka Peninsula in 1854. In spite of this "encirclement," Russian troops after the fall of Sevastopol won a signal victory against the Turks at Kars in Asia. In the final analysis, the Crimean War demonstrated rather clearly how ineffective was naval power without the backing of huge armies, when pitted against a great land power. At no time did Anglo-French military forces penetrate more than a few miles beyond the Crimean coast. For classic literature on this war, the reader will do well to consult *Sevasto-*

pol, three sketches by Leo Tolstoy, who himself took part in the Crimean campaign.

All the belligerent nations suffered heavily in the war, although Russia's loss of a quarter of a million men was the greatest. The French lost 80,000 men and the English 22,000. In view of the fame of Florence Nightingale, whose name is ordinarily associated with the care of the wounded in this war, it is perhaps worth while to note that the famous Russian surgeon, Nicholas Pirogov (1810-1881), did much to promote the development of antiseptic surgery in the field, established first-aid stations behind the Russian lines, and organized an order of nursing sisters to tend the Russian wounded. One of these nurses, Darya Sevastopolskaya, became as celebrated in Russian annals as Florence Nightingale in England. The Treaty of Paris destroyed at one stroke the results of two centuries of effort on the part of Russian rulers. While Sevastopol remained in her possession, Russia temporarily lost control of the Black Sea. She was also compelled to relinquish her exclusive protectorate over Orthodox Christians in the Near East, all the great powers sharing the responsibility for Christian residents in Turkish lands. By the cession of southern Bessarabia Russia was likewise excluded from the mouth of the Danube. In addition the Bosporus and the Dardanelles were closed to the armed fleets of all nations. Thus the military prestige which Russia had built up under Suvorov and Kutuzov, and the stabilizing influence she had been able to exert throughout Europe since 1815, were swept away. The Treaty of Paris sounded the beginning of the end of tsarist expansion in Europe. More important still, Russia remained isolated from the Concert of Europe, while, in the years that followed the Treaty of Paris, the balance of power in the West was completely upset by the rise of Germany and Italy as national states.

7

From Liberator to the Last Emperor (Alexander II to Nicholas II)

1855-1894

REIGN OF EMPEROR ALEXANDER II (1855-1881)

ALTHOUGH Alexander became emperor by the death of his father on March 2, 1855, the continuation of the Crimean War and the events following its conclusion delayed his coronation until the next year. Because of the noteworthy and beneficial reforms which he introduced into his distracted country, he was very much praised by subsequent generations, who bestowed upon him such titles as the White Tsar, the Liberator, the Great Reformer, the Abraham Lincoln of Russia. At the beginning of his reforms the Westernizers rejoiced greatly in his liberalism.

Born in St. Petersburg on April 29, 1818, Alexander became emperor at the age of thirty-six. Whereas his father, Nicholas I, had received no special training for the responsibilities of an emperor, inasmuch as his accession had seemed remote, all of Alexander's training was directed with a view to preparing him adequately for his high office. His education had been most liberal and his experience in statecraft most adequate by the time he was called upon to assume the reins of government. One of his tutors was the poet Zhukovsky, who translated the *Iliad* and the *Odyssey* into Russian and whose nobility of character was generally recognized. At the age of twenty-three, he married Maria Alexandrovna, Princess of Hesse-Darmstadt. They had eight children, six sons and two daughters.

ALEXANDER II ANNOUNCING TO HIS COURT
THE EMANCIPATION OF THE SERFS

INTERNAL REFORMS

It is no secret that shortly before his death, Nicholas I, with unusual honesty and recognition of fact, admitted to his son that he had erred in his Slavophile and autocratic policies. The crumbling of the Russian defense before a Western European attack had made it clear that a government of such extreme autocracy as that which Nicholas I had instituted was suited, if at all, only to Asiatic peoples. This was generally admitted even by enthusiastic Slavophiles. Thus Aksakov affirmed that "Sevastopol fell that God might reveal all the rottenness of the system of government." Yet another ardent Slavophile, Samarin, said: "We have fallen, not before the forces of the Western Alliance, but as a result of our own internal weakness."

Nicholas advised Alexander, therefore, to follow more liberal methods upon his accession. Although publicly Alexander expressed diplomatic vindication of his father's policy and attempted to smooth over the humiliating terms of the Treaty of Paris, he lost no time in instituting a different policy of his own, devised to repair the ravages of past mistakes. The day of his coronation was marked by the issuance of a manifesto of thirty-eight articles. Among its provisions was an amnesty for surviving Decembrists of the 1825 uprising and for Polish conspirators of the 1831 revolution. Moreover, children who had been forcibly inducted into the army and navy were to be returned to their families and permitted to make their own choice of a profession.

With these beginnings, Alexander II undertook at once the major problems which confronted him and, in the course of time, instituted reforms in respect to the following: serfdom, zemstvos, court procedure, and universal military service. We shall now proceed to consider his reforms in order, beginning with the one which he considered of major importance.

At the time of Alexander's accession, the population of Russia was about 70,000,000. Of this number 47,000,000 were living in a more or less arduous condition of serfdom. Some of them, to be sure, were free in everything but name. These were the 20,000,000 Crown peasants, who had become dependents of the state by the process of redemption previously mentioned. In addition to these, there were 4,700,000 on appanages, or *Udyely*. These peasants had their own communities, wherein they exercised a degree of self-government and managed their private affairs in accordance with their own traditions. The problem which they presented to the state was comparatively easy to handle, consisting as it did of little more than official confirmation of the freedom which they already enjoyed. By the middle of 1858, an edict of the government made them free in law as well as in fact.

The cancerous spot in the system of serfdom, which required the most diplomatic treatment to effect its cure, was to be found in private ownership of serfs; actually some 22,400,000 peasants were virtually slaves of individual landowners. The bondage of the 1,400,000 of these who served as domestic servants (*Dvorovie* or *Kholopy*) was especially strict; Alexander II directed his efforts, therefore, toward the abolition of this type of servitude.

He was obliged to move with caution and circumspection, for, although a large majority of the people was in favor of freeing the serfs, there was an opposing faction, composed of rich landowners and reactionary public officials, who were both influential and powerful. It was necessary to secure their support before a drastic reform could be instituted with any hope of success. The emperor, therefore, sought to win the co-operation of these classes by an appeal to practical reasoning. In an address delivered before their leaders in Moscow, he pointed out succinctly that it was much better for them to handle the problem while it was still under their control, than to wait until their hands were forced by uprisings, which would result in destruction of property and loss of life. "Better that the reform should come from above than wait until serfdom is abolished from below." This made a great impression, for the owners of the serfs could not fail to recognize the soundness of his reasoning. Every effort was made to convince the landlords that the existing system of land tenure was becoming economically more unprofitable and prevented the adoption of more up-to-date agricultural methods. Whereas this situation had long been apparent to many impoverished landlords, those who had serfs out on the *obrok* system, working in factories or at some trade, and who derived a handsome income thereby, were particularly hard to convince. Even those landlords converted to emancipation were likely to hold out for compensation in order that they might use the capital so acquired to modernize their farm equipment and agricultural methods.

The minister of the interior, Count Sergei Lanskoy (1787-1862) and the adjutant-general, Y. I. Rostovtsev (1803-1860), took an active part in the preparations for emancipation. Committees established in each province submitted recommendations, which were in turn examined by the Tsar's General Committee. Alexander himself toured the provinces to get a first-hand picture of conditions and spent hours in session with his General Committee. The main issue to be decided was whether to grant the peasant his personal freedom, without land, as in the case of the Baltic Provinces (1816-1819), and thus create a huge landless proletariat in Russia, or to grant the peasant both freedom and land, a procedure which, unless accompanied by compensation for the landlord, might well lead to the ruin of the latter. The state treasury, following the Crimean War, was scarcely in a position to shoulder the financial burden. It was therefore concluded that if the peasant was to receive the land, he himself must pay for it. Practical considerations for the handling of the matter necessitated long discussions, deliberations, and adjustments, but finally on March 3, 1861, the sixth anniversary of his accession, the emperor issued the manifesto abolishing serfdom from Russia. If the reign of Alexander had been distinguished solely by the issuance of this manifesto it would merit a place of importance in Russian annals, and he himself would be entitled to the gratitude accorded him by his subjects.

Despite the emancipation, however, the peasant problem was far from solved. The solution adopted was essentially a compromise, by which the landlords received no formal compensation for services lost but retained the ownership of the land. The peasants continued to live on the land and till the soil, but as freemen they were obliged to pay for these privileges either in money, produce, or services. Provision was made whereby the liberated peasant could purchase land and pay for it over a period of years. The system of redemption was, however, highly complicated. Where the peasants agreed to take one-quarter of their allotment, the issue could be settled with the landlords direct. If they had 20 percent of the purchase price available, the state would advance the balance to the landlord in the expectation of collecting from the peasants later. In accordance with these arrangements, the Crown peasant received an *average* allotment of twenty-three acres, the appanage peasant one of fifteen acres, and the privately owned serf nine acres. Although circumstances varied considerably in different parts of the country, except in the north and west the liberated serfs obtained less land than they had tilled prior to emancipation, and they were often handicapped by lack of pasturage, hayfields, wood, and even water. In the majority of cases the transfer of the land was not accompanied by any move to consolidate the strip holdings of the peasant, and an already antiquated system of cultivation was therefore perpetuated. By the death of Alexander in 1881, however, more than 80 percent of the landowners had sold out to the peasants.

One further aspect of the process of emancipation deserves some consideration, since it helps to explain much of Russia's later economic and social difficulties. The land thus acquired by the peasants did not belong to them individually but was held in communal ownership by the *mir*, or village commune, an institution of peculiarly Slavonic origin. It was the *mir* that assumed responsibility for the payment of the peasant's redemption dues, his taxes, and his forced labor. The peasant soon found that his hard-won liberty was qualified by the fact that the authority of his local *mir* had superseded the authority of his former landlord.[1] Although theoretically the principle of equality prevailed among the village peasants who comprised the *mir*, in practice the institution came to be dominated by its more aggressive and well-to-do representatives. The resentment of the peasant, who was often compelled to pay more than the market value for land he regarded as his own in the first place, and who was in the process subjected to restrictions imposed upon his household by the *mir*, was amply demonstrated by the more than 2000 peasant uprisings which occurred in the country from 1861 to 1863. In view of later developments in Russia, it is important to emphasize here that, although each peasant member of the *mir* shared in the responsibility of paying off the purchase price of the land, none of it became his private possession. It is apparent that such an arrangement closely resembled a Soviet *kolkhoz*, or collective farm, of the 1920's and in fact served as the best possible training for subsequent economic developments.

It should be recognized that the problem of land-ownership was not efficiently handled and that the failure to do so without doubt precipitated the Revolutions of 1905 and 1917. What could have been done to produce more general satisfaction and thereby avoid the aforementioned social catastrophies? It has been most ably demonstrated that there were two possible solutions, either of which would in all probability have prevented later misfortunes.[2] The government might have elected to give the peasants merely their personal freedom and to assist individuals, rather than groups or communes, to purchase the land from the original owners. As a second mode of procedure, the government might have taken over the land with suitable compensation to its former owners and then parceled it out among the peasants, again on an individual basis. In either case, by the year 1917, there would have been in Russia millions of *farmers* instead of millions of *peasants*, who would

---

[1] See Maynard, Sir John, *Russia in Flux*, N. Y., 1948, Chapter II, "The Peasant in the Nineteenth Century," pp. 22-38. On the whole subject of peasant conditions from the emancipation to 1917, see Robinson, G. T., *Rural Russia Under the Old Regime*, N. Y., 1932, pp. 64 ff.

[2] In this matter the author concurs entirely with George Vernadsky. See *A History of Russia*, New Haven, Yale University Press, 1930, pp. 154-155. See also Maxwell, B. W., *The Soviet State*, 1934, pp. 258-259.

have constituted a conservative, agricultural middle class. It was for the purpose of developing such a class that Premier Stolypin instituted his reforms of 1906-1911, but it was then too late. There is no doubt that the success of Russia's social revolution was due to the lack of a middle class.

The stability of any country is in a large measure dependent upon the middle class, and in proportion as this class is strong and well established, the danger of a social revolution along communist or fascist lines is lessened. The capitalist, with extensive schemes and high ambitions, may risk his entire capital in a speculative venture. He may lose everything, but on the other hand, his gains may exceed all dreams of avarice. He enjoys playing for a great stake. The laborer, especially in Europe, has very little to lose while he may gain much by a change in the social order. Hence a revolution becomes his speculative venture. A member of the middle class, however, is in an entirely different position from either of these representatives of two social extremes. He possesses a little property or a small capital, which has cost him years of toil and self-denial to accumulate. He has become accustomed to some modest comforts. A revolution would rob him of all of this and plunge him into an abyss of destitution and privation. He has nothing to gain and everything to lose, hence he is conservative in the extreme. Any government which takes cognizance of its middle class and furthers its interests has little to fear in respect to revolution and communism. This is the case in the United States where the middle class is very large and has a somewhat high standard of living. The chief reason why other European countries did not go communistic after World War I, as did Russia, is to be found in their possession of a relatively large middle class. This explains also why the Soviet government in pursuance of its communistic ends was so ruthless in its treatment of the *kulak* farmers, a product of the Stolypin reforms, 1906-1911. In passing, "If Russia had had a middle class of any size," says Maurice Hindus,[1] "the Bolshevik Revolution might never have become an active fact, or, if it had, it surely would have failed."

The emancipation of the serfs in Russia in 1861 inevitably calls to mind the parallel emancipation of the slaves in the United States in 1863 and invites comparisons. Whereas in the United States the Negroes achieved their freedom only as a result of the prolonged and bloody Civil War (1861-1865), in autocratic Russia the change was inaugurated peaceably after years of investigation and preparation. It is im-

---

[1] *The Great Offensive*, N. Y., 1933, p. 357. See also pp. 357-368. See Chamberlin, W. N., *Russia's Iron Age*, 1934, pp. 228-229.

portant to note that, while in the United States the liberated population constituted a racial minority of Negroes, in Russia the liberated serfs were Russians and no racial antagonism complicated the search for a solution.[1] Aside from this fact, emancipation in Russia was productive of more profound and far-reaching consequences, since the 22,400,000 Russian serfs constituted approximately one-third of the population and were scattered throughout Russia proper, whereas the 3,500,000 Negroes amounted to somewhat less than one-ninth of the population of the United States and were located in one region, the South. Although in both countries the aftermath of liberation involved untold hardship and suffering, in Russia, which remained basically an agricultural country, the effects were perhaps more profound than in America where the rapid industrialization of the North offset in part, for the country as a whole, some of the dislocation that accompanied emancipation. In Russia a considerable number of liberated serfs had been engaged, under the *obrok* system, in manufacturing and trade, and a few had accumulated wealth even prior to their liberation.

With the abolition of serfdom, a change in rural government soon became necessary. Previously the nobility of a province had governed in behalf of all freemen residing therein. In 1864 a form of representative government, known as the zemstvo (from *zemlya,* land), was introduced into thirty-four provinces. Under this order, all property owners were allowed to participate in local affairs, although the nobility had precedence in all respects. By representative vote an "Executive Committee" or "Zemstvo Committee" was elected for a term of three years. This body took charge of the local affairs of a province. By 1870 town government was managed by a similar system. The zemstvos could levy taxes and had the supervision of roads, public charity, public health, and schools. The central government, which had a veto in all matters, was careful to restrict the zemstvo to local affairs and often interfered even in this field. This was especially true in regard to the schools, which, as directed by the zemstvos, were usually more liberal than the government desired. Hence there was considerable governmental supervision of the teaching body. Yet often, in spite of the interference of the government, the zemstvo schools produced noteworthy results in their efforts to banish ignorance from the rural districts. Both the provincial zemstvo and the town government were responsible for much material and cultural progress previous to the Revolution of 1917. If this had not been the case, the Revolution would have been

[1] See pp. 202-203.

marked by even more horrors and bloodshed. In 1914 the expenditure
of the zemstvos of forty-three provinces was in the neighborhood of
400,000,000 rubles. Of this, the sum of 106,000,000 rubles was devoted
to public education. There were 50,000 zemstvo schools employing
80,000 teachers and furnishing instruction to 3,000,000 children. All
of this came to an end in 1917.

Of equal importance to the reforms in local government were the
reforms in the judiciary in 1864. The most outstanding of these were
an alteration and improvement in court procedure, the introduction of
trial by jury, and the organization of lawyers into a formal bar. Thus
strengthened, the courts operated with a considerable degree of efficiency. Their prestige was enhanced by the recognition of their independence from administrative interference, by provision for better pay
and improved training for judges, whose appointment was permanent,
and by regulations requiring public hearings in cases that came before
these courts. The principle of equality before the law was recognized.

Another important reform of the reign of Alexander was the introduction in 1874 of compulsory universal military service. However, it
was by no means so rigid and autocratic as it had been under Nicholas
I. Thus the long term of service was shortened to six years, and family
ties and responsibilities were respected. An only son, an only grandson, or a son who was the sole support of a family, registered in what
was known as the reserve of the Second Category (*Vtoroye Opolt-
chenie*). This reserve, previous to World War I, was never called into
active service. Likewise recruits possessing a secondary education received consideration in respect to term of service, promotion, and certain privileges. Although the officers of the Guard were drawn exclusively from the aristocracy, the rest of the army was the most democratic institution in all Russia. Here the diverse races and creeds of the
great expanse of the empire met on a footing of equality and began to
develop a better understanding of each other.

Much of the harsh, restrictive legislation of Nicholas I was repealed,
and a more liberal, humanitarian policy adopted. In the army and the
imperial tribunals, corporal punishment was legally abolished, although
sometimes resorted to, nevertheless. In the peasant tribunals it still
remained in force. Censorship of the press was relaxed in its vigilance,
and soon there sprang up in St. Petersburg and Moscow periodicals
which had a brisk circulation. By 1860 full civil rights were granted to
foreign residents, in conformity with the practice followed by other
European countries. This did much to break down the barriers which
the policy of Nicholas I had created between Russia and her neighbors.

Restrictions were removed from the universities. The number of students was no longer limited to 300; the cost of tuition was lowered, and scholarships were offered for the encouragement of talent and ability.

Alexander II likewise extended many privileges to the Jews. On March 16, 1857, and November 27, 1861, he enacted laws which permitted Jewish scholars, university graduates, wholesale merchants, and manufacturers to reside outside the Pale of Settlement. In 1865 this privilege, with certain restrictions, was also granted to artisans. The emperor would have been glad to abolish the Pales entirely, but he dared not oppose the bureaucracy. The Jews were fully cognizant of his good will, and his policy did more to Russianize them than all previous resorts to force and compulsion. Indeed if the Jews had continued to enjoy these privileges and had been allowed to associate with other citizens on a basis of freedom and equality, by 1917 many of them would have been completely absorbed by the Russian people. The pogroms, following the reign of Alexander II, once more set them apart and made them keenly aware of their Judaism.

In pursuance of his policy of liberalism, Alexander II tried to calm the seething unrest in Poland by granting the country self-government. He appointed Grank Duke Constantine Nikolayevitch as viceroy, because of the latter's Polish sympathies and liberalism, and established complete local autonomy under him. Poland, however, responded to the overtures of the emperor by an outbreak of rebellion in January 1863. Russian garrisons in Poland and Lithuania were attacked, and the revolt began to assume formidable proportions. The seriousness of the situation was further intensified by the possibility of interference by Austria, France, and England on the basis of the international settlement at Vienna. The reactionaries now took the opportunity to charge that the reforms had been carried to extremes and were the cause of all sorts of confusion and disaster. The emperor yielded to their insistence, suppressed the revolt without mercy, and then deprived the Poles of local autonomy. In order to gain some support in the rebellious territory, he granted privileges to the peasants at the expense of the nobles.

Among his other problems Alexander confronted serious financial difficulties, some of which emanated from the huge expenditures and wholesale graft that occurred during the Crimean War, some from the excess of imports over exports subsequent to the war, as a result of which there was an alarming depreciation of the ruble. The emperor secured an able financial administrator in M. Kh. Reutern (1820-1890), who directed his efforts toward economy at home and the increase of exports abroad, especially the export of wheat. With this last object in view, he encouraged the construction of railways to Russia's leading ports on the Baltic and Black Seas. Incidentally, the export of Russian grain to western Europe adversely affected American farm prices and contributed to an agricultural depression in the United States. The Russian economy was continually handicapped, however, by the difficulty of attracting foreign capital, and Russia was forced in the main to fall back on her own resources. As previously indicated, there were only 13,000 miles of railroad in Russia by 1875, as compared with the 35,000 miles in operation in the United States at the close of the Civil War. It is significant that even the $7,200,000 secured from the sale of Alaska to America in 1867 were earmarked by Reutern for railroad construction. Although by dint of great effort Reutern succeeded temporarily in stabilizing the financial situation in Russia by 1875, the renewal of war with Turkey in 1877 threatened to undo much of the good he accomplished.

FOREIGN POLICY

The defeat of Russia in the Crimean War by no means put an end to Russian efforts in the direction of territorial expansion. It was scarcely to be expected that Russia, which held more than 1000 miles of coastline on the Black Sea, would accept indefinitely the unrealistic provision in the Treaty of Paris that excluded her fleet from that sea and forbade the construction of fortifications along its shores. Russians likewise regarded their exclusion from the mouth of the Danube as intolerable. Alexander II merely awaited a favorable opportunity to dispose of "these two nightmares." Moreover, Anglo-French success in "blocking" Russian expansion in the direction of the Mediterranean in 1856 merely deflected the tsarist program of expansion to the Middle and Far East, with the result that England, in particular, soon had further occasion for anxiety.

The favorable opportunity Alexander sought was afforded by the Franco-Prussian War (1870-1871). Under the circumstances it was greatly to Bismarck's advantage to promote discord between England and Russia, while Germany settled her score with France. In October 1870, therefore, with the prior consent and perhaps even at the instigation of Bismarck, Prince Alexander Gortchakov, the Russian foreign minister, announced Russia's unilateral denunciation of the Black Sea clauses of the Treaty of Paris. In return for the "benevolent neutrality" of Russia during the Austro-Prussian War (1866) and the Franco-Prussian War, Prussia at once refused to join England in any protest against Russian action. As a result, the offensive clauses were formally repealed by the signatories of the Treaty of Paris at a conference held in London in 1871. At the same time, in a face-saving gesture, the powers reaffirmed those clauses which provided for the closing of the Straits to the warships of all nations, except at the invitation of the Sultan of Turkey.

Meanwhile, news of Russian expansion in Central Asia began to arouse concern among the European powers, especially England. After the successful completion of the conquest of the Caucasus in 1859, the Russian army continued its efforts to revive the military prestige of the Tsarist Empire by new victories in Asia and to establish a defensible frontier there. In a rapid succession of victories during the next twenty years the Russians captured the Uzbek city of Tashkent (1865) and made it the capital of the new province of Turkestan, occupied Samarkand (1868), the famous capital of the Empire of Tamerlane, and converted the Khanate of Bokhara into a Russian protectorate. England, greatly alarmed at the strides the tsarist forces were taking in the direction of India, proposed the recognition of a series of "buffer states," including Afghanistan. Although Russia somewhat tentatively accepted this proposition, the instability of conditions in Central Asia and the absence of a natural frontier led to the occupation of Khiva (1873) and of the Khanate of Kokand (1876), thereby extending Russian frontiers to the mountainous northwest borders of China. Russian forces then proceeded to subjugate the warlike Turkoman tribes in the Trans-Caspian region. Thus Russia carved out for herself a new and rich Asiatic empire. In the wake of Russian armies came merchants and traders. It was not long until American cotton was being cultivated in Central Asia. About the same time Russian relations with Persia assumed a new aspect, when in 1878 the shah requested the Russian government to undertake the training of the Persian armed forces.

Before the Crimean War, official Russian opinion was divided as to the wisdom of expansion in the Far East. Such expansion as took place was mainly the product of individual initiative. As a result of the Russian defeat in Europe, however, the monarchy lent official sanction and support to prominent and colorful Russian expansionists like Count Nikolai N. Muraviev (1809-1881). Indeed Muraviev may be said to have established the pattern for a Russian foreign policy in the Pacific, based upon two premises: cultivation of friendship toward the United States and expansion at the expense of China. Judging by materials extant he was the first to suggest, as early as January 1853, the cession of Russian America, including Alaska, to the United States as a guarantee against any future clash between the two countries. As a result of his energy and activity Russia's territorial gains in the Far East were considerable. By the Treaty of Aigun in 1858 the Amur region, which had been abandoned to China in 1689 by the Treaty of Nertchinsk, was regained. In the same year the Treaty of Tientsin conferred upon Russia the extraterritorial privileges already acquired by other Western powers. Two years later, in 1860, Russia acquired the Maritime Province as a result of the Treaty of Peking. The Chinese government recognized the right of Russia to engage in free trade in Mongolia in 1862. Within another ten years there was a flourishing seaport and naval station at Vladivostok on the Sea of Japan. Nor was Russian expansion confined to the mainland in the years that followed. In 1875 Russia entered into an agreement with Japan, whereby she exchanged the Kurile Islands for the southern half of the Island of Sakhalin.

Realizing the hostility of the European powers, Russia from time to time had sought a *rapprochement* with the United States. The suspicion and dislike which both countries felt for England and a certain similarity in their social problems of serfdom and slavery made a mutual understanding not improbable. Nevertheless the *rapprochement* did not progress beyond the lending of moral support upon a few occasions. For instance, the United States demonstrated its good will to Russia at the time of the Crimean War. In return for this the Russian government came out openly in favor of the Union forces during the critical stage of the Civil War. The dispatch of units of the Russian fleet to New York and San Francisco in the fall of 1863 may have been motivated by self-interest, in view of Anglo-French hostility toward Russia during the Polish insurrection, but it led Gideon Welles, Secretary of the United States Navy, to exclaim in all sincerity: "God bless the Russians!" Admiral Popov's sojourn in San Francisco during the winter of 1863-1864 served to discourage any hostile action on the part of Confederate cruisers against that port. The pro-Russian sentiment which swept the Union at this time played an important role in connection with William H. Seward's purchase of Alaska for $7,200,000 in 1867.[1] However, Alexander's policy of imperialism won no approval in the United States, and American diplomacy was, as yet, definitely committed to the policy of avoiding "foreign entanglements." Therefore Alexander abandoned any effort to bring about a closer understanding with the United States and in 1872 joined with William I of Germany and Francis Joseph of Austria in the Three Emperors' League.

In 1875 the Near Eastern question came once again to the fore, with

---

[1] See Farrar, Victor J., *The Annexation of Russian America to the United States*, Washington, 1937, p. 61.

the outbreak of disturbances, first in the Turkish provinces of Bosnia and Herzogovina, and later in Bulgaria, in protest against Turkish oppression. The Bulgarian massacres that marked the suppression of the revolt aroused public opinion throughout Europe, and among the Slavic peoples in particular. Although the signatories of the Treaty of Paris had assumed the role of protectors of the Christian peoples under Turkish domination, they failed to take any decisive action in the face of Turkish atrocities. England had acquired a vested interest in Turkey, having extended loans to that country amounting by 1875 to some £200,000,000, and although Gladstone made political capital out of the Bulgarian atrocities, Disraeli, the prime minister, refused to act in concert with the powers. Bismarck, estranged by Alexander's intervention to forestall a preventive war on the part of Germany against France in 1875, rejected Gortchakov's proposal to call a conference and pursued a policy calculated to embroil England with Russia, thereby fanning the flames of war in the Near East.[1] In 1876 the small Balkan states of Serbia and Montenegro made war on Turkey, and the former placed its army under the command of an able Russian general. The Serbs were, nevertheless, confronted with the certainty of overwhelming defeat, when, on April 24, 1877, Russia took unilateral action and declared war on Turkey.

Although the Turkish forces were supplied with up-to-date English equipment, the outcome of the war soon became apparent, as the Russian army continued its relentless march on Constantinople. Although war hysteria ran high in England, Disraeli did not wish to fight alone, and his efforts to secure active Austrian intervention proved futile. France was more concerned with the German menace than with Turkey. As Russian troops approached Constantinople, England dispatched a fleet to the Sea of Marmora, and the hostile Anglo-Russian forces faced one another for a time at San Stefano. Since Austria joined England in threatening to break off diplomatic relations with Russia in the event that Russian troops occupied Constantinople, the tsar, anxious to avoid a general conflict, halted his army just outside the city. On March 3, 1878, the Turks made peace with Russia by the Treaty of San Stefano.

The terms of this treaty bore witness to the overwhelming defeat of the Turks. They provided for the creation of a new and greatly enlarged principality of Bulgaria, the independence of Montenegro, Rumania, and Serbia, and administrative reforms in Bosnia and Herzogovina. For her share, Russia regained the mouth of the Danube,

---

[1] See Potemkin, Academician V. P., Editor, *History of Diplomacy* (in Russian), Moscow, 1945, Vol. II, pp. 30-39.

which she had lost in 1856, together with Batum, Kars, and Ardahan
in Transcaucasia, and a financial indemnity. In demanding so much
from Turkey Alexander committed a diplomatic error. He aroused the
envy and fear of other powers having interests in the Balkans, namely
England and Austria. Since, in 1875, in response to the urgent appeal
of Queen Victoria, Alexander had exerted pressure upon Germany to
prevent the renewal of war against France, he had assumed that both
England and France would allow him a free hand in the Balkans. This
did not prove to be the case. Austria, seeking compensation in the
south for what she had lost to Germany, joined England in demanding
a European conference to settle the whole problem of peace in the Balkans. For a time a general European war seemed imminent. However, Germany took the initiative through her chancellor, Bismarck,
who assumed the role of an "honest broker" and called a conference at
Berlin in 1878 to revise the Treaty of San Stefano.

At Berlin, Gortchakov confronted an anti-Russian bloc, with the
result that Russia lost by diplomacy a large part of what she had gained
by force of arms. The provisions of the Treaty of San Stefano regarding Bessarabia, the Dobruja, and the independence of Montenegro,
Serbia, and Rumania were allowed to stand. The territory of Bulgaria
was, however, drastically reduced. Macedonia was restored to Turkey,
and the remaining region was divided into two parts, namely, Bulgaria
and Eastern Rumelia, both of which were reduced to dependencies of
Turkey. Austria was permitted to occupy Bosnia and Herzogovina
"temporarily," as well as to station troops in the Sanjak of Novibazar.
Since the Russians insisted on retaining Kars, Batum, and Ardahan in
Transcaucasia, England took Cyprus as "compensation."

Thus although Russia, in spite of her complete isolation by the great
powers at Berlin, retained her own territorial gains, she once again lost
her sphere of influence in the Balkans, and with it her prestige among
the Slavic peoples of that area, who felt that their interests had been
sacrificed. Alexander II, like Nicholas I before him, had failed to settle
the Turkish question by unilateral action. As for the "defenders" of
Turkey, Austria and England, without having fired a shot in the war
they participated in what actually amounted to another partial partition
of the Ottoman Empire. Bismarck's support of Austria's interests over
and above those of Russia at the Congress of Berlin effected a breach
in the Three Emperors' League. Moreover Russia's isolation in Europe was still further emphasized by the establishment of the Triple
Alliance of Germany, Austria, and Italy (1879-1881). As in the case
of the Crimean War, Russia turned her back upon Europe and proceeded

to concentrate upon further expansion in Asia, especially in the Far East.

The diplomatic defeat at Berlin led to increased criticism of Alexander II at home. Had he succeeded in winning Constantinople, or even in preserving intact the terms of the Treaty of San Stefano, public criticism would have been in large measure silenced, especially among the conservative Slavophiles. The reactionaries had long raised the cry that his domestic reforms were undermining the very foundations of the government. They now claimed that his foreign policy had humiliated Russia in the eyes of the world. The liberals, too, had long accused Alexander of procrastination in instituting reforms, which, when they came, proved to be halfway measures. Many of the more radical intellectuals had already preached Nihilism,[1] as did Michael Bakunin (1814-1876) from his refuge in Switzerland, or anarchism, like the scholarly Prince Peter Kropotkin (1842-1921), and regarded revolution as the only solution. Young intellectuals were distributing revolutionary and seditious literature among the people. In 1877, during the Turkish War, some 183 Nihilists had been arraigned in St. Petersburg for sedition, and were regarded by many as martyrs to the cause of liberalism. In 1879, however, an abortive attempt was made on the life of the emperor. When it was learned that the tsar had been condemned to death by a secret society with widespread affiliations, the government struck back with blind fury and conducted a campaign of repression throughout the country. Several other attempts were made upon Alexander's life before he was finally assassinated on March 13, 1881, by a member of a terrorist organization known as "The Will of the People."[2] Ironically enough, Alexander was assassinated immediately following his acceptance of a constitution for Russia—a constitution on which a Preparatory Committee, headed by Count Loris-Melikov (1825-1888) had been working since 1880. His son and heir, Alexander III, rescinded the constitution and the *ukaz* of Alexander II, which had been signed, was never proclaimed.

REIGN OF EMPEROR ALEXANDER III (1881-1894)

The entire country was shocked by the assassination of Alexander II, with the result that the stage was set for a general reaction against liberalism. The accession of Alexander III coincided with a period of

---

[1] See pp. 206-207.
[2] A graphic account of the conspiracy against the life of Alexander II is to be found in fictionalized form in Mark Aldanov's novel, *Before the Deluge*, N. Y., 1947.

economic depression (1880-1885)—an aftermath of the European slump of 1876—which affected prices and led to industrial strikes of weavers, railwaymen, and dock laborers. This depression likewise contributed to the impoverishment of the landowning nobility, many of whom had to sell their estates and move to the towns. Here they agitated incessantly for a return to a more autocratic policy in government under a strong, reactionary ruler. Such a ruler Alexander III proved to be.

All Alexander's governmental measures were directed toward the restoration of absolute autocracy and the suppression of everything which savored of liberalism and revolution. Privileges were curtailed, and former restrictions revived and intensified. In this favorable atmosphere religious persecution began once again to make itself manifest, as if it had been merely biding its time in anticipation of such an opportunity. Since in Russia, autocratic government has always been closely associated with the Church, it occasions no surprise that the emperor's former tutor, Constantine Pobyedonostsev (1827-1907), Procurator of the Holy Synod from 1880 to 1905, was the directing spirit behind much of the reign of terror which broke out shortly after the accession of Alexander III. Pobyedonostsev was a former Professor of Civil Law at the University of Moscow and a jurist of some repute, the author of a *Course of Civil Law* (1868-1875). In his political philosophy, however, he was the advocate of autocracy and an uncompromising opponent of constitutional reform. In Russia his name became synonymous with black reaction and religious persecution under the guise of Russification.

Whereas all non-Orthodox peoples and dissenters in general suffered from this campaign, it was the Jews who were especially singled out for bitter and relentless persecution. Within a few weeks of the accession of Alexander III a series of atrocities were committed against the Jews in some 170 places in the southern parts of European Russia. These pogroms, as they were called, had the official sanction of the government and elicited no protest from the Orthodox Church. They were devised to distract attention from certain revolutionary movements that were threatening tsardom, and since some Jewish youths had joined their Gentile compatriots in a movement against autocracy, the government pointed to the pogroms as an indication that the Russian people "had given vent" to their fury against revolutionaries and like enemies of the emperor.

As already indicated, religious persecution was not confined to the Jews alone, Roman Catholics and Protestants also being subject to it.

In their case, however, the persecution consisted more in a curtailment of liberties, with the purpose of forcing religious conformity and achieving Russification. Thus throughout Poland further restrictions were placed on the acquisition of land by Poles, and the Bank of Poland was replaced by the Bank of Russia. Even in Finland a campaign of Russification was begun. In the Baltic Province an attempt was made to eradicate German cultural influence, the German language being replaced by Russian in the courts and schools. In the Caucasus Tartars and Georgians were subject to corresponding restrictions.

Against political offenders the law became so severe that all radicalism and terrorist organizations like "The Will of the People" were driven underground. The following excerpt from the law on political offenses signed by Alexander III in 1881 affords eloquent testimony of the conditions which existed in Russia at this time:

Section 249. All persons who shall engage in rebellion against the Supreme Authority—that is, who shall take part in collective and conspirative insurrection against the Gossudar (the Emperor) and the Empire; and also all persons who shall plan the overthrow of the Government in the Empire as a whole, or in any part thereof; or who shall intend to change the existing form of government, or the order of succession to the throne established by law; all persons who, for the attainment of these ends, shall organize or take part in a conspiracy, either actively and with knowledge of its object, or by participation in a conspirative meeting, or by storing or distributing weapons, or by other preparations for insurrection—all such persons, including not only those most guilty, but their associates, instigators, prompters, helpers, and concealers, shall be deprived of all civil rights and be put to death. Those who have knowledge of such evil intentions, and of preparations to carry them into execution, and who, having power to inform the Government thereof, do not fulfill that duty, shall be subjected to the same punishment.

Section 250. If the guilty persons have not manifested an intention to resort to violence, but have organized a society or association intended to attain, at a more or less remote time in the future, the objects set forth in Section 249, or have joined such an association, they shall be sentenced, according to the degree of their criminality, either to from four to six years of penal servitude, with deprivation of all civil rights (including exile to Siberia for life) . . . or to colonization in Siberia (without penal servitude), or to imprisonment in a fortress from one year and four months to four years.[1]

Under such a system parents were exiled because their children were engaged in revolutionary activity. Even the well-known Russian novel-

---

[1] See Kennan, George, *Siberia and the Exile System,* Vol. II, p. 509.

ist, Vladimir Korolenko (1853-1921), after having been reprieved from exile in Siberia due to an official error, was banished again when he refused to betray friends and acquaintances who opposed the government. In 1885 an American by the name of George Kennan, who had been in Russia on previous occasions, undertook for *The Century Magazine* to make a study of the exile system. His classic two-volume report (*Siberia and the Exile System,* New York, 1891) so aroused public sentiment in the West that it even led to the adoption of some reforms in Siberia.

It naturally follows that government censorship permeated every phase of life. The press and the universities, which were reorganized in 1884, were stripped of every semblance of liberty. There was outright interference with the courts, especially as regards the independence of judges and the jury system. The police exercised a supervision and operated with a license unheard of even in the days of Nicholas I. Political prisoners were regarded as having lost all rights and were subjected to shocking brutality. A greater contrast to the liberalism of Alexander II could not well be imagined than that presented by the absolutism of Alexander III. In 1887 a plot to assassinate Alexander III was uncovered by the police. The leaders of the conspiracy were executed. Among them was Alexander Ulyanov, Lenin's eldest brother.

While the baleful influence of political reaction hung over the country like a pall, important advances were made in the economic development and industrialization of Russia. In order to free the country from economic dependence on Germany, Professor Ivan Vyshnegradsky, minister of finance, in 1891 inaugurated a policy of tariff protectionism, which served as a spur to domestic industrial enterprise, especially the production of such items as iron, coal and cotton. Banks were established to aid in the rehabilitation of the destitute nobility and to care for the needs of the peasants. Certain labor legislation was also enacted by which exploitation of employees by employers was somewhat limited. The state derived huge profits from the establishment in 1893 of a government monopoly of the sale of intoxicating liquors. Of particular importance were the steps taken in the direction of the stabilization of the ruble, which led in 1897 to the adoption of the gold standard, thereby facilitating business at home and abroad.

The outstanding material accomplishment of the period was the construction of the Trans-Siberian Railway, decided upon in 1885 and actually begun from both Vladivostok and Tchelyabinsk in 1891. Whereas in the United States railway construction ordinarily preceded the population of a region, in Russia it had served heretofore to open up

FROM LIBERATOR TO THE LAST EMPEROR 149

to trade and industry many areas that were thickly populated. Already by 1880 the railroad had crossed the Volga and reached the Urals. Although it was well known that a railway across Siberia would promote the economic development and settlement of the country, the project was delayed by failure to agree on a suitable route across the Urals. Rumors of a Chinese railway project under English auspices finally galvanized the government into action.[1] The Trans-Siberian Railway was constructed by the state between 1891 and 1904 at a cost of 400,000,000 rubles. Although in its inception the project was primarily economic rather than strategic in design, after 1891 its strategic importance became ever more apparent. In reality this railroad made Siberia an integral part of the Russian Empire. Moreover, as events were soon to prove, it outflanked the British fleet in the Pacific.

Much of the success of the new national economic policies referred to above must go to Count Sergei Witte (1849-1915), who succeeded Vyshnegradsky as minister of finance from 1892 to 1903. Adopting as his own the policy of tariff protectionism inaugurated by his predecessor, Witte secured a favorable commercial treaty from Germany in 1894, thereby ending a tariff war between the two countries. Witte's primary objective was the economic development of Russia by means of industrialization and railroad construction, which he placed ahead of agrarian reform. Perhaps the secret of his success was that he left the delicate agrarian problem strictly to the emperor to handle, while he devoted himself to business and avoided arousing the antagonism of the landlords. In Russia, where agriculture was still the backbone of the nation, the interference of the government in the affairs of the landlords was likely to be as productive of trouble as government interference in business in the United States.

Witte was perhaps the first trained economist to be able to make his policy felt in the Emperor's Council to the extent that it superseded for a time that of the militarists and strategists. The impression is that he was tolerated rather than fully appreciated. Since he spoke the language of the industrial European nations, he was able to obtain much-needed foreign loans for the development of domestic industry. With his good neighbor policy he accomplished more, especially in the Far East, than his successors who pursued a policy of imperialistic expansion. The only man who has rivaled Witte in internal affairs, although his emphasis was on agrarian rather than industrial development, was Peter Stolypin (1862-1911), who was prime minister under Nicholas II,

---

[1] See Mayor, James, *An Economic History of Russia*, N. Y., 1914, Vol. II, pp. 226-228.

1906-1911. Both men subordinated foreign affairs to domestic well-being, and, although their methods differed, under both the country enjoyed a modicum of prosperity. In both cases their successors proved unable to check the imperialistic struggle for aggrandizement, and Russia was plunged into war in 1904 and 1914 respectively.

Under Alexander III, Russia, for the most part, stood aloof from European affairs and ceased to interfere in the concerns of other nations. This policy of "hands off" had come increasingly into favor following the Congress of Berlin in 1878. The emperor trusted no foreign power, had an especial hatred for England, and tolerated no outside meddling as a return for his own noninterference. During his reign, Russia but once had resort to arms. This was the conflict on the Kushk River with the Afghans in 1885. At its conclusion Russia came into possession of the Merv and Pendeh Oases.

Alexander III was nevertheless responsible for what turned out to be a momentous reorientation of Russia's foreign policy in the West. The formation of the Triple Alliance in Central Europe following the Congress of Berlin had aroused serious misgivings in Russia due to the clash of Austrian and Russian interests in the Balkans. In 1886 the prominent Russian publicist, Katkov, inaugurated a violent anti-German campaign in the Russian press, comparing Russian pilgrimages to Berlin with those of the Golden Horde, and called for a French alliance. Although the Three Emperors' League was renewed, with some recognition of Russia's primary interest in the Balkans, by the Reinsurance Treaty of 1887, this dynastic link was permitted to lapse after the fall of Bismarck in 1890. The new course of German policy under Kaiser William II, together with Bismarck's blunder in excluding Russian loans from the German market, which led to economic strife between the two countries, led Alexander III with reluctance to seek both security and economic aid elsewhere.

In 1888 the first of a series of French loans, which by 1891 amounted to three and one-quarter billion francs, paved the way for a realignment of Russian foreign policy. The French government promoted better feeling by arresting, at the request of the Russian ambassador, a group of Russian Nihilists in Paris. In 1891 a French squadron entered Russian naval waters for the first time since the Crimean War and was enthusiastically received at the Russian naval base at Kronstadt, where the tsar climaxed the official welcome by ordering the Russian band to play the hitherto forbidden French national anthem, the *Marseillaise*. It was during this visit that a Franco-Russian *rapprochement* was effected.

The Dual Alliance between Russia and France in 1891, by which both powers agreed to confer and to take concerted measures in the event of a threat of aggression, brought an end to Russian isolation in Europe. It remained only to implement the alliance by a military convention defining the terms of aid, which was accomplished in 1893. Although the existence of the alliance was not proclaimed until 1895, following the accession of Nicholas II, it remained an open secret in Europe. The Franco-Russian alliance was a significant event both for Russia and for Europe. From France Russia was able to secure the capital necessary for the construction of the Trans-Siberian Railway which changed the balance of power in Asia. In Europe it eventually paved the way for the division of the continent into the two armed camps which clashed in 1914 in World War I.

8

The Last of the Romanovs (Nicholas II)

REIGN OF EMPEROR NICHOLAS II (1894-1917)

NICHOLAS II came to the throne on November 1, 1894, and was crowned in Moscow on May 14, 1896. He lacked both the temperament and the training necessary for an able ruler. His unyielding obstinacy alternated with a weak vacillation. At times he was very susceptible to influence, but almost invariably seemed to yield to that which was most pernicious. While fairly well versed in the field of general literature, he had only the most inadequate and incorrect knowledge of the science of government. Like the majority of Russian princes and grand dukes, he had received an early education which had served to implant in him unreasoning and stubborn prejudices toward certain races and individuals.

In November 1894, he married a German princess of the House of Hesse, who accepted the Orthodox faith, and assumed the name of Alexandra Fyodorovna. From the first the new empress was very unpopular. Since her first appearance among the Russians coincided with the elaborate funeral ceremonies of Alexander III, she came to be known as the "funeral bride." [1] Because of her lack of Russian sympathies and her inability to adapt herself to Russian life, she was constantly the object of suspicion and distrust. Many people resented the fact that she refused to speak Russian unless obliged to do so, and made English and French the preferred languages at court. Her influence over Nicholas II was believed to be great, hence she received the blame

---

[1] At the height of the coronation festivities a horrible tragedy occurred. Thousands of spectators, who were waiting for the royal cortège, suddenly broke through the police lines. A panic ensued, in which some 2000 persons were crushed and trampled to death. In spite of this disaster which plunged the city into mourning, the usual state ball was held in the evening at the French Consulate. This was a great blunder on the part of the sovereigns and contributed much to their unpopularity.

for many reactionary measures. It is true that she was even more prejudiced and narrow-minded than he and, upon occasion, prevented him from making much-needed concessions. However, on his own responsibility Nicholas made it extremely plain shortly after his accession that he intended to follow the policy of his father. This he did by tightening government control and censorship in all fields where independent thought or action might be suspected of making an appearance.

As previously indicated, Alexander III had succeeded in re-establishing autocratic rule, which had been somewhat weakened by the reforms of Alexander II. He was able to do this because he very carefully kept out of foreign entanglements which were likely to weaken his prestige and authority at home. On the other hand, Nicholas II permitted himself to become involved in foreign affairs to his and to the country's exceeding disadvantage. The failure of his foreign policy was largely responsible for the social disorders which marred his reign.

Despite the recent financial and political ties with France, Nicholas II realized that Russia's position was by no means secure. In addition to being constantly pressed for money, he had an army, which was but poorly equipped as compared with the military forces of his European neighbors. In consideration of these facts, he took the initiative in calling for a conference of the Great Powers in the interests of international peace. The first Peace Conference convened at The Hague in 1899. In 1907, when Russia was much weakened by the Japanese War and the Revolution of 1905, the second Hague Peace Conference was called. Although the second Conference assembled at the invitation of Nicholas II, the suggestion for it came from President Theodore Roosevelt. Neither conference succeeded in bringing about any practical and lasting adjustments. The Great Powers were much too distrustful and jealous of one another to render any understanding possible. England resented the Franco-Russian alliance, Germany was wary of England, and Russia was suspicious of all of them.

Although international peace was of supreme importance to all Europe, no country stood in greater need of it than Russia. Even before the first Hague Conference in 1899, a group of farsighted statesmen, under the leadership of Witte, had seriously urged the abandonment, at least temporarily, of the policy of territorial expansion in favor of an economic expansion in the markets of the Middle and Far East. This, they believed, would contribute materially toward the establishment of internal stability; for the attainment of this end, however, there must be guarantees of external peace. A step in this direction was the understanding with France, which was much to the interest of both countries in view of Germany's growing militarism.

Germany, for her part, maintained peace with Russia and rendered her rather valuable assistance in European politics, because it was to her own interests to do so. She particularly favored Russia's activities in the Middle and Far East for two reasons. Her own immediate objectives in the *Drang nach Osten* were in the Near East, in Turkey. If Russia were occupied further afield, she would not meddle with Turkey, and at the same time would draw away the attention of England from the region in question. Russia's pretensions in the Far East were, at that time, of no particular interest to any nation but Japan, and hence were not as yet a factor to be considered in European politics. The mutual rivalry of Russia and Austria in the Balkans alone threatened to lead to immediate hostilities in the course of adjustment. To be sure, Alexander III had been strongly in favor of leaving the Slavonic peoples of the Balkans to their fate after Bulgaria and Serbia had demonstrated their "ingratitude" following the Congress of Berlin. After his death, however, there was a revival of interest in the "tradition" of the Near East. Germany again came to the fore and prevented a clash between Russia and Austria by engineering a *modus vivendi* between them with with respect to the Balkans.

Nicholas II, whose accession to the throne in 1894 coincided with the Sino-Japanese War, had a particular interest in the Far East. As heir apparent he had traveled widely in Asia, including Japan. On his return trip he laid the foundation stone for the eastern terminus of the Trans-Siberian Railway and subsequently became chairman of the committee on the construction of this road. Thus he was the first Russian monarch to have acquired first-hand information of Siberia and the Far East,[1] and the experience kindled his imagination. When, after a brief but decisive war, Japan defeated China and seized part of Manchuria and the Liaotung Peninsula, Nicholas, supported by Witte, secured the collaboration of Germany and France to force Japan to revise the Treaty of Shimonoseki (1895) and relinquish the conquered territory. On July 6, 1895, Russia, together with France, loaned China 400,000,000 francs to pay the Japanese indemnity. England and Germany also made loans to China, amounting to £16,000,000 each. In gratitude for this assistance, China was persuaded by Witte to make a treaty with Russia (June 3, 1896), whereby the latter secured permission to build railroads in Manchuria across the Provinces of Heilung-

---

[1] Gurko, V. I., *Features and Figures of the Past*, Stanford University, 1939, p. 256.

kiang and Kirin in the direction of Vladivostok. The Chinese Eastern Railway Company was organized and financed with the aid of France and Germany. According to the original plans, this railroad was to connect Tchita and Vladivostok and to operate only in northern Manchuria. In return for this concession, Russia guaranteed to come to the aid of China in case the latter was attacked by a third party. It was understood that this clause was aimed at Japan.

Russia had now laid a firm foundation for a policy of peaceful, economic penetration of China, which policy, if continued, would have redounded very considerably to her material advantage and averted the disastrous conflict with Japan in 1904-1905. Unfortunately Nicholas II and his advisers had more imperialistic aims. When Germany, after openly advocating the occupation of Chinese ports by European nations as a guarantee of their financial interests, took the lead and seized Kiaochow, Nicholas was persuaded, against the advice of Witte, to take parallel action. Russian warships appeared at Port Arthur a week later, and on March 27, 1898, Russia by resort to bribery forced China to surrender to her on a twenty-five year lease the Liaotung Peninsula, the very territory that Japan had been forced to evacuate after the peace of Shimonoseki, while France occupied Kwangchowan and Great Britain took Weihaiwei "for so long a period as Port Arthur shall remain in possession of Russia." It is worthy of note that like the Liaotung Peninsula, Weihaiwei had also been occupied by Japan during the Sino-Japanese War but had been voluntarily relinquished. Thus the good results of the Russo-Chinese Treaty of 1896 were entirely destroyed. China was bitterly resentful toward all the European powers, but most of all toward Russia for her breach of friendship. The situation was not improved when in 1900 Russia and other European countries intervened for the purpose of suppressing the Boxer Rebellion. Russian troops occupied Manchuria and committed many acts of violence against the Chinese civilian population in this region.

Many causes contributed to the deterioration of relations between Russia and Japan. As a matter of course, Japan had deeply resented Russia's interference in 1894-1895. Then the latter's occupation of the Liaotung Peninsula in 1898, and of Manchuria in 1900, had aroused throughout Japan the most serious fears of a further extension of Russian imperialism. From 1900 on Nicholas II fell more and more under the influence of an irresponsible group of adventurers, whose reckless policy led Russia to drift into war with Japan. The so-called Bezobrazov Circle, which in addition to the ambitious schemer, A. M. Bezobrazov, included Admiral Alexeyev, whom Nicholas in 1903 appointed his Vice-

roy in the Far East, and Admiral Abaza, a representative of the Yalu
Company for the development of the forest resources of Northern Korea,
favored a policy of outright expansion and intervention in Manchuria
and Korea. They vigorously opposed Witte's policy of caution and
peaceful penetration. Hence Japan not only feared severe economic competition with Russia, especially in Korea, but she was likewise apprehensive lest this region fall a prey to Russian expansion. The Japanese
felt that their very existence was at stake. Moreover Admiral Alexeyev
pursued a policy in regard to Japan which, by reason of its domineering
tactlessness, tended to render the situation more and more acute. By
1902, the construction of the Trans-Siberian Railroad, by means of
which Russia outflanked the British fleet in the Far East, led to the
conclusion of an Anglo-Japanese Alliance directed against Russia. Before the construction of this railroad, Eastern Siberia was little more
than a distant Russian hinterland. The advent of the Trans-Siberian
route, however, indicated clearly enough to both Britain and Japan that
Russia intended to become a leading Pacific power—a situation they
were anxious to prevent. It is significant to note, however, that prior to
signing an alliance with Great Britain the Japanese statesman, Prince
Ito, tried ineffectually to reach an understanding with Russia regarding
Korea.

Meanwhile the Russian government, dominated as it was by the
expansionists after the removal of Witte in 1903, felt the necessity of
"a small victorious war," which would unite the people and divert their
attention from unsatisfactory internal conditions. For some time, as an
outgrowth of the repressive policies of V. K. Plehve (1846-1904), minister of the interior, and an inveterate opponent of Witte, there had
been mutterings of a revolutionary nature, and nothing could be better
calculated to check these than a brilliant victory in some foreign field.
The country was in no condition to engage in a test of strength with any
European power, but Russia had never yet lost a war with a non-Euro-
pean nation. Hence the situation in regard to Japan seemed to be made
to order.

England also was much interested in the possibility of a struggle
between Russia and Japan. In such an event, Russia would be drawn
away from the Middle East, where she had long been a thorn in the
flesh to Great Britain. Moreover, the latter, in common with other
European powers, had become more and more interested in the Far East,
and Russia's expansion in that direction, which a few years earlier had
been of no especial importance to her, was now regarded by England
with the most lively concern.

England and Japan, it should be said, were not the only countries alarmed by Russian expansion in the Far East. The United States, which, following the Spanish-American War (1898), watched with growing concern the tightening of the Russian grip on Manchuria, was vitally interested in the opening up of this region to American investment. While John Hay's call for the preservation of the Open Door in China (1899-1900) was not aimed solely at Russia, the American secretary of state was motivated largely by his fear that Russia would obtain exclusive rights in Manchuria to the detriment of American interests. For similar reasons the United States government regarded with satisfaction the Anglo-Japanese Alliance of 1902, which recognized Japan's special interests in Korea. In fact, less than a month before the outbreak of hostilities between Russia and Japan the United States assured the Japanese government of its "benevolence" in the event of war. Thus by 1904 Russian policy in the Far East had not only alienated China and brought about an alliance between England and Japan, but it had led the United States to lend moral support to Japanese expansionism in order to counteract that of Russia.

Under such circumstances, all that was needed to precipitate a crisis was some excuse or overt act. This Japan furnished on February 8, 1904, when without warning her fleet attacked Russian warships moored in the outer harbor of Port Arthur. A declaration of war by Russia followed, and the struggle was on. In its initial stages, the Korean Peninsula was the locale of land fighting between the Russians and the Japanese. In fact, Russo-Japanese rivalry for the control of Korea was a leading casus belli in this conflict.

The war did not go well for the Russians. Although the incompetent Alexeyev was superseded as commander-in-chief by the minister of war, General Kuropatkin, the former remained viceroy in the Far East, with the result that there was no real co-ordination of effort, such as was displayed by the Japanese. In September 1904 the Russians were defeated in the important Battle of Liaoyang. On January 1, 1905, General Stoessel, in what practically amounted to treason, surrendered Port Arthur without calling a Council of War, although the garrison still had a three months' supply of food and more than 2,000,000 rounds of ammunition. The defense of this important port cost the Russians more than 28,000 men and the Japanese more than twice that number. With reinforcements from Port Arthur, the Japanese were able to win the Battle of Mukden in March 1905, although in the course of two weeks' fighting both sides lost 70,000 men. Whereas the main forces of the Russian army were never sent to the Far East, Admiral Rozhdestvensky sailed the Baltic fleet halfway around the world, only to meet

with overwhelming defeat at the hands of Admiral Togo in the Battle
of the Tsushima Straits in May 1905. The Russians lost thirty out of
forty-seven ships, and only three managed to reach Vladivostok.

   This disastrous turn of affairs naturally produced internal results
far different from those which the Russian government had anticipated.
The Russian people had never been particularly interested in the war,
seeing no good reason why they should fight Japan for Chinese territory when China herself remained consistently neutral. The series of
defeats produced financial disturbances, which in turn provoked internal disorders. Far from diverting popular attention from revolutionary
activities, the war provoked an uprising. The Russian government was
ready to secure peace on almost any terms, so that the army might be
used to crush internal revolt. The Japanese were not unaware of the
collapse of their foe, but they themselves were well-nigh exhausted and
were too eager for peace to press very far the advantage which their
victories gave them. At this critical juncture, President Theodore
Roosevelt tendered his good offices, with the result that a treaty of peace
was signed on September 5, 1905, at Portsmouth, New Hampshire.

   Throughout the war American public opinion had remained overwhelmingly favorable to Japan. Roosevelt's own pro-Japanese stand is
clearly indicated in a letter which he sent to his friend Cecil Spring-
Rice, the British ambassador in St. Petersburg:

   As soon as this war broke out, I notified Germany and France in the
most polite and discreet fashion that in the event of a combination against
Japan to try to do what Russia, Germany, and France did to her in 1894
(*sic*) I would promptly side with Japan and proceed to whatever length
was necessary on her behalf.[1]

The American press represented the Japanese war effort as a struggle
for self-preservation against "a vicious despotism," as well as for the
maintenance of the Open Door and the integrity of China. It was even
claimed that Japan was fighting America's battle in the Far East and
stood for the preservation of Anglo-Saxon civilization![2] Anglo-American loans practically financed the Japanese war. As the conflict pro-

   [1] Quoted in Zabriskie, *op. cit.,* p. 104.
   [2] For an interesting analysis of American public opinion during the war and the
peace conference, see Thorson, Winston B., "American Public Opinion and the Portsmouth Peace Conference," *American Historical Review,* Vol. LIII, No. 3, April 1948,
pp. 439-464; and by the same author, "Pacific Northwest Opinion on the Russo-
Japanese War of 1904-1905," *Pacific Northwest Quarterly,* XXXV (October 1944),
pp. 305-322.

gressed, Roosevelt became somewhat concerned lest Japanese victories should lead to Japanese predominance in the Far East and constitute a threat to American interests. He visualized a long war, with the ultimate exhaustion of both belligerents, as most likely to redound to the interests of the United States. The official Russian press, for its part, openly blamed the United States for instigating the war and speculated about American designs on Eastern Siberia. It was largely in the expectation that Roosevelt might use his influence with Japan to secure reasonable peace terms that the Russians agreed to his mediation and the holding of the peace conference in the United States.

Nicholas II, anxious to secure the best possible terms, wisely appointed the previously discredited Witte as the head of the Russian delegation, with instructions not to pay "a kopeck of indemnity or yield an inch of land." At Portsmouth the Japanese demanded (1) an indemnity of $750,000,000, (2) the cession of the entire island of Sakhalin, (3) the lease of the Liaotung Peninsula, and (4) the limitation of Russian naval power in the Far East. A deadlock ensued, but since both powers stood in dire need of peace and could float no more loans in the foreign market to carry on the conflict, pressure was brought to effect a compromise. By the terms of the Treaty of Portsmouth Japan secured only the southern half of the island of Sakhalin and Russia's lease of the Liaotung Peninsula, including Port Arthur. Since the Russians to the bitter end remained obdurate on the subject of paying "tribute" to an Asiatic power, the Japanese finally abandoned their demand for a cash indemnity. Since Japan acquired important political, military, and economic concessions with regard to Korea, thereby replacing Russia, and the two belligerents agreed to evacuate Manchuria and return it to China, the United States government felt reasonably satisfied that the balance of power had been restored in Asia. Whether or not President Roosevelt was influenced by considerations unfavorable to Japan, the fact remains that he tendered a service of inestimable value to both combatants. In Russia, however, the "favorable" terms of the treaty were attributed, not to him, but to the leader of the Russian delegation, Sergei Witte, who received the title of "Count" as a reward for his services.[1] The Japanese, in spite of their very considerable gains, resented the fact that they had been deprived of the just "fruits of victory" and regarded the treaty as "a national disgrace." There was little or no indication at the time, however, that Japan and Russia would soon join forces to curb American expansion in the Pacific.

---

[1] See, however, Lobanov-Rostovsky, Andrei, *Russia and Asia*, 1933, p. 234.

POLITICAL PARTIES AND THE REVOLUTION OF 1905

In Russia the emergence of political parties was obstructed by the reaction that marked the period from the closing years of the reign of Alexander II until 1905, during which all political as well as terrorist organizations were driven underground or of necessity found asylum abroad. George Plekhanov (1857-1918), for example, a one-time exponent of "The Will of the People," fled to Switzerland, where he adopted Marxism and in 1883 founded the first Russian group of avowed Marxists under the name, "Liberation of Labor." Its members translated into Russian the works of Marx and Engels and distributed them secretly in Russia. By 1893 the term "Social Democrats," borrowed from Germany, was being applied to Russian Marxists. One of their number, Nikolai Lenin (Vladimir Ilyitch Ulyanov, 1870-1924), who had joined a Marxist group in Kazan, where he was expelled from the University for engaging in subversive student activities, in 1895 organized among the workers' circle of St. Petersburg a League of Struggle for the Emancipation of the Working Class. Similar leagues were formed in other cities, and the most immediate result of their activities was an increase in strikes.

Against the background of a severe economic crisis, a secret convention of nine delegates was held in Minsk in 1898 to unite these leagues into a Russian Social Democratic Workers' Party, an avowedly Marxist group, such as Plekhanov had advocated. Lenin, first in Munich and later in London, edited its first newspaper, *Iskra* (*The Spark*), which was smuggled into Russia, where as the foremost revolutionary sheet of its time it exercised an important influence on the Revolution of 1905. Another revolutionary, Leon Trotsky (Lev Davidovitch Bronstein, 1879-1940), joined the editorial staff of *Iskra* in London. In 1903, when these Social Democrats held a second congress in Brussels and London, their deliberations resulted in a Party split. The minority, or Mensheviks, lost in the balloting by only two votes (25:23). It was their contention that the social revolution must be achieved only after a careful and intensive preparatory campaign of education had trained the masses for a democratic regime. The majority, or Bolsheviks, had no patience with such deliberate methods, but favored an abrupt overthrow of the existing social and political order by a resort to force. Lenin was the leader of the Bolsheviks, while Plekhanov, and for a time, Trotsky, supported the Mensheviks. Both groups aimed at the overthrow of tsarist autocracy and the organization of socialist revolution. The difference between them was one of methods rather than of aims. Not until 1912, at a conference in Prague, were the Mensheviks expelled from the Party. In the same year the now well-known newspaper, *Pravda* (*Truth*), was founded as the organ of the Party.

The Social Revolutionary Party was organized about the same time (1901-1902) as that of the Social Democrats, the latter's activities perhaps serving as an impetus to their own. The S.R.s, as they were called, were, however, primarily concerned with the interests of the peasants, in contrast to the S.D.s who championed the cause of the workers in the city. They drew inspiration from the *Narodniki* (Populists) of the 1870's and sought to develop political consciousness among the peasants, contending that the land should belong to those who tilled it. Like the S.D.s they stood for the socialization of the land rather than for private ownership. Aroused by the appalling famine on the Volga, 1891-1892, and the unsatisfactory agricultural conditions in general, they encouraged agrarian disturbances. Moreover, a minority among them sought to arouse popular feeling against the government by a series of terroristic acts, whereas the S.D.s sought the same end by somewhat less violent means, such as strikes and popular demonstrations. One of their number was responsible for the assassination of Dmitry Sipyagin, minister of the interior, in 1902, while another killed the highly unpopular Plehve in 1904, and still another disposed of the Grand Duke Serge, uncle of the emperor and governor-general of Moscow, in the spring of 1905. The S.R.s did not accept Marxism in its entirety, being influenced in part by the "Utopian" School of Socialism in France, and by the thinking of some Russian novelists and literary critics. As in the case of the S.D.s, a wide divergence of opinion among the membership caused them to separate into "Right" and "Left" wings. The S.R.s soon became the largest political party in Russia. Both the S.D.s and the S.R.s had a following among university students and included in their membership representatives from the professions of law, medicine, and education. The leaders of both parties of necessity had to live abroad.

The Constitutional Democratic Party was composed of both conservative and liberal members of the intelligentsia, who disapproved of the radical theories and practices of the earlier groups. Its members advocated a policy of liberalism, which gradually and by peaceful means would displace absolute autocracy by a constitutional government, modeled upon the parliamentary system of England or France. The most learned men of the nation and many liberal landowners either belonged to this party or sympathized with its aims. The party, although organized in 1903, did not begin to make its influence felt until 1905. Prior to that time it was, like all other political parties, banned by the government and was obliged to work in secret. No group was more influential throughout the country during the years from 1905 to 1917. The party came to be known as the Kadets, or the K.D.s, from the first letters of the Russian words for Constitutional Democrats.

Inasmuch as all parties thus far considered had as their common aim the abolition of autocracy in favor of a representative government chosen by the people, the tsarist regime was absolutely without popular support. To repair this lack and offset the activities of the various social reform groups, a counter-revolutionary organization known as the Black Hundred was built up at the initiative of the government and secretly under the direct patronage and protection of Nicholas II himself. Its members were drawn from the ranks of the Orthodox clergy and from the most reactionary elements of the country. While there were sincere and upright monarchists among them, there was also present a most vicious and undesirable element. This was made up of ordinary hoodlums, who delighted in pogroms and similar atrocities and who took advantage of the government immunity to indulge in all forms of lawlessness and violence against the "enemies of the emperor." Their propaganda often incited the rabble to take violent action against non-Russian elements in the population, such as the Poles, Armenians, and Jews. Their connection with the notorious Kishinev pogroms of 1903 brought discredit to the government both at home and abroad. However when the more decent monarchists ventured to call the attention of the emperor to these abuses, both he and the empress refused to listen to their protests.

By the outbreak of the Russo-Japanese War in 1904, in spite of all the efforts of the government to wipe out subversive activities, there existed a rather widespread revolutionary movement. Under the police department's direction, government agents, or spies, were instructed to join the various revolutionary groups to obtain evidence against their leaders. Although many such leaders fell victims to the machinations of these agents, some of the latter became so active in revolutionary circles that the government was in doubt as to their real affiliations and sympathies. The government made various and fruitless efforts to divert the attention of the revolutionaries. The failure of the war with Japan in this connection has already been mentioned. With every defeat abroad the revolutionary movement at home gained momentum and became more threatening. At the instigation of both wings of the Social Democrats, strikes broke out on a large scale and spread with an unprecedented rapidity. At one time in 1905 there were 1,834,000 workmen engaged in major strikes, the largest number ever participating at one time in such demonstrations. The years 1903 to 1917 witnessed fifteen major strikes in Russia.

The peasants, likewise, had become disaffected under the influence of propaganda spread by the Social Revolutionaries. They demanded land on a large scale and on the basis of strictly private ownership. In the old days of serfdom, they had been accustomed to say to the landowners, "We are yours, but the land is ours." Now their terror-istic cry had become: "Kill the landowners and seize the land." There-upon they fell upon many of the rich landowners, murdered them, and looted and burned their property.

Although the majority of the leaders among the clergy gave their support to the reactionary forces, which were endeavoring to suppress popular dissatisfaction either by violent or subtle means, there were others among them who felt that the Church had a duty to perform toward the people. It was their belief that the clergy should assume the leadership of the hundreds of thousands of illiterate and misguided workers in the towns and on the farms and direct them toward con-structive efforts, by which they and the country at large would be benefited. Most prominent among these ecclesiastical leaders was Father George Gapon. Many conflicting opinions have been expressed in regard to this man's character and deeds, but we may assume that he was absolutely sincere in his efforts to procure by religious means that adjustment of social conditions, which government oppression and revolutionary activities had alike failed to accomplish. He began to hold meetings for the workingman, opening and closing each gath-ering with prayers for divine guidance. He begged the workers to refrain from violence and seek redress of their wrongs through peaceful measures. He told them that the emperor did not know what condi-tions were really like since he was misinformed by deceitful advisers, who were responsible for all the sufferings of the people. Great crowds flocked to hear him preach his simple logic which was comprehensible to a simple people.

By tireless efforts and ceaseless persuasion he convinced large numbers of workers that they should abandon the revolutionary and socialistic organizations and cast their lot with him. Then he decided that the time was ripe for a personal appeal to the "Little Father." Sunday, January 22, 1905, was selected as the day for this appeal. Thousands of workingmen with their wives and children assembled for a religious service, after which the entire multitude marched to the Winter Palace with Father Gapon at their head. Reverently bearing aloft portraits of the emperor and members of the royal family and singing hymns, they presented the aspect of a devout religious procession. Anything less like a revolutionary demonstration cannot well be imagined. Father Gapon had told them that the emperor would no doubt receive them himself and instructed them to fall upon their knees when he appeared in token of their loyalty and submission.

It is difficult to believe that Nicholas II was not well informed by his various spies of the spirit and purpose of this march.[1] Had he or one of his representatives afforded the marchers a brief hearing, they would in all probability have dispersed quietly with that gratitude and respect in their hearts which might have served later to save the life of Nicholas II, if not his throne. With a blind obtuseness of judgment, which finds few parallels in history, soldiers and Cossacks were ordered to open fire without warning upon the assembled crowd. Estimates of the number of victims range from 70 to 500 or more killed, and 250 to 3500 wounded. Whatever the numbers, the government had committed an unpardonable blunder, the repercussions of which were felt throughout the country. No words can depict the terror and the wrath of the people over the horrors of Bloody Sunday. Those who had lost friends or relatives vowed an undying vengeance, the intensity and fervency of which only increased with the passing years. Wrath also fell upon the Church, because the people were fully convinced that they had been betrayed and entrapped by its emissaries. From this time forth the workers aligned themselves wholeheartedly with revolutionary and socialist forces. "Bloody Sunday" marked a crisis in the revolutionary movement.

On the evening of Bloody Sunday, Maxim Gorky led Father Gapon to the rostrum of a protest meeting, where the priest spoke as follows:

Dear blood brethren, the bullets of the Imperial soldiers have killed our faith in the Tsar. Let's take vengeance on him and his entire family. Vengeance on all his ministers and all the exploiters of Russian soil. Go, pillage the imperial palaces! All the soldiers and officers who killed our innocent wives and children, all the tyrants, all the oppressors of the Russian people, I herewith smite with my priestly curse.

---

[1] For a different account of Bloody Sunday, see Alexander Grand Duke of Russia, *Once a Grand Duke,* New York. See also Walsh, E. A., *The Fall of the Russian Empire,* N. Y., 1931, pp. 74-76, and General P. G. Kurlov, *Fall of the Russian Empire* (in Russian), Berlin, 1923, pp. 16, 36.

BLOODY SUNDAY, JANUARY 22, 1905

Father Gapon was forced to flee to Switzerland, from whence for a time he directed bitter philippics against the Russian government. His later movements are something of a mystery. He met his death in a small village in Finland, where he was murdered by workingmen who denounced him as a "provocateur."

Throughout the country there was prompt reaction to Bloody Sunday. In Poland a general strike was proclaimed. In western Georgia Russian officials were ousted, and the inhabitants organized and maintained their own government for a period of several months. Widespread peasant uprisings took place throughout European Russia. Disorders and strikes occurred in cities from St. Petersburg to the Caucasus, with workers and members of the intelligentsia demanding a Constituent Assembly and an eight-hour day. When news arrived of the destruction of the Russian Baltic Fleet in the Battle of Tsushima, workers called for the end of the war, and the crew of the battleship *Potemkin,* anchored off Odessa, mutinied and escaped to a Rumanian port. In brief, over a wide area of the country, government authority ceased to function.

Under the pressure of military reverses and internal revolt, the government decided to make a gesture in the way of political reforms. This indicated a belated and withal limited recognition of a principle confirmed by historical facts that a government which would continue must never yield to a mob but should take due cognizance of any demands made by a considerable number of reliable citizens. On August 19, 1905, the Government's own plan for a Duma was announced. Since this plan envisaged only a consultative body, to be chosen by indirect election on the basis of a narrowly restricted franchise conferred chiefly upon landowners, it completely failed to quell the dissatisfaction of all those who demanded a constituent assembly with broad legislative powers. Here again the Imperial government of Russia missed an opportunity of taking measures to avert its downfall.

The internal situation grew more and more critical. The agitation of the Social Democrats resulted in bringing about a general strike among public utility workers. Railroads ceased to operate, and cities were without electric lights and without water. At this juncture a new organization came into being in St. Petersburg, the Soviet of Workers' Deputies. *Soviet* is the Russian word for "council." Originally its members were drawn from all Socialist groups, but the Bolsheviks comprised only an insignificant minority. This organization was in the nature of a representative council of socialist groups and workers.

Its first chairman or president was Khrustalev-Nosar, a lawyer by profession. His importance, however, was soon overshadowed by that of the vice-president, who then went by the name of Bronstein, but who is better known as Leon Trotsky. Trotsky was at that time a leader of influence among the Mensheviks (Moderate Socialists), who controlled a majority in the Soviet. This council was regarded with much disfavor by the Bolsheviks, who repeatedly warned the Mensheviks that there was no safety in the latter's policy of deliberate methods and co-operation with the government. The Bolsheviks demanded rapid action and complete severance from a government which would only "double cross" them in the end.

It is uncertain what the Soviets might have instituted or accomplished at this time, for they were forestalled by the government before they had a chance to become very numerous or very powerful. According to Witte, the peasant disorders, which wrecked some 2000 estates in 1905, caused more concern in government circles than the Soviet of Workers' Deputies and its general strike. Nicholas II and his advisers had finally become thoroughly alarmed, in view of the relentless advance of the revolutionary forces and the threatened collapse of the government. Count Witte, who was noted for his liberal ideas, and Grand Duke Nicholas Nicholayevitch, Jr., succeeded in exerting sufficient influence and pressure to produce a Manifesto for the instituting of political reform. This Manifesto, which was issued on October 30, 1905, startled even the most radical of the socialists by its liberal provisions. It granted practically everything for which the Liberals and moderate Socialists had been asking, that is, freedom of speech, freedom of assembly, universal suffrage, and a representative and legislative Duma. It clearly aimed at winning over the liberal groups among the revolutionaries, who would be rendered powerless by the loss of their most able members. Count Witte was made prime minister and given the power to select his own cabinet. Promptly he invited the co-operation of the Liberals. This was a remarkable opportunity for them, which, if it had been accepted, would have given them almost absolute control of the government and redounded much to their prestige. However in this year, 1905, they failed, as they did later in 1917, by exhibiting a deplorably weak hesitation and vacillation when the time came to act. Despite the excellence and thoroughness of their campaign for just such reforms as the October Manifesto offered, they did not respond to any extent to the invitation of the prime minister, and the psychological moment passed.

The radical Socialists, after recovering from the first surprise occasioned by the Manifesto, expressed their disapproval of it as a halfway measure, for now nothing short of a social upheaval would satisfy them. The Bolsheviks came out strongly against it under the leadership of Lenin, who had just returned to Russia. Despite its failure to win the support of the various parties, the Manifesto gave a moral victory to the government and saved it from an immediate collapse. The general public was pleased with the liberalism of the document and lost for the time being the desire for revolt. The Manifesto of 1905 came to be regarded as even more important than the Manifesto of 1861, abolishing serfdom.

Disappointed at the lukewarm reception accorded the Manifesto by the Liberals, the government turned to other means of suppressing revolutionary activities. Using as an excuse the well-known fact that certain Jews had become affiliated with the various organizations sponsoring revolt, another series of pogroms was instituted. The atrocities which followed were the most ghastly in the history of pogroms, largely because the worst element of the Black Hundred participated and was chiefly responsible for all that occurred. In Odessa, for example, where seven hundred were killed, the Cossacks of the Black Hundred bayoneted women and children and threw some of the latter from fifth and sixth story windows. The victims were almost entirely innocent persons, who had no idea of engaging in any activities against the government. The real Jewish revolutionaries for the most part managed to escape.

Armed insurrection broke out in Moscow toward the end of December 1905. The government knew that such a demonstration was threatening and for that reason, as has been previously mentioned, was very anxious to end the war with Japan and get the troops home. They began to return immediately following the Peace of Portsmouth in September, so that by December the majority was available. In comparison with their losing fight with the Japanese, the suppression of an internal revolt seemed very simple and easy. Moreover, inasmuch as the Manifesto had satisfied many influential persons, the revolt did not become as widespread as in 1917. Nevertheless, the second Russian Revolution of 1905 caused the death of thousands, the wounding of tens of thousands, and the exiling of many more. Between 1905 and 1909 the number of political prisoners rose from 85,000 to 200,000 annually.

The Revolution of 1905 shook the autocracy to its very foundations. The concessions made in time of dire emergency in the direction of a constitutional regime, although whittled down in the process of the counter-revolution, could never be scrapped entirely. The government, jarred into action, attempted in the years that followed to tackle some of the basic problems that confronted Russia, such as the agrarian issue, mass illiteracy, and military reorganization. The time available for what amounted in some respects to a revolutionary transformation of the country was, as events were to prove, all too short. At least a generation of peace was needed. World War I overtook Russia before the fundamental changes under way could be expected to produce the desired results, and the monarchy, which unknowingly faced its last great test following the Revolution of 1905, went down to defeat amid the chaos of 1917.

THE DUMAS; STOLYPIN

When the Revolution of 1905 had been crushed, a general assembly was called in accordance with the provision of the Manifesto of October 30, 1905. This was the first of a series of four Dumas which were called before 1917. The term, "Duma," which is derived from the verb *dumat,* meaning "to think," was linked in Russia with the traditions of the past. The *Boyarskaya Duma,* a consultative council which had made recommendations to the tsar, and which was replaced by the Administrative Senate under Peter the Great in 1711, was never in any true sense of the word a legislative body. Although Nicholas II would have preferred that the new Duma should perform a similarly restricted function, the emergency had forced him to make greater concessions. Although hedged about by many restrictions, the Imperial Duma was nevertheless a legislative body, chosen by indirect, but very nearly universal male suffrage for a period of five years.

Although the October Manifesto had provided the forms of Western democracy, including the five freedoms of person, conscience, speech, meeting, and association, it remained to be seen how they would take root in the alien Russian soil. Witte's additions to the fundamental laws, enacted on the very eve of the inauguration of this experiment in constitutional government, arbitrarily placed the army, navy, and foreign loans outside the competence of the Duma, thereby violating the spirit, if not the letter, of the October Manifesto, which provided that "no law can obtain force without the consent of the State Duma." Witte likewise made good use of his reputation abroad to secure a large loan from France, which served at a most critical time to make the administration independent of the new Duma. It was not an auspicious beginning.

The First Duma, convened on May 10, 1906, which was boycotted by the radical Socialists, included, in the words of Sir Bernard Pares, "the cream of the Russian intelligentsia." [1] Of its 478 members, 187 were Constitutional Democrats (Kadets), and 85 represented the moderate Labor Party. Among the 204 peasants elected, only two were recorded as illiterate. The session was opened by the emperor in person, and S. M. Muromtsev, a lawyer and author, as well as a member of the Kadets, was elected President. The members promptly turned to the discussion of such controversial issues as the activities of the Black Hundred in connection with the pogroms, the desirability of an amnesty for revolutionary offenders, the abolition of capital punishment even for political offenses, the end of the extraordinary courts and the passport system, and compulsory expropriation of the land. They even passed a vote of censure on the emperor's ministers, although the principle of executive responsibility to the legislature had not been conceded by the Manifesto. Although Article 14 of the Statute of the Duma and Article 26 of the Statute of the State Council guaranteed freedom of speech, Nicholas II could not endure the criticism of governmental policies resorted to by the delegates, and with the approval of reactionary bureaucrats he arbitrarily dissolved it on July 21, after a session of seventy-two days, and with a total disregard for its five-year term. From Finland, where some 200 of the disillusioned Kadets and Labor members sought refuge, was issued the Viborg Manifesto, which protested the dissolution of the Duma, called for civil disobedience to the government, and nonrecognition of foreign loans negotiated without the consent of the Duma. The country, weary of revolution and violence, failed to rise to the support of the Duma.

The Second Duma, which convened on March 5, 1907, and which was selected in accordance with the same franchise, fared no better than the first. All those who had participated in the Viborg Manifesto were barred from re-election. Lenin had reversed his earlier position in regard to the boycott of the Duma, and the new assembly included 180 Socialists, who proved to be far more hostile to the government than their predecessors. Unfortunately they dissipated their energies by making denunciatory speeches, instead of undertaking worth-while reforms. When the police uncovered two plots in which both revolutionary parties, the S.D.s and the S.R.s, were implicated, the Second

---

[1] See Pares, Bernard, *The Fall of the Russian Monarchy*, p. 94.

Duma was dissolved unceremoniously on June 16 for plotting against the emperor.

Peter Stolypin, who had been appointed prime minister by Nicholas II on the eve of the dissolution of the First Duma, had already made arrangements for a drastic revision of the electoral law, as a result of which the Third Duma, which met in the fall of 1907, could no longer be said to represent the people as a whole but mainly the conservative propertied classes among the Great Russians. Even the peasant members of the Third Duma, it was claimed, were elected by the gentry. An illustration of how drastic was the restriction of the franchise is provided by Sir Bernard Pares, who was informed by one member of this Duma that all his constituents could be assembled in one room.[1] The Third Duma, nevertheless, included some able men, and since the monarchy had no occasion to question their loyalty, they were able, through the organization of special commissions, to effect important agrarian and military reforms and to remain in session for the full term of five years.

Sir Bernard Pares, already mentioned above, who spent some time each year in Russia from 1904 to 1919, and observed the operation of the Dumas at first hand, has commented on them as follows:

. . . The Duma had the freshness of a school, with something of surprise at the simplicity with which differences that had seemed formidable could be removed. One could feel the pleasure with which the Members were finding their way into common work for the good of the whole country. In the First Duma peasants had picked out as their chief impression the realization that Russia was a great family, that there were so many others with thoughts and hopes like their own. "It went past like a dream," one of them said to me. The Second Duma was fast growing more and more into a family when it was prematurely dissolved. The Third Duma, though its horizon was much more limited, did come to stay, and its membership was better qualified to take practical advantage of the education which it offered. Some seventy persons at least, forming the nucleus of the more important commissions, were learning in detail to understand the problems and difficulties of administration and therefore to understand both each other and the Government. One could see political competence growing day by day. And to a constant observer it was becoming more and more an open secret that the distinctions of party meant little, and that in the social warmth of their public work for Russia all these men were becoming friends.[2]

[1] Pares, *op. cit.,* p. 103.
[2] *Ibid.,* pp. 117-118.

Much of the credit for the handling of the agrarian situation must go, however, not to the Duma, but to Peter Stolypin, who served as Nicholas II's prime minister from 1906 to 1911. Stolypin had had much practical experience in politics, having served as Governor of Saratov Province, as well as minister of the interior. Although less brilliant than Witte, he was straightforward, honest, courageous, and energetic in his efforts to improve domestic conditions in Russia. Having achieved the restriction of the franchise and suppressed the revolutionaries by establishing a series of military courts, he turned to more constructive measures, especially to the agrarian situation. During the First Duma the Constitutional Democrats had introduced a bill advocating that the government take over the large estates upon the payment of suitable compensation to the owners and then allot the land to the peasants. Stolypin opposed such abrupt measures, which were sure to antagonize the large landowners, and substituted his own solution for the agrarian problem. By a truly revolutionary decree of November 22, 1906, he provided for the abolition of the peasant commune, or *mir,* in favor of individual ownership and the consolidation of peasant holdings. Stolypin's objective was to transform Russia from a nation of peasants into a nation of farmers. Each peasant, he insisted, was entitled to a farm of his own, as well as to government aid in financing it. Hence reforms were effected in the Peasants' Land Bank to facilitate the financing of this program. Peasants in the overcrowded Black Soil areas were encouraged to migrate to Siberia. Better agricultural methods, including the use of machines and fertilizers, were fostered. Stolypin's program was first introduced by imperial *ukaz,* over the protests of the Duma, and did not actually become law until it was ratified by the Third Duma on June 14, 1910. In the meantime, however, Stolypin continued to carry on his reforms. No doubt the success of the program was due in part to the fact that for a decade following 1907 Russian agriculture produced bumper crops, and the country enjoyed almost unprecedented prosperity.

By 1911, Stolypin's reforms had brought into existence from one to two million such peasant farms, the owners of which were later known in Soviet Russia as "kulaks." If Stolypin had been permitted to continue this work, the number of these farms would have doubled and trebled, with the result that the Revolution of 1917 might have taken an entirely different course. Unfortunately for the peasants, Stolypin was assassinated on September 14, 1911. The assassination was the work of a young lawyer, Bogrov by name, a Social Revolutionary. It occurred in the Kiev Opera House in the course of a performance given in honor of a visit of the emperor. Stolypin's harsh methods in dealing with political opposition were given as a cause. Nearly 3000 persons are said to have been executed during the five years that he was in power. Although the more radical peasants may not have appreciated his efforts on their behalf, he nevertheless contributed much to their welfare, and his death operated as a distinct check to reforms in their favor.

The election of the Fourth Duma in 1912 was accomplished with an even greater disregard for the right of popular suffrage. The Procurator of the Holy Synod, Sabler, a strong reactionary, desired that certain members of the clergy should serve as deputies in the Duma. In order to make their election certain, the minister of the interior arbitrarily rearranged electoral districts. While the First Duma had 6 clergymen, and the Second Duma 13, including two bishops, the Third included 45 and the Fourth 46. Thus once more the clergy evinced its willingness to co-operate with the government in restricting the liberties of the people. The Fourth Duma startled the people by the course of its procedure. It was this Duma which brought about the overthrow of the Romanov dynasty.

Very powerful in directing the election of the Duma was the so-called "Mad Monk," Rasputin (1871-1916). Beginning with 1905, when his influence first began to be felt, he exercised almost unlimited authority in the appointment of public officials and the shaping of foreign policy. There are few stranger tales in history than that dealing with the career of this man. He was neither a priest nor a member of any religious order but was a mere wanderer, who combined the characteristics of a picaresque rover with those of a pilgrim. He did not even go by his right name, which was Novikh, but adopted the epithet, which his fellow peasants in his native Siberian village had bestowed upon him because of his well-known course of immorality and crime. His chief claim to superiority apparently consisted in the possession of a personal magnetism of such force that he was able to bend many persons to his will and even bring healing to the sick. It is said that in his capacity as a "healer" he attracted the attention of a wealthy lady, who was responsible for his coming to St. Petersburg and for his subsequent introduction to the empress. Since he appeared to benefit the sickly Prince Alexis [1] as no doctor had been

---

[1] Alexis, the long-awaited heir to the throne, was born August 12, 1904. When he was three years old, he fell while playing and received an injury which began to bleed. When the court physician was unable to check this bleeding, the empress sank in a swoon. She realized that she had transmitted to her only son the disease known as hemophilia, which had afflicted males of her father's family for 300 years.

able to do, the empress believed that he was possessed of divine power and surrendered entirely to his direction. The emperor, likewise, came under his influence, so that the licentious adventurer was for a time the real ruler. Bitter protests came from all sources, but neither Nicholas nor the empress would listen to them. At last members of the nobility took matters into their own hands, and Rasputin was assassinated in December 1916, by the wealthy Prince Felix Yusupov, whose wife was a niece of Nicholas II, and his fellow conspirators, the Grand Duke Dmitry Pavlovitch, a cousin of the emperor, and the ultra-reactionary, Vladimir Purishkevitch.

POLITICAL, SOCIAL AND ECONOMIC CONDITIONS ON THE EVE OF WORLD WAR I

Disturbed by the Anglo-French *Entente Cordiale* of 1904, which was an outgrowth of Russia's involvement in the Far East, Nicholas II promptly sought to re-establish better relations with Germany. In July 1905, while the Russo-Japanese War was still in progress, the German emperor and the tsar reached a secret agreement at Bjorko, which virtually amounted to a Russo-German alliance. Since this private "deal" constituted, for all practical purposes, an abrogation of the Franco-Russian alliance of 1894, the ministers of Nicholas II forced him to annul it. Not the least of the reasons for avoiding a break with France was Russia's constant need of money, in view of her struggle against internal disorder and her reverses in the war. When on April 16, 1906, France, in return for Russia's support against Germany at Algeciras (1906), extended to her a huge loan, this aid came at a most critical and opportune moment and did much to bind Russia more firmly to France.

The *rapprochement* with France, together with the outcome of the Japanese War, led the Russian foreign minister, A. P. Izvolsky, to seek improved relations with Great Britain. In an agreement with the latter country in August, 1907, known as the Anglo-Russian Entente, Russia materially modified her claims upon territory in Central Asia, thereby relieving the uneasiness of England in respect to India. By this agreement, Russia recognized Afghanistan as a British sphere, both powers consented to maintain a "hands off" policy in Tibet, and each retained a sphere of influence in Persia—the Russians in the north and the British in the south. A famous cartoon in the English magazine *Punch* portrayed the British lion and the Russian bear mauling the Persian cat! Inasmuch as the Japanese War had all but ruined Russia's pretensions in the Far East, Great Britain had gained all her ends. Her hostility, therefore, was considerably abated, and the way was paved for a better understanding between the two powers.

The second Hague Peace Conference of 1907 and its failure to accomplish disarmament have already been mentioned. Russia would have been glad to devote the French loan ($400,000,000) of 1906 to internal improvements rather than to armament. However her recent defeat by Japan and the fact that other European countries, especially Germany, were armed to the teeth, made her position extremely precarious and her need of armament imperative. It was these considerations which led her to take the initiative in calling a Peace Conference in the hope of averting future wars. The failure of this earnest attempt on the part of Russia was a great disaster to her. It had, however, a very significant result, that is, the alignment of Germany and Austria against the Triple Entente made up of Russia, Great Britain, and France. The course of European politics was such that Great Britain soon began to fear Germany far more than she ever had feared Russia. The events growing out of the Turkish revolution, 1908, intensified this fear and also served to cement more firmly the alliance of the Triple Entente against Germany. The aforementioned revolution brought a pro-German government into power in Turkey. In October of the same year, to the consternation of the Triple Entente, Austria suddenly annexed Bosnia and Herzegovina, which she had occupied temporarily in 1878. Although Germany's part in the annexation was clearly discernible, the Russian government was in no position to do anything about the matter, and the Triple Entente accepted perforce the *fait accompli*. The fact was that Izvolsky, in trying to make a deal with Austria whereby he might secure Austrian support of Russian interests in the Straits, had been completely outwitted by the Austrian foreign minister, Aehrenthal. Worse still, the Bulgars, obviously acting by preconcerted arrangement with Austria, seized this opportunity to proclaim their final independence from Turkey. The upshot of the Balkan crisis of 1908, which has sometimes been termed a dress rehearsal for 1914, was that Pan-Slav sentiment in Russia was thoroughly aroused, Serbia looked to Russia for aid against Austria, and the Triple Entente was further consolidated by its opposition to the new *Drang nach Osten* on the part of the Central Powers.

Germany's next move came in the summer of 1911, when the German gunboat *Panther* was sent to Agadir, ostensibly to protect German interests in Morocco but really for the purpose of attempting once more to secure a foothold in that territory. Powerful Arab leaders of South Morocco were entertained by the officers of the *Panther,* who promised German assistance if they made an attempt to throw off French control. As in 1905-1906, at Algeciras, French diplomacy won the victory. France's right to a protectorate in Morocco was recognized, November 4, 1911, but in return she ceded to Germany some 250,000 square kilometers of her possessions in the northern Congo.

There was no reason to believe that the Central Powers would be satisfied with the outcome of the Agadir affair, and European relations became tense. Inside Russia, German-Austrian diplomacy had long been active in increasing the tension existing between the Russian people and their government. For example, Austria sedulously fostered Ukrainian "culture" in her territory of Galicia, from whence it spread to Russian territory and exerted a subversive influence. The purpose of this was to create among Ukrainians a sentiment of good will toward the Central Powers and a desire to separate themselves from Russia. In retaliation for this propaganda, Russia brought about the union of Serbia, Bulgaria, and Greece against Turkey in the First Balkan War, 1912-1913. This was intended as an indirect blow against Austria. The Central Powers, however, succeeded in stirring up dissension among these minor powers, which, after defeating Turkey and stripping her of most of her European possessions, divided their allegiance, Serbia turning to the *Entente,* and Bulgaria seeking the patronage of the Central Powers. In the Second Balkan War (1913), Bulgaria was defeated by the combined action of Serbia, Greece, and Rumania. But the Germans, at the request of Turkey, dispatched a military mission under General Liman von Sanders to Constantinople to reorganize the Turkish army. While Germans dreamed of a Berlin-to-Bagdad railway, Russians regarded the German interest in the Near East as a direct threat to Russian interests at the Dardanelles. The Balkans remained a veritable powder keg. It required only a slight pretext to cause the mutual hostility to explode, and this was afforded by the events of the summer of 1914.

In Russia internal conditions on the eve of World War I could hardly have been worse. Not only was there an alarming lack of political stability, but economic conditions were in a precarious state. The strikes alone were almost as universal and involved almost as

TSAR NICHOLAS II REVIEWING HIS BODYGUARD AT KRASNOY SELO IN AUGUST 1911

many persons as in 1905. There were 1,059,000 workmen engaged in strikes as compared with 1,843,000 in 1905. The government sought desperately to divert public attention from the rotten politics and wretched economic conditions and eagerly seized upon a means offered it by the Black Hundred in the city of Kiev. This organization had brought charges against Mendel Beilis, a Jew, of the ritual murder of a Gentile boy named Andrey Yushtchinsky. A conviction would have resulted in a series of pogroms against the Jews, whereby the authorities hoped to exhaust the people in an orgy of blood. Instead of diverting popular attention, this farcical trial merely brought into glaring prominence the entire rottenness of the system of government. The people were much aroused over the manifest injustice of the accusation against Beilis. Protests poured in not only from organizations in Russia but also from foreign countries, including the United States. Despite this, the case dragged on for two years, from July 1911 to November 1913. However public opinion and especially world opinion were too strong to be disregarded and in the end Beilis was acquitted. Russian officials were of the opinion that German-Austrian diplomacy utilized this famous case to further several ends: first, to stir up unrest among Russian Jews; second, to injure Russia's world prestige; and finally, to divert Russia's attention from German militarism.

There were, however, lights as well as shadows in the picture presented by Russia prior to World War I. Heroic efforts of Liberals in the Duma had resulted in significant achievements, one of the most important being in the field of education. On May 16, 1908, a law was passed which provided for four years of elementary instruction for all children between the ages of eight and eleven. By 1914 there were 149,000 elementary schools, in which about half the children of school age were enrolled. Educational authorities estimated that by 1922 more than twice that number of schools would be needed to accommodate the increasing school population. Despite the obstructive measures of a reactionary government and the opposition of the Orthodox Church, there is little doubt that the hopes of the Liberals for universal education would have become a reality by 1922. The war and the revolution of 1917, however, interrupted the educational campaign.

As a result of the reforms of Stolypin, the bulk of the peasants was in possession of full civil rights and enjoyed a fair degree of prosperity. Whereas agriculture was, as always, the basic industry in Russia, it was not especially well developed because of antiquated tools and methods. Thus, although large areas were under cultivation,

Russia ranked fourth in the world production of grain. Hours of work in the various trades and occupations had been shortened, a working day now averaging from ten to twelve hours. For this the worker received on an average about $150 a year, which according to Russian standards, was a very fair wage. The country's chief source of income came from the alcohol monopoly introduced by Witte, which in 1913 yielded a revenue of $335,000,000. Since the building of the great Trans-Siberian Railway, previously mentioned, the number of railroads had steadily increased, supplying work for many and making some progress toward uniting the scattered settlements of Russia's vast expanse of territory. The area of Russia at this time was 8,764,586 square miles, almost three times that of the United States. This supported a population that approached 180,000,000, which represented 169 ethnic groups with as many dialects.

The support of the royal family cost the country 11,000,000 rubles (about $5,450,000) annually. In addition the emperor derived an income equal in amount from estates known as *Udyely* belonging to the royal family, and from deposits which he kept in banks in England and Germany. In London banks he had £20,000,000, which, according to the Grand Duke Alexander, he is said to have devoted in its entirety to charity during the years 1915-1917. The imperial family also possessed rare jewels valued at $80,000,000. These jewels had been collected during the three centuries of Romanov rule.

In view of all that has been said of strained European relations, it may seem strange that there was not an earlier outbreak of hostilities. As a matter of fact a general war was delayed solely by the race for armament, each country seeking to oustrip the other. Of course this in itself increased international tension, but each nation hoped to gain military superiority before the advent of the inevitable combat. As has been indicated elsewhere, Russia was behind other European countries in the matter of armament but had, nevertheless, made considerable progress. The improvements had given the Russian junkers a most exaggerated idea of their ability. They thought they could fight anyone and burned with a desire to recover the prestige lost in the war with Japan.

Despite the machinations of Germany, which have been discussed earlier, it would be unreasonable and unfair from a historical standpoint to attribute to her the entire responsibility and blame for World War I. A careful study of all phases of the situation leads to the conclusion that the war was a divided responsibility, and that all the major powers of Europe had a hand in precipitating the catastrophe. To be sure,

THE NEVSKY PROSPECT, ST. PETERSBURG, ABOUT 1910

Germany was eager to carry out the Moltke Plan,[1] and Austria dreamt of domination in the Balkans. On the other hand, however, French resentment over the outcome of the Franco-Prussian War and the loss of Alsace-Lorraine was as alive as ever, and France never relinquished her hope of retaking this territory. Moreover she wished to put an end to German interference in her African colonies and protectorates, especially in Morocco. It is a well-established fact that French emissaries in various parts of the world had disseminated propaganda against Germany in the early 1890's. England, indeed, did not want war in 1914 and tried very hard to prevent it. The efforts of Sir Edward Grey to avert hostilities are well known. Nevertheless, England regarded Germany as a dangerous competitor, whose power she wished to see curbed. This Grey hoped to do without actual participation in the war but by acting in the capacity of a powerful neutral country, which would be in a position to dictate terms.

As for Russia, we may say by way of recapitulation, that the governmental authorities were exceedingly anxious for war, inasmuch as the Beilis case and the failure of Russian diplomacy in the Balkans in 1912 had brought them into exceedingly bad repute with the people. Foreign propaganda, such as that disseminated by Austria and the fomenting of strikes by various and sundry agitators and agencies contributed to the unrest among the masses. The upper classes, for their part, were disgusted and alienated by the power given to Rasputin. The government was tottering, and a brilliant military campaign was urgently needed to restore its prestige and stability. Thus when war loomed, the country was plunged into the conflict with the speed of lightning by officials who were making one last desperate effort to maintain their sway over the Russian people. General Lukomsky, who had charge of Russian mobilization, proceeded with incredible rapidity. Whether he did so with the encouragement of France or under the influence of Russian jingoists is uncertain. In any event, the speed with which the Russian army was mobilized had much to do with hastening the outbreak of the war.

The immediate cause, or rather pretext, for the war was the assassination of the Austrian archduke, Franz Ferdinand, on June 28, 1914, in the heretofore unimportant town of Sarajevo in Bosnia. Austria, alleging that the assassination had been perpetrated with the

---

[1] The Moltke Plan originated with General Helmuth von Moltke, Chief of the German General Staff, 1906-1914. He had detailed topographical surveys made of all neighboring countries, especially of Russia, France, and Belgium. These surveys were studied by officers in preparation for possible wars.

sanction of the government of Serbia, issued an ultimatum to the latter country on July 23, 1914. One clause of the ultimatum demanded the participation of Austrian officials in the investigation of the murder and the apprehension of the conspirators. No doubt Serbia was correct in believing that, if permitted, this Austrian "participation" would lead to an occupation of a part of Serbian territory by Austrian troops on the pretense that the investigating officials must be protected. The occupation of Serbian territory would in turn lead to absorption by Austria. Even so, Serbia might have yielded to the demands of a stronger country, especially since she was on bad terms with Bulgaria, who had been plotting for revenge ever since the Balkan War in 1912. However Serbia, certain of Russia's support, gave only a qualified acceptance to the Austrian ultimatum. In consequence, Austria, in spite of German pressure to the contrary, declared war upon Serbia on July 28, 1914, and immediately invaded Serbian territory.

In view of the two opposing systems of alliance that had been established German hopes for the "localization" of the Austro-Serbian conflict proved untenable. Russia and France refused to permit Austria to have a free hand in Serbia. Because of the Parliamentary situation in England, Sir Edward Grey found it inadvisable or impossible to align his country unqualifiedly with either side or to exert sufficient pressure on Germany to prevent the latter from granting Austria a *carte blanche* against Serbia. Russian bureaucrats, including Minister of Foreign Affairs S. D. Sazonov, fearful that a delay in Russian mobilization would result in an undue advantage for the highly mobile German armies, induced the tsar to resort to general mobilization, which, in view of the terms of the Franco-Russian alliance, was practically equivalent to war. It culminated in a German declaration of war against Russia on August 1, followed by similar action against France two days later. German violation of the neutrality of Belgium brought England into the war on August 4, followed by her ally, Japan, on August 22. Turkey entered the conflict on the side of the Central Powers in October, thereby closing what might have been an important allied supply route to Russia. Thus the great powers blundered into World War I.

RUSSIA AT WAR, 1914-1917

Once Germany had declared war, Nicholas II called upon all Russians to rally to the defense of their country. His appeal met with an immediate and enthusiastic response from all classes of the people, especially as the governmental policy was approved by the Fourth Duma and the zemstvos. The participation of England and France did much to win popular support of the war in Russia and avert those disorders which Germany had hoped, not without reason, would follow the mobilization of the Russian army. Even the radicals saw hope for the future of Russia if she took part in a war in which France, a republic, and England, a true democracy, were opposed to monarchial Germany. They felt that if Russia associated herself with these countries as an ally, she too might be able in the end to secure a democratic form of government. For this reason many volunteered without waiting for their turn to be called to arms. However, in those early days few in Russia or elsewhere believed that the war would be of long duration. It was thought that the regular army alone would be engaged in the actual conflict. Therefore the readiness to take up arms meant nothing more than an expression of loyalty to Russia. There was another reason for popular support of the war. In his appeals for the co-operation of the people, Nicholas II emphasized the element of Slavonic emancipation. An address by the emperor to the Duma on August 8, 1914, contained the following statement: "We are not only defending the dignity and honor of our country, but we are also fighting for our Slavic brothers, the Serbs, our coreligionists and kinsmen, and at this moment I behold with joy how the Union of all the Slavs with Russia is being strongly and unremittingly carried to consummation." Poland was also guaranteed the restoration of her ethnic boundaries under Russian suzerainty.

The war enthusiasm was, however, of short duration in Russia. Within a few weeks it had been greatly lessened by fear. On August 17, 1914, upon the insistence of her allies, Russian forces under General Rennenkampf entered East Prussia. They were thus the first allied forces to set foot on enemy soil, a factor of great psychological importance. Troops under General Samsonov followed up this offensive. This army numbered about 200,000 men and represented the very flower of the Russian military system. It was, nevertheless, destined for defeat, because German strategy had carefully laid a trap in the invaded region. General Hindenburg, with Ludendorff as chief of staff, attacked the Russian forces on August 31, 1914, at Tannenberg. The battle resulted in an overwhelming defeat for Russia. The Germans drove their foes into the Mazurian Swamps of East Prussia. Here 30,000 were either drowned or bayoneted, and 90,000 were taken prisoners. This disastrous defeat struck terror to the heart of the Russian masses. The German front was regarded as impregnable, and an order to report to this front was looked upon by many as a sentence of death. Whereas the blow to Russia was irreparable, France profited exceedingly by the Battle of Tannenberg, inasmuch as it withdrew six divisions of German troops and one cavalry division from the Western Front. This reduction of the invading forces made it possible for the French and English to check the German advance at the first Battle of the Marne and thereby change the entire course of the war.

The military plans worked out in advance of the war by Russian strategists had called, first of all, for the invasion of the Austro-Hungarian Empire and the destruction of its not so formidable military might. Only when that was accomplished did the Russian General Staff plan to undertake an offensive against Germany. Furthermore, the Schlieffen-Moltke plan of operations likewise envisaged a German offensive against France before the German armies would be called upon to face the slow-moving Russians. Thus the allied appeal to Russia for an offensive against Germany in August 1914 not only disrupted Russian strategy but likewise that of Germany.

In the light of what happened in World War II, it is now clear that it was Russia that provided the "second front" for the allied armies in the first world war. Whenever the situation on the Western front became threatening, the Allies invariably demanded that Russia come to their aid by launching a counter-offensive against Germany. On the other hand, in 1915 when Russia was sorely pressed, and in dire need of support because of the retreat of her army and the collapse of Serbia, the Allies did not stage any large drives on the Western front, which would have drawn off the armies of the Central Powers. To be sure, the Allies tried to render assistance at the Dardanelles and thereby put an end to the isolation of Russia, but with no results. In the spring of 1915, however, "the immemorial and sacred dream of the Russian people" appeared to be near fruition, when Russian Foreign Minister Sazonov reached a secret agreement with England and France whereby, in the event of an Allied victory, Constantinople and the Straits zone would be annexed to Russia. The entrance of Italy into the war in May, 1915, was productive of no benefits to Russia. For the most part she was left to her fate. Yet despite her defeat by the Germans, Russian man power rendered valuable service to the Allies, aside from serving as a means of diverting attention from the Western Front.

While the armies of the Western Allies bogged down in France and Belgium and failed to reach enemy soil until 1918, Russia launched four armies against Austria-Hungary in 1914 and occupied Austrian

Galicia. The Russian army likewise carried on offensive operations against Turkey on Turkish soil, seizing large slices of Armenia and Eastern Anatolia in 1915. In fact British success against Turkey under General Allenby later in the war was greatly facilitated by Russian action against the Turks in the Caucasus. Russian man power not only played an important role against Austria and Turkey, but in accordance with a Franco-Russian deal of December 19, 1915, five Russian brigades were dispatched via the Chinese Eastern Railway and the port of Dairen to the Western Front and Salonika.[1] In return France promised Nicholas II badly needed supplies of munitions.

The losses and failures, which marked the year 1915, greatly weakened the morale of the army and the people at large, which in turn led to serious political problems. The army had been found most inadequately prepared to meet the Central Powers, whose men were equipped with the most modern and deadly machinery of warfare. This was not due solely to the fact that prior to the war Russia had not been able to keep pace with her neighbors in armament. Graft and treason among high officials had criminally reduced army equipment. Upon the occasion of the Russian retreat from the Carpathian Mountain region, when a hail of sharpnel was descending upon the troops, the following order was issued: "Do not fire unnecessarily and take the ammunition from the killed and wounded." One of the officials, who was found to be chiefly responsible for the inadequate equipment of the Russian Army was General Sukhomlinov. He was dismissed in August 1915.

As the year 1915 advanced, the Duma and the emperor were increasingly unable to agree. Finally the Duma demanded a new cabinet composed of responsible leaders who would restore public confidence. The emperor did not want to yield to this demand and in order to avoid doing so assumed the command of the Russian army. The former commander-in-chief, Grand Duke Nicholas, was transferred to the Caucasian front. All this was done at the suggestion of Rasputin, whose influence was also responsible for the unreasonable supplanting of one ministry after another. The Duma wished to continue the war and hence had the support of the Allies in all its disagreements with the emperor. Certain influential government officials, however, were in favor of making a separate peace with Germany. Their first step was to win over Rasputin, who brought about the dismissal of Minister of Foreign Affairs Sazonov who was pro-Ally.

[1] See *Red Archives*, No. 2 (99), 1940, and *Ibid.*, 4 (101), 1940, pp. 228-235.

His place was taken by B. V. Sturmer, whose pro-German sympathies were well known. Naturally this aroused the suspicions of the Allies.

As for Nicholas II, he found himself in a most unusual and precarious position. Almost within his very palace, there was a strong combine using every means in its power to bring about a separate peace with Germany. The Duma was pro-Ally and hence opposed to a separate peace, but its policies were so at variance with his own that they were constantly at loggerheads. Moreover the military situation was becoming progressively worse. Russian armies had won successes against the Austrians and Turks only to meet defeat at the hands of the Germans under General Mackensen. In 1915 Germany had conquered Poland, Lithuania, and part of Latvia, thereby constituting a potential threat to the Russian capital. As compared with eighty-four divisions on the Western Front, where the Allies remained on the defensive, the Germans had massed one hundred sixty-one divisions against the Russians by the fall of 1915.

By the winter of 1916-1917, the Duma's dissatisfaction with the emperor had reached a high pitch. The empress also became the object of its displeasure, and at the November session several speeches were made, openly charging her with exerting a pernicious influence. Nor were the charges groundless. She was constantly urging her husband with all the eloquence at her command to defy the Duma and crush those who opposed him. In a letter written to him while he was at the front in 1916, she advised that the premier be hanged and that several high officials be exiled to Siberia. In all the words and deeds of the sovereigns the influence of Rasputin was evident, but even after his assassination on December 29, 1916, their stubborn temper did not change and they made no concessions to the demands of the representatives of the people. It was then that a plot began to develop in court circles, approved and supported by members of the Allied corps, which had as its aim the deposition of the emperor in favor of some other member of the royal family.

The situation in Russia on the eve of the Revolution was briefly as follows. There was an army of about 15,000,000 men, counting the reserve troops in the rear and the wounded, as well as those in active service at the front. All of them were discouraged and heartily sick of the war which seemed to drag on indefinitely. Among them were some 600,000 Jewish soldiers, whose loyalty and sacrifices had won the praise of even the greatest reactionaries at the beginning of the war. Nevertheless, they were in constant terror for the safety of their families